FORMER CHILD STARS

FORMER
CHILD STARS

JOAL RYAN

ECW PRESS

CANADIAN CATALOGUING IN PUBLICATION DATA

Ryan, Joal
Former child stars : the story of America's least wanted

ISBN 1-55022-428-X

1. Television actors and actresses — United States — Biography.
2. Child actors — United States — Biography 3. Child actors —
United States – History. I. Title.

PN1992.4.A2R92 2000   791.45'028'092273   C00-931716-3

Cover and text design by Tania Craan
Layout by Mary Bowness
Front cover photo: Zimmerman/Shooting Star
Back cover photo: G. Seminara Collection/Shooting Star;
Viacom/Shooting Star; Photofest; Photofest
Printed by Transcontinental

Distributed in Canada by General Distribution Services,
325 Humber Blvd., Toronto, Ontario M9W 7C3
Distributed in the United States by LPC GROUP,
1436 West Randolph Street, Chicago, Illinois, U.S.A. 60607
Distributed in Europe by Turnaround Publisher Services,
Unit 3, Olympia Trading Estate,
Coburg Road, Wood Green, London N2Z 6TZ
Distributed in Australia by Wakefield Press,
17 Rundle St., Kent Town,
South Australia 5071

Published by ECW PRESS
2120 Queen Street East, Suite 200,
Toronto, Ontario, M4E 1E2
ecwpress.com

The publication of *Former Child Stars* has been generously
supported by the Government of Canada through the Book Publishing
Industry Development Program. Canadä

PRINTED IN CANADA

ACKNOWLEDGMENTS

This book had a rather roundabout gestation, so here's as simple a chronological rendering as I can come up with.

Thanks to: (1) my father, John T. Ryan, for executive producing (read: paying for) the movie (*Former Child Star*) that became the e-zine that became the Web site that became this book; (2) the cast and crew of *Former Child Star*; (3) Rodney Allen Rippy, the erstwhile Jack in the Box kid (and upstanding adult) who bailed me out and informed my movie with his own real-life kid-in-Hollywood experiences; (4) the original seventy-five subscribers of my e-zine, *Former Child Star-Palooza* (well, all right, you didn't subscribe – I subscribed *you* – but I appreciate that most of you didn't *un*subscribe); (5) Chris Gore, who gave my fledgling e-zine a plug in *Film Threat* (www.filmthreat.com) and made it a little less fledgling; (6) Paul Petersen (*The Donna Reed Show*), for blazing trails with A Minor Consideration (www.minorcon.org), becoming one of my subscribers, and, later, letting me pick his brain for this book; (7) Greg Bulmash, of the belated WASHED-UPdate, who out of the blue (and from the kindness of his heart) offered to give *Former Child Star-Palooza* an early Web home; (8) *Entertainment Weekly*, the *Boston Phoenix, Newsweek, Movieline*, and CNN *Newsstand*, for plugging away on the redubbed Former Child Star Central site (www.formerchildstar.net); (9) Peter Rubie, my agent, for diligently pushing this book even when no one was getting it; (10) Jack David, Jen Hale, and everyone at ECW Press for finally getting it (and demonstrating extreme patience in *waiting* to get it); (11) Raechel Fittante, who doesn't think she helped but *did* by making some early (and worthy) research trips to the Margaret Herrick Library of the Academy of Motion Picture Arts & Sciences; (12) Michael Ryan, Alice Ryan, and, again, John T. Ryan, for additional research assistance; (13) Pat Ryfle, for not going mad as she transcribed my interview tapes; (14) Todd Fuller, of the fine Sitcoms Online (www.sitcomsonline.com) Web sites, for saving me from *Diff'rent Strokes* ignorance and providing me with some killer episodes; (15) Stuart Ross, for his editing expertise; and, (16) all the Former Child Star Central readers (and subscribers) for hanging in there, even though the Web site went cobwebby as I finished off this tome.

Very special thanks to the ex-kid actors whom graciously agreed to share their experiences in interviews for this book: Brandon Cruz, Jeremy Licht, Stanley Livingston, Steven Mond, Paul Petersen, Jon Provost, Shavar Ross, Glenn Scarpelli, and the aforementioned Mr. Petersen. Special thanks also to Don Stroud, who shared memories of his onetime stepfather Jackie Coogan, and William Peter Blatty, who did what he could to recall some obscure info regarding the casting of *The Exorcist*.

Thanks to other ex-kid actors who I interviewed from 1997 to 2000 for other articles and publications (and from which I have culled certain quotes and info for the following pages): Gary Coleman, Danny Bonaduce, Tony Dow, Billy Gray, Billy Mumy, the late Dana Plato, Robbie Rist, Johnny Whitaker, and Barry Williams. And to Bryan Madden of the Leave Gary Coleman Alone!! Web site (http://members.aol.com/Broken225/garycoleman.html), who granted me an interview for my Web site.

Assorted thanks to: Richard Horrmann of Hollywood.com, Judy Ryan of Glendale, and Hawk of the cage in our kitchen. No thanks to Marmoset Man.

And to Steve Ryfle who told me (and told me) to write this book before somebody else did – and then read it when I did.

Thanks to all.

TABLE OF CONTENTS

INTRODUCTION

HOW I STARTED OUT MAKING A SMART-ALECK MOVIE AND ENDED UP WITH A SERIOUS-LIKE BOOK

Gary Coleman, Adam Rich, Dana Plato. Former occupations: TV child star. Current occupations: Human punch line, police-blotter entry, suicide statistic. How'd they get here from there? That's what we want to know, right? Enquiring minds and all.

Great, except what this book wants to know is why we even care. Why we buy the tabs. Why we watch the talk shows. Why we revel in the rumors. Why we tell the jokes.

As for myself? All I really knew about former child stars I learned watching TV – a fact, I believed, that made me eminently qualified to make a movie on the subject. In the end, it was a quality that left me – the journalist cum would-be auteur – with a pair of dusty film canisters, a three-volume edition of film-festival rejection letters, and an ego the size of a partially dissolved baby aspirin.

In 1996, I wrote, directed, and just-about-everythinged a no-budget comedy called *Former Child Star*. The project began with the most ignoble of intentions – namely, to make fun of all those "losers" I grew up watching on TV. The concept was genius, I congratulated myself: a former child star rejected by society on account of her, you know, former child stardom strikes back with a crime spree only to fall in love with one of her victims, a smitten ex-fan. Fabulous. It was the Dana Plato story with laughs – make that, *planned* laughs. I was heady with my wit, my keen powers of observational humor, and my daddy's money. Now, I didn't exactly think this flick was going to play the Mann's Chinese, but I was pretty sure I was going to make the right kind of people (i.e., the rich kind of people who make movie deals) laugh. A comedy about former child stars? How could I botch that? It'd be like making an animal movie that didn't make you misty-eyed. Some things just are. Bunnies are cute, guys in black are bad, former child stars are *funny*.

Then I had to go mess it all up by caring.

It started the day I thought it might be a good idea to have a real former child star appear in (hey!) *Former Child Star.* Fabulous. And deadly. Not knowing any real former child stars on whom I could call and goad into lampooning, I was left to do the producerly thing and grovel. To the computer I went, printing out very personal, ultra-respectful form letters to the likes of Gary (*Diff'rent Strokes*) Coleman, Erin (*Happy Days*) Moran, and the guy who played Jim-Bob on *The Waltons.* (The Jim-Bob thing was an admitted long shot. Even today, I'm not convinced I sent the letter to the *right* David W. Harper of Los Angeles. In case I didn't, I'd like to thank the *other* David W. Harper of Los Angeles for not turning me in to the postal police.)

In my headhunt for a real former child star, I even placed a couple of phone calls. I tracked down an address for Tina (*Family Ties*) Yothers via a tabloid story. I called 411. Got a number. Dialed it up. Being ever so much the chicken, I purposely rang the number on a weekday afternoon, figuring the odds were with me that the answering machine would pick up.

It was the perfect scenario: I could leave my pitch; Tina could decide whether or not to call me back; I could go on about my day pretending I'd accomplished something. Problem was, Tina Yothers answered the phone. Criminy. Now what was I supposed to do? Writing letters was one thing; actually talking to Tina (*"Family Freakin' Ties"*) Yothers was another. You know the part where I was heady with my wit and my keen powers of observational humor? A distant memory. Instead, I mumbled, stumbled, and apologized my way through a low-prestige, non-paying job offer. ("Gee, um, Miss Yothers, would you, um, want to, uh, you know, be sorta in my movie? For, uh, free?") And you know the part where I wanted to make fun of real former child stars? I backtracked, retracted, and apologized my way out of my script. ("It's, you know, really a sort of different take, um, on the whole former-child-star-joke thing.") Not that any of this suddenly contrite behavior worked on Yothers, mind you. She listened – politely – and told me – patiently – that she didn't consider herself a "former" anything.

Oh, I said.

I don't want to say that Tina Yothers haunted me, but she certainly ruined me. The smart aleck was dead, replaced shortly thereafter by the all-new, all-empathetic Oprah. Soon after the Yothers incident, I found myself shooting off a memo to the actress playing my "reel" former child star on the subject of how I was no longer convinced we were making a comedy. Rather, I wrote, I was starting to think we were making a tragedy, or at least a sympathetic portrait of a used, abused, and confused woman. I drafted my leading lady a weepy, two-hanky character backstory. I made her a character-mood tape – with cuts by Nina Simone ("Little Girl Blue"), Chet Baker ("Someone to Watch Over Me"), and, of course, Judy Garland ("I'm Always Chasing Rainbows"). To sum up, I had lost my mind. Not to mention my comic nerve.

Damn you, Tina Yothers.

Midway through production, I finally and definitively stopped wanting to make a movie that made fun of all those losers I grew up watching on TV. Why exactly were they losers, I now thought. Because they'd made more money at age eight than I'd made my entire life? Because they'd reached the top of their professions (if only for thirteen weeks), and I hadn't (for even six minutes)? Who was the loser? Was I a better person because I'd never achieved renown? Were they worse persons because they didn't make the cover of *TV Guide* anymore?

By the time I sat down to interview our one bona fide real former child star (Rodney Allen Rippy of 1970s burger-commercial fame) for a videotaped cameo, I was more than wracked with guilt – I was really, really full of it, too. If Rodney had said "Boo," I might have dissolved into sobs. The result of my suddenly mixed – or, mixed-up – emotions was evident on the screen. (As was my lack of foresight to hire a production designer, make the camera guy use another lens, or get a clue as to how to frame something, but that's another story.) In the end, *Former Child Star* was a well-meaning miscue of a little film in which jokey, cartoony characters vented real feelings and real emotions about real-world plights. (For what it's worth, my daddy wants all you readers out there to know that he thinks *Former Child Star* is much better than *Citizen Kane*. So, you can, like, buy a copy from us if you want. No kidding. And now, back to the book. . . .)

In January 1997, I launched a former-child-star e-zine. The venture was a shameless promotional tool for the film, of course, but one that provided real, semi-useful information. If you wanted to know, say, what became of the guy who played Molly Ringwald's love interest in *Sixteen Candles*, I dug around and eventually replied that Michael Schoeffling was last spotted doing carpentry work in Pennsylvania. (Really.) If you had a

Danny Bonaduce sighting to share with the world, I posted it. The tone of the e-zine was fun, not mean. Tina Yothers would have been proud. (I hoped.)

And then a funny thing happened – the thing clicked, much more so than the movie. People who didn't care a whit about *Former Child Star* did care about, you know, former child stars. I got write-ups in *Newsweek, Entertainment Weekly,* and *Movieline,* not to mention a CNN news crew in my apartment. I got e-mail from readers thanking me for the info, not so much, I think, because they *needed* to know what happened to that kid from *The Courtship of Eddie's Father,* but because they actually cared. Empathy – it happens to the best of us.

And so the e-zine grew into a Web site (www.formerchild-star.net) grew into this book. And because of my particular former-child-star journey, this book isn't so much about what it's like to be a child star (former or otherwise), or about whether being a kid in Hollywood is a good, bad, or evil thing. Rather, it's about why I – why we – are stopped by the words *former child star.* It's about why I – why we – tend to think of the whole subject as one of life's big jokes. It's about why everything former child star sells tabloids, punches up *Tonight Show* monologues, spikes talk-show ratings, and encourages the breathless likes of the *E! True Hollywood Story.*

If I had to settle on a thesis (and, sadly, after much delay, I did), it's this: this is the story of how we – the audience – came to obsess over kids who used to live in prime time, and how that obsession became the real curse of the former child star. The story behind the creation of America's least wanted, if you will.

For the most part, this book distinguishes between kid actors who found stardom through TV and those who found stardom through film, focusing on the television contingent. (So if you're looking for some juicy Macaulay Culkin stories, you'll have to stoop elsewhere.) We're about the Kid Who Played

Chip on *My Three Sons* or the Kid Who Played the Orphan Boy on *One Day at a Time*. In any case, the operating theory here is that a TV kid makes a more personal impression than a movie kid – and, in the end, becomes more bedeviled by our perceptions and expectations. How does this happen? TV kids work on shows aimed at other kids; movie kids work in projects aimed at adults. Think about it: how many newly minted twenty-somethings or thirtysomethings do you know who over whatever- happened-to stories about, say, Justin (*Kramer vs. Kramer*) Henry? Now think about how many peers you know who absolutely devour whatever-happened-to tales of Gary Coleman. The difference? We grew up with Coleman. We (maybe) caught a glimpse of Henry at the Oscars. One was our virtual peer; the other, a movie star. One appeared attainable; the other not.

Granted, this theory doesn't always hold up. Everybody, frankly, wants to know what's up with Macaulay Culkin. On my Web site, the most popular question was (and still is) the one about Michael (*Sixteen Candles*) Schoeffling. But we're sticking to TV kids here because (1) they're as good a case study as any, and, frankly, a better one because no one's really done them in detail before; and, (2) they're a way to avoid contributing another MGM-destroyed-Judy Garland recap to the annals of literature, leaving us more time to recap how a curse destroyed the lives of the cast of *Diff'rent Strokes*.

I once broached my line about how it's "harder" to be an ex-TV kid star than an ex-kid movie star to Paul Petersen, the activist and undisputed king of the former-child-star sound bite – and he pretty much didn't buy it. An exploited kid is an exploited kid, he said. The problems are the same across the board – TV kids, movie kids, stage kids, sports kids, whatever. But then again, his perspective is that of the insider. He's the one who grew up on a set (*The Donna Reed Show*). I'm the outsider.

I've interviewed former child stars and I've researched former child stars and I've thought (somewhat deeply, I admit) about former child stars, but all I really know is what I've watched on the couch-and-living-room-table side of the box.

The former child star experience belongs to the former child star – the Gary Colemans, the Adam Riches, Dana Platos, the Paul Petersens. There's some detail here about what it was like to grow up on a set, about what it was like to be famous, about what it was like to not be famous, but it can hardly be called the definitive account. That is for the former child star to write. This book's specialty is us – how *we* processed what they did and, over time, assigned our own motives, causes, prejudices, and punch lines. That's pretty much it, then. This is a TV former child star book about the people who grew up with the TV former child star. See, all I still really know about former child stars is what I learned watching them. I'm just smarter about the whole thing now. Or so I think – and hope.

This one's for Tina Yothers.

THE CAST

A thumbnail guide to the book's key recurring characters (and their key credit/credits):

Danny Bonaduce (1959–   ) Danny Partridge on *The Partridge Family*, 1970–74.

Lauren Chapin (1945–   ) Kathy "Kitten" Anderson on *Father Knows Best*, 1954–60.

Todd Bridges (1965–   ) Willis Jackson on *Diff'rent Strokes*, 1978–86.

Gary Coleman (1968–   ) Arnold Jackson on *Diff'rent Strokes*, 1978–86.

Jackie Coogan (1914–1984) *The Kid, Peck's Bad Boy, The Addams Family*.

Brandon Cruz (1962–   ) Eddie Corbett on *The Courtship of Eddie's Father*, 1969–72.

Jodie Foster (1962–   ) *Taxi Driver, The Accused, Silence of the Lambs*.

Billy Gray (1938–   ) Bud Anderson on *Father Knows Best*, 1954–60.

Rusty Hamer (1947–1990) Rusty Williams on *Make Room for Daddy*, 1953–65.

Ron Howard (1954–   ) Opie Taylor on *The Andy Griffith Show*, 1960–68.

Anissa Jones (1958–1976) Buffy Jones on *Family Affair*, 1966–1971.

Trent Lehman (1961–1982) Butch Everett on *Nanny and the Professor*, 1970–71.

Emmanuel Lewis (1971–   ) Webster Long on *Webster*, 1983–87.

Stanley Livingston (1950–   ) Chip Douglas on *My Three Sons*, 1960–72.

Steven Mond (1971–   ) Robbie Jayson on *Diff'rent Strokes*.

David Nelson (1936–   ) David Nelson on *The Adventures of Ozzie & Harriet*, 1952–66.

Ricky Nelson (1940–1985) Ricky Nelson on *The Adventures of Ozzie & Harriet*, 1952–66.

Jay North (1951–   ) Dennis Mitchell on *Dennis the Menace*, 1959–63.

Paul Petersen (1945–   ) Jeff Stone on *The Donna Reed Show*, 1958–66.

Mackenzie Phillips (1959–   ) Julie Cooper on *One Day at a Time*, 1975–80, 1981–84.

Dana Plato (1964–1999) Kimberly Drummond on *Diff'rent Strokes*, 1978–86.

Jon Provost (1950–   ) Timmy Martin on *Lassie*, 1957–64.

Tommy Rettig (1941–1996) Jeff Miller on *Lassie*, 1954–57.

Adam Rich (1968–   ) Nicholas Bradford on *Eight Is Enough*, 1977–81.

Shavar Ross (1971–   ) Dudley Ramsey on *Diff'rent Strokes*.

Glenn Scarpelli (1966–   ) Alex Handris on *One Day at a Time*, 1980–83.

Ricky Schroder (1970–   ) Ricky Stratton on *Silver Spoons*, 1982–87.

Johnny Whitaker (1959–   ) Jody Davis on *Family Affair*, 1966–71.

CHAPTER ONE

THE PEOPLE VS. GARY COLEMAN

Q: "I wouldn't think there were people out there who genuinely don't like Gary Coleman."

A: "Yeah, you really wouldn't expect it, [but] there's people out there."

— BRYAN MADDEN, "LEAVE GARY COLEMAN ALONE" WEB SITE

She said, well, that's why you're a washed-up child star. And then, give or take a beat, he socked her in the eye.

Gary Coleman's timing, as usual, was impeccable.

Criminal or moral implications aside, the punch, thrown during an autograph-request-gone-wrong exchange, was the perfect blow for the cause of the former child star — the kick-me loser of our TV times. And it was delivered by the perfect emissary — the walking, talking punchline of his generation.

There was a downside, of course. The punch landed the onetime *Diff'rent Strokes* star in an Inglewood, California, courtroom on trial for misdemeanor assault and battery. If convicted, he stood to lose his license as a security guard – the mall-policing business being his most recent means of a paycheck. In a karmically just world, the judge would have tossed the criminal complaint and ruled that the fan, at fault or no, had it coming. That we *all* had it coming. That Coleman was the wronged party. That Coleman was the one due make-good compensation. That Coleman was a class-action suit unto himself. Because if not every former child star is Gary Coleman, then Gary Coleman surely is Every Former Child Star.

He is the frustrations, the failures, the slights. He is the successes, the riches, the fame.

He is them.

He used to be us, too. Once upon a time, he was just a kid. Just like us.

So, how come we sorta hate him?

We didn't always, you know. We used to need him. *Diff'rent Strokes*, canned sitcom or no, helped kill a perfectly boring Thursday (and, later, Saturday) night. If you were too young to drive, date, or drink, Gary Coleman was your man. In the late 1970s, he was the kid world's representative at the big people's table. There was nobody with more juice. Nobody higher paid. Nobody more ubiquitous. Gary Coleman was the Shirley Temple of the sitcom world. The all-timer. Everybody else was just an Emmanuel Lewis-style knockoff.

Put simply, he was the state-of-the-art TV child star.

And less than a decade later, he was the state-of-the-art TV former child star.

What happened?

We grew up, and he didn't.

He got older, too, sure, but he didn't look or act older. And besides, as of the mid-1980s, he was still on that stupid – yes, stupid, we could say now – *Diff'rent Strokes*. What was up with that? Give it up, Arnold, okay? Or at least get out of the sixth grade before you, like, grow a mustache. Geez.

Once you got to drive, date, and drink, you definitely did *not* need *Diff'rent Strokes*. You did *not* need Gary Coleman. And so we haven't needed Gary Coleman for almost twenty years.

But what about Gary Coleman? What is he supposed to do with that? Disappear?

> "I long for days where I'm not recognized. I look forward to days when I'm not recognized. But since I've been [on TV] in practically every English and other-speaking country in the world there's really no place that doesn't know me." (Gary Coleman)

And there it is – the Gary Coleman Paradox, the Former Child Star Dilemma. When their time is up, when their shows are canceled, we want them to go away. We want them to disappear.

But they can't. Reruns assure otherwise; our TV-burned memories assure otherwise. We don't need to see another second of another *Diff'rent Strokes* to know that Gary Coleman *is* pint-sized Arnold Jackson Drummond from Harlem. Now and forever. He can't go away; *they* can't go away.

And for that, we make them pay.

The TV former child star is the kid brother or kid sister who keeps tagging along. Keeps pestering us. And, most of all, keeps dragging us back to the stupid little kid *we* used to be. Keeps returning us to that night, that living room, when we had nothing better to do than lie around and watch some rich-and-famous, *TV Guide*-cover kid – some jerk our age – make an entire live studio audience laugh. Is it too melodramatic to suggest that one day, we vowed, we'd show him? We'd show them all. We'd grow into cool jobs and, consciously or no, we'd enforce strict standards for our former TV buddies:

Get a new TV show – or go away.

We don't need you anymore.

The occasional autograph excepted.

THE AUTOGRAPH

California Uniforms sells shirts and pants and shorts and hand-cuffs. It's a tidy supply shop on a tidy boulevard in a tidy middle-class business district in tidy Hawthorne, California. It's across the street from a Denny's and next door to a kids' dentist. The scene is all so perfectly perfect in a perfectly ordinary sort of way (except maybe for the part about the handcuffs). About two thousand miles east is a K-Mart in Zion, Illinois – another bastion of the would-be perfectly ordinary. The K-Mart (there's actually two in Zion these days) is where Gary Coleman once said he might have ended up, happily, had he not gone to Chicago to make commercials in the mid-1970s, or moved to Hollywood in the late 1970s to do a sitcom. But Gary Coleman didn't end up at the Zion Big K. He ended up here. At California Uniforms. Living out the defining Former Child Star Moment.

It was July 31, 1998. A Thursday afternoon. Coleman, then thirty, stopped by the shop for a bulletproof vest. He needed one on account of his line of work – he was a security guard at the nearby Fox Hills Mall in Culver City, California. It could be argued he also needed one for his other line of work – being the most recognizable, most targeted former child star on the planet. But Gary Coleman was in no mood to argue. He was in a hurry.

While browsing in the store, Coleman was approached by another customer, one Tracy R. Fields, a five-foot-six, 205-pound municipal bus driver. She'd come by California Uniforms to buy a pair of shorts. Then she saw Gary Coleman. And she did what people are wont to do when they see Gary Coleman. She went, "Oh, my God! There's Gary Coleman!"

Fields didn't want trouble; she wanted the man's autograph. Red-hot famous or no, security guard or no, lovable or no, Gary Coleman is Gary Coleman is Gary Coleman. You don't run into the genuine article too often. And Tracy R. Fields wanted Gary Coleman's autograph – because, well, "Oh, my God! There's Gary Coleman!"

> "As long as [fans] call me by my name, they got my attention. Normally people are very quick and candid with their words and then they're gone. You know, 'Thank you very much, I love your work,' and, you know, that's all I ever need." (Gary Coleman)

At California Uniforms, Coleman apparently did not get what he needed. What happened was either:

(A) Fields politely asked Coleman for his autograph. He scribbled his signature on a piece of paper and handed it to Fields. She asked him to personalize the TV-land memento for her son. He flipped out, ripping up the autograph, "calling her numerous derogatory names," and (inexplicably) charging, "You black people are all alike." Then, give or take a beat, he punched her in the eye.

(B) Fields rudely accosted Coleman, shouting, "Can I have your autograph?" The affable, careful Coleman obliged. He scribbled his signature on a piece of paper and handed it to Fields. Unsatisfied, she countered (loudly), "Ain't you gonna put something nice on it?" He decided she didn't deserve his autograph and tore it up. Fields turned "scary" and "ugly" – the heft of her breasts alone enough to corner Coleman's four-foot-eight, "eighty-six pounds of nothing" frame. Then, give

or take a beat, he punched her in the eye. (The better to
distract her from hitting him first.)

Story A was Fields' version of events (corroborated by eye-
witness accounts). Story B was Coleman's version of events.
About the only point that the two parties agreed on was a line
of conversation – delivered by Fields after Coleman destroyed
the vaunted autograph – that definitively upped the incident
from the annals of a quickly forgotten trash-talk fest to a fist-
flying, on-the-criminal-dockets melee.

The line went something like this:

Well, that's why you didn't make it as a successful actor as an
adult.

Well, there it is, isn't it? The bane of Gary Coleman, the
bane of the former child stars, indeed, the very reason we call
them *former* child stars: "Well, that's why you didn't make it as
a successful actor as an adult."

Game, set, match.

In court, Coleman would say, "She made sure everybody in
the store heard it and it was embarrassing – quite hurtful."

And so Coleman made Fields hurt.

"When she told him, 'No wonder you're a washed-up star'
. . . he came from over the counter all the way over here and
punched her," store owner Rosemary Jones said. Before the
incident was over, Fields claimed, she suffered at least $1.25
million worth of severe mental and emotional distress, as well
as physical pain from repeated blows to the face, neck, stomach,
and aforementioned bosom. "Despicable conduct," her resulting
civil lawsuit concluded.

In between the dis and the starter punch, there were a few
choice exchanges (Fields: "Fuck you, and I'm not going to
watch you on TV no more"; Coleman: "No, fuck *you*, lady."),

but those were throwaways – a little gratuitous R-rated cussing to keep things interesting for the audience. In a good movie, a director would have recognized the insults for extraneous lines and cut straight to the heart of the matter: fan insults ex-child actor; ex-child actor slugs fan. But, then again, when was the last time Gary Coleman was in a good movie?

Cue the laughtrack.

> "Gary Coleman's trial is under way. He's accused of punching a woman who asked him for an autograph. And today the judge ordered the woman to undergo a psychiatric exam to find out why the hell she was asking Gary Coleman for his autograph."
> (Jay Leno, *The Tonight Show*)

THE PLEA

Gary Coleman blew his nose. His legal counsel patted his shoulder, pushed him a box of Kleenex. It was winter 1999. And it was over. He was copping a plea.

In the case of the people vs. Gary Coleman, the defendant didn't wait to hear what the jury had to say. Why bother? He was, after all, Gary Coleman. Did he have any reason to suspect they'd cut him a break?

> "Oh, Gary, stop while you're ahead."
> "Gary, you have no self-respect obviously."
> "Gary, why don't you go out and get a job like everybody else?"

That's what we – TV anchors, morning-radio callers, general all-around people – say publicly about Gary Coleman. We sorta hate him, remember?

Maybe Gary Coleman remembered. Maybe he didn't want to run the risk of a year in jail. Maybe he didn't want to chance a record-staining conviction. Maybe he simply didn't want to leave his future up to a jury of his peers. (Honestly, why would he have wanted to do that?)

And, so, in that Inglewood courtroom on February 4, 1999, shortly after the completion of closing arguments, a teary Coleman, wearing the white suit that should have made him look like the good guy (but left him a dead ringer for a 1980s-club-going relic), short-circuited his own due process, pleading no contest to a misdemeanor count of disturbing the peace. Coleman was dinged with a ninety-day suspended jail term, a $400 fine, a $1,180 so-called "penalty fee," and ordered to complete fifty-two sessions of an anger-management course.

The former child star – who figuratively, if not literally, fought for the cause, for the respect, of the former child stars – lost.

How appropriate.

After all, that's what former child stars do, right? They lose. They're losers. They're cursed. People who *used to be* popular? *Used to be* rich? *Used to be* on TV? Please. Welcome to today: we're a plugged-in, hard-wired, satellite-equipped culture of TVs and VCRs and computers and DVDs and maxed-out power strips. If it doesn't happen on a screen (preferably on one of the Big Three networks), it doesn't happen. If *you* don't happen on a screen, you don't happen.

The former child star doesn't happen. The former child star is obsolete.

And so that is how Gary Coleman, would-be comic genius, devolves into Gary Coleman, joke. It happens to the best of 'em.

> "There's nothing I can do — it's public domain. People have the right under the federal government to joke about me or my situation or my name or anything about me. I can't stop that."
> (Gary Coleman)

And he won't stop it. It's not his to stop. This train has been running a lot longer than Gary Coleman's been running (or stumbling). As big as Gary Coleman is (or was), he's not bigger than this. We knew — or thought we knew — how his career was going to implode before it barely began. It's like that Chris Rock line about (and delivered to) the 1990s-era bubblegum boy bands: "Don't you know how this movie's going to end?"

Exactly. Don't they? And how could they not? Are we the only ones watching all those people-used-to-think-I'm-cool-but-now-I'm-really-bitter-that-I'm-not *Behind the Music Biography About the True Hollywood-Story* TV specials?

If Gary Coleman hadn't, say, sued his parents, gone bankrupt, toiled as a security guard, socked a fan, and ended up on trial, we would have been shocked. Instead of asking him how come he's not on TV anymore, we would have asked him (with equally annoying regularity): So, how come you're not cursed like all the other former child stars?

How come you're not robbing banks?

How come you're not broke?

How come you're not bitter?

Oh, make no mistake, the Gary Colemans of the world *are* a people doomed to failure — not always by their actions, but by our expectations. You get arrested, you're a loser. You settle into a comfortable, if obscure, existence, you're a loser. You attempt an ill-fated comeback, you're a loser. You score a prime time comeback, you're special. You don't, you're not.

And *that's* the curse of the former child star. So maybe Gary Coleman shouldn't take this national-joke thing personally. Maybe he shouldn't wish himself into the checkout register at the Zion Big K. Maybe he should accept his tribulations as destiny.

And maybe he should take heart. He won't be the last once-beloved kid personality blindsided by his would-be fans and protectors.

He was not the first.

CHAPTER TWO

THE
FIRST KID

"He is a fine little fellow and a gold mine for us."

— JOHN H. COOGAN, ON SON JACKIE COOGAN

The first was Jackie Coogan. A long time ago, before there was Gary Coleman, before there was *Diff'rent Strokes*, before there was TV, there was Jackie Coogan.

And while we said we were going to talk about TV kids – not movie kids – we'll make an exception for Jackie Coogan. Because he was the first.

The first child star. The first former child star. The first former child star to make headlines for merely being a former child star.

And that's why we're here, right? To talk about the origins of "the curse." To talk about how America's least wanted were goners from the start.

Try this for an opener: Jackie Coogan was asleep when he first met Charlie Chaplin – or, rather, when Chaplin first met Jackie. Snoozing Jackie was unconscious, unknowing, unwitting. And that's how the child star was born.

The scene couldn't have been any more apt if Chaplin had picked Coogan's pockets. Chaplin, of course, didn't. But not to worry. Someone else did.

The rest of Jackie's story goes something like this . . .

John Leslie "Jackie" Coogan, Jr., a veteran performer and impossibly cute tyke, was born on October 26, 1914, in Los Angeles. Charles Spencer "Charlie" Chaplin, a veteran silent-era screen star and critically certified comic genius, was born on April 16, 1889, in London. Their paths crossed in 1919. Coogan was four, Chaplin about thirty. Acting on a tip from moviehouse owner Sid Grauman (or so one story went), the genius caught the tyke's act at the Orpheum Theatre, then one of Los Angeles' leading meccas for mirth and general vaudeville merriment. (The genius remembered it like this: he needed a break and went to catch a show.) Jackie had been earning his keep (or, at least, contributing to the Coogan family coffers) since he was a toddler. He made his first stage appearance at sixteen months, crashing his parents' act at Keith's Riverside theater in New York. By the time Chaplin happened upon Jackie, the Banged One had long since become a regular bit in the family act, which was led by his father, John H. "Jack" Coogan, and mother, the former Lillian Dolliver. The Coogans' specialty was clog dancing – a simple, folkloric rite, not to be confused with the latter-day *Lord of the Dance* spectacle/mess. The talent had kept the New York-born Jack Coogan in showbiz since he was a kid himself, and it eventually landed him and his on the vaunted Orpheum circuit. After moving West, the elder Coogan even earned bits in several films. Make no mistake, though: Jack Coogan was not a star. Nor was Lillian, nor Jackie. They were working vaudevillians.

Enter Charlie Chaplin.

If it wasn't love at first sight (and, by Chaplin's own account, it was not – Chaplin, he wrote in his autobiography, did *not* immediately know he needed any kid, much less Jackie, for a new film project), then it certainly was intrigue at first sight. Legend has it that the night after the Orpheum show, Chaplin arranged to meet the Coogans at the Alexandria Hotel in Los Angeles' downtown theater district. Chaplin himself wrote that he didn't even think of Jackie for a good week after the performance. The indisputable fact is that Jackie *did* make an impression on the screen star. While Chaplin found Jack Coogan's routine "nothing extraordinary," he saw something in the little kid who'd come out at the close of the gig, bowed, done a couple of dance steps and then "knowingly," Chaplin wrote, waved at the audience. Far from obnoxious or cloying, Chaplin found the little kid "charming." And so came about the fabled Alexandria summit. It was about 11 o'clock, the story went, and Jackie was tired. By the time Chaplin showed, Jackie was asleep in a chair in the lobby. He was roused to talk with the iconic film star – and he did so, briefly.

And then – iconic film star, or no – Jackie fell back asleep. Jackie was, as the *New York Times* put it a couple of years later in recounting this insta-legend, "unaware of the impression he had made on the bothersome stranger."

In short time, the bothersome stranger called on Jackie for his two-reeler *A Day's Pleasure* (1919), a look at a family outing in slapstick form. Chaplin had been moved to sign Jackie after he heard (erroneously, it turned out) that big-screen rival Fatty Arbuckle wanted the boy for a movie of his own. About a week after the Orpheum show, Camp Chaplin contacted Camp Coogan and asked if Jackie was available to do a picture. "Why, of course," Jack Coogan replied, according to Chaplin, "you can have the little punk." In *A Day's Pleasure*, an unbilled Jackie played the younger of the Little Tramp's two sons. The gig was reputedly a screen test – to see how Jackie looked on-screen, a curious notion since the miniature Jackie, to audiences at least, was barely on view. The gig was also reputedly a bonding test – to see if the genius and the tyke got along. Whatever the case, whatever the criteria, Jackie apparently passed.

"A PICTURE WITH A SMILE — AND PERHAPS, A TEAR"

At age four, Jackie Coogan was a development deal waiting to happen. He had the sort of big, brown saucer eyes that rightfully belonged to puppy dogs. He had the sort of soft brown hair that arguably belonged to girls – but rightfully belonged to him (the better to frame those eyes). And he had a smile that could rip your heart out. He also had tear ducts that responded on command – the resulting sobs of which could also rip your heart out.

In short, Jackie Coogan was the standard-issue kid star before there was such a thing.

Then, as now, the one thing a star needed above all was a star vehicle. And with Chaplin's *The Kid*, Jackie had his vehicle. When the project started in 1919, Jackie was about four and a half and the film was called *The Waif*. By the time it was completed in 1920, Jackie was five and a half and the film was called *The Kid*.

In between was a long, strange, trip that seemed to make little sense to anyone but Chaplin himself. The film was, Jackie said, "little vignettes that . . . hung together by a small gossamer web." He might have been too specific. By all accounts, Chaplin made up *The Kid* as he went along. There was comedy (the Kid hurling rocks through windows so his Little Tramp of a dad could fix them – for a fee), there was melodrama (the Kid being hauled away – tearfully – from the duo's hovel by the authorities), there was fantasy (the Tramp being reunited with the Kid in heaven, or at least a courtyard where everyone wears wings).

If the set seemed crazed, the process jumbled, well, then that was filmmaking. And up until *The Kid*, Chaplin had not made a film. He'd made shorts. Two-reelers. Three-reelers. By comparison, *The Kid*, which eventually clocked in at about sixty minutes, was an epic. Amazing what a kid's face – a kid's expressive face – could do for an artist's range.

Jackie's role amid this chaos (a chaos that included Chaplin trekking to Utah with the reels to prevent estranged wife Mildred Harris from absconding with his filmic baby during a nasty divorce battle) was simple: to be the kid in *The Kid*. That was about it (excepting the time Chaplin called on Jackie to unleash his most adorable, irresistible little-boy moves – the dance steps, the smiles, the pratfalls – at an impromptu performance to quell backers who were uneasy over the behind-schedule project). Any of the traumas later associated with the Hollywood child star was not present on *The Kid*. There were no nefarious threats to shoot pets (the better to make 'em cry). There were no studio-prescribed pill-popping sessions (better to keep 'em peppy). That sort of stuff just didn't happen.

Jackie thought well of Chaplin, remembering him as a director who, despite the imperious perks granted the all-powerful person on a set, patiently coached him through their routines. For his part, Chaplin found Jackie "as inattentive to his work as any normal child of his age would be" – a high compliment, actually, from a filmmaker who very much needed a "normal child" to help sell his sentimental, uncharacteristically un-cartoony tale.

If Jackie was unaware of the machinery at work, his parents were not. They knew Chaplin wanted and *needed* their kid for *The Kid* – and they weren't thrilled by the original offer of $40 a week. Chaplin acquiesced. Jackie got $75 a week. On paper, anyway.

The Kid opened in January 1921. Jackie got third billing (as

"Jack Coogan"), after Carl Miller (seen briefly as the deadbeat dad) and Chaplin regular Edna Purviance (as the mother). Chaplin, whose name was all over the credits from the first flickering flames, took what would be called a modest fourth billing (until you noticed his name was ever so slightly larger than the others). The audience and critics, meanwhile, had their own ideas as to who deserved star treatment.

To say *The Kid* was an "instant hit" is to confuse 1920s-era Hollywood for Y2K-era Hollywood. Seventy years ago, "instant hits" essentially didn't – couldn't – exist. Movies didn't "open wide" – there were no five thousand prints to be screened in five thousand theaters across the country. Movies opened in one city – maybe a few cities – before venturing out to the hinterlands (i.e., the stuff outside of New York and Los Angeles). But as much as any 1921 film could be deigned an "instant hit," *The Kid* was just that. ("All precedents broken!! The greatest picture of its kind ever made," local theater ads of the day blared.) In New York, the film debuted at a benefit gala at Carnegie Hall – and it was all uphill from there. "A source of immense delight," judged the *New York Times*, which took pains (as did other reviews) to note the "wonderful youngster" name of Jackie Coogan. Said our nation's newspaper of record, "He is The Kid, and he will be remembered in the same image with Chaplin."

That about nailed it.

Jackie *was* The Kid. (Jackie "Kid" Coogan, in fact, fast became his newspaper-blurb moniker.) And Jackie *was* remembered for being in the same "image" with Chaplin. The one-sheet ad for *The Kid* said it all (in photo-form): Chaplin, in full Tramp regalia, peering around a corner; little Jackie, in full Kid regalia (ragamuffin overalls and floppy hat), peering around the same corner (if not peering out from under Chaplin himself). That was *The Kid* in a visual soundbite – and it was an image that was repeated and reproduced and replayed.

For three years after its initial release, *The Kid* played non-stop, working its way through fifty countries – and through each of them, Jackie "Kid" Coogan was there, peering out from beneath the great one. Actually, in short time, it became hard to tell: who was the great one? Even if there weren't really "instant hits," Jackie Coogan was an outright "instant star." Judged the *New York Times* in February 1921, "Jack Coogan . . . has achieved cinemagraphic fame more suddenly and at a younger age, probably, than any other screen player. . . ." More astonishing (and impressive), he did it without Web sites, direct-mail campaigns, *Entertainment Tonight*, or any modern-day advertising conveniences. Jackie's fame was a phenomenon. From the night at the Alexandria in 1919 to early 1921, he went from scraping by on $75 a week to being presented with a $5,000 thank-you bonus from Chaplin and Co., to pulling down $62,000, and, later, a reputed $300,000 a year making even more movies for Associated First National (née First National), the studio behind *The Kid*.

By April 1921, Jackie was rating headlines for coming down with bronchitis – an illness that prompted fellow stars to wire good-luck grams, newly converted fans to send him jars of homemade jelly, and slugger Babe Ruth to visit him at his New York hotel room, twice. "Other boys went to see Babe Ruth," Jackie would say. "Babe Ruth came to see me."

What was the attraction? What was the hook?

The cutes.

Chaplin might have been impish, Mary Pickford might have been sweet, Douglas Fairbanks might have been heroic, but Jackie Coogan had the cutes. He was the entire package – in a tiny, adorable, cute, little package. Maybe he couldn't outduel Fairbanks at swordplay, but he had heart and cunning and the audience just knew he'd acquit himself nicely by the final reel. Even if he had to cry himself the advantage.

Plus, he had the cutes.

Hollywood hadn't been the first to realize that audiences were suckers for little kids – the first guy who put a preschooler and a puppy dog on a stage and noticed the surge on the applause meter figured that one out. The first kid who escaped a spanking for breaking something he shouldn't have broken on account of he said something funny at dinner got the idea, too.

Sooner rather than later, some kid was going to be *the* kid of the movies. The ticket-buyers were primed. The people with the cameras just needed to direct their lenses in the right direction. Jackie Coogan just needed to hit his marks. Smiling, crying, dancing, looking cute on cue?

Cinchy.

It was all the other stuff that got hard.

THE "PRIZED THEATRICAL PROPERTY"

No one quits while they're ahead. No one goes, "You know, I've just done this great little piece of work – something that'll stand up through the years. I think that's enough. More than I can ask for, really. I'm done." No one says, "No, please don't write me that check."

Why would Jackie Coogan be the first? Besides, what was there to say no to? Fame, money, fun? This was prime time, babe. Jackie was a road-tested showbiz kid. Performing is what he did. It's what he enjoyed. The movie-star lifestyle stuff that went along with the career wasn't bad, either. After *The Kid*, Jackie's family, which as of 1925 also included younger brother Robert, purchased a ranch in Pine Valley, California, near San Diego. When Jackie wanted milk, he said, he drank milk from one of his ranch's cows. Back in Hollywood, the Coogans had a fancy spread along Wilshire Boulevard. The house came complete with a rare-for-its-day swimming pool. And when Jackie wanted swimming lessons, he said, he got swimming lessons – from the three-time, gold-winning Olympic medalist next door, Duke Kahanmoku.

The money was piling in (as much as $22,000 a week). The credits were piling up (a dozen pictures in a half-dozen years: the aforementioned *Peck's Bad Boy*, *Trouble*, *Oliver Twist*, *Daddy*, *Circus Days*, *Long Live the King*, *A Boy of Flanders*, *Little Robinson Crusoe*, *The Rag Man*, *Old Clothes*, *Johnny Get Your Hair Cut*, *The Bugle Call*, *Buttons*).

In a dismissive review of Jackie's *Kid* followup, *Peck's Bad Boy* (1921), the *New York Times* snidely found it "inevitable that the boy should become a prized theatrical property and be exploited for his box office value."

The paper didn't get it.

In an unprecedented 1923 deal with Metro, Jackie didn't just make movies, he made money *off* movies – a sixty-forty split of a film's profits went *his* way. True, his parents kept him on a strict (if generous for the time) $6.50 weekly allowance, but that was to keep him in touch with his kid self. The important thing was, Jackie Coogan Productions was in business. "Now let's get this straight," Jackie would say, by way of illustrating his pull back in the day, "Wallace Beery [his *Trouble* costar] – everybody – worked [for] *me*. We hired people. The only person I ever worked with was Charles Chaplin."

So, was Hollywood, as the newspaper review charged, really exploiting Jackie Coogan? Sure. But he was exploiting right back. He was making millions. In 1923, he was the No. 1 box-office star in the United States – ahead of Rudolph Valentino and that Fairbanks fellow.

Then came puberty.

If Jackie Coogan was Hollywood's first child star, then he was also the first child star to try to ride out the onslaught of hormones that tend to make a cute little kid a not-so-cute, gangly teen. To be sure, the Coogan camp – in a pre-Madonna, Madonna-esque way – *did* try the image-makeover thing. Jackie's 1927 film *Johnny Get Your Hair Cut* featured just that – Jackie getting a haircut. His trademark bangs and longish locks were shorn onscreen. If not yet a man, then at least Jackie was no longer "The Kid." And that was the problem.

Being "The Kid" – the adorable, huggable kid with the cutes – had been Jackie's hook. Image-conscious movie stars, even a supposed morph queen like Madonna, never *really* radically alter their looks. John Wayne always looks like John Wayne always acts like John Wayne. (Same goes for Madonna, minus a hair-color change or three.) But – damn that nature – Jackie Coogan could not always look (or act) like Jackie "Kid" Coogan. He couldn't help it. Child stars can't help it. They get new faces. They get new voices. And their new selves have to go stand in the job line like everybody else.

Jackie was no different. After a golden, nearly decade-long run, his time was up. His moneyed Metro deal ended – conveniently, for the studio – when he was a not-so-cute thirteen. Pioneering the hideout technique, Jackie took a break from the big screen. Went to England. Did some stage work. He returned to Hollywood in 1930, at age sixteen, to star in the first film adaptation of Mark Twain's *Tom Sawyer*. It was Jackie's first talkie – and, as it turned out, one of his last star vehicles. The new look wasn't working. At least, not enough to land him glamorous, name-above-the-title gigs.

It was, as Jackie's manager Arthur L. Bernstein told the press in 1935, a "difficult age" – too old for kid parts, too young for romantic leads.

"A difficult age?" Arthur Bernstein had no idea.

Or, then again, maybe he did.

THE BEGINNING OF THE END
(OR THE END OF THE BEGINNING)

In the mid-1930s, Jackie Coogan's whirlwind life switched into reverse. It was still whirlwind – it was just a *bad* whirlwind.

MAY 4, 1935: Jackie and four buddies – his dad included – leave Hollywood, bound for the Coogan ranch in Pine Valley. In the car with the Coogans are Junior Durkin, a twenty-year-old up-and-coming actor featured in Katharine Hepburn's *Little Women*; Robert Horner, a playwright; and Charles Jones, foreman at the Coogan ranch. About fifty-five miles east of San Diego, the car – driven by John Coogan – is said to be forced off the road by a passing vehicle. The Coogan car careens down an embankment, crashes into rocks, and rolls over four times. Jackie, riding in the rumble seat, is thrown clear. Seriously injured, he lives. He is the only one. The headline in the next day's newspaper adds psychic pain to the physical toll: "Junior Durkin Dies As Crash Kills 4." Jackie takes second billing in a subhead.

JUNE 21, 1935: Jackie is named in a pair of lawsuits worth $250,000 by the families of Junior Durkin and Robert Horner. The complaints charge the ex-child star should have commandeered the wheel from his father prior to the accident because the elder Coogan was (1) driving too fast and (2) drunk. By July, Jackie faces a total of three lawsuits stemming from the crash. They seek a combined $600,000. (The legal mess isn't cleared up until April 1936, when a court finds John Coogan had *not* been drinking at the time of the crash, and that Jackie was not liable for the resulting deaths.)

OCTOBER 26, 1935: Jackie turns twenty-one, "thereby [becoming] the possessor of the first portion of the million dollars, more or less, that he earned as a child movie star years ago," the Associated Press reports. The newly minted millionaire, however, sounds a less-than-enthusiastic note. "So, I'm a man now," Jackie says. "I don't know whether I like it or not."

DECEMBER 1935: Jackie announces his engagement to nineteen-year-old starlet Betty Grable, but the couple's plans to wed the following June are quickly scuttled when RKO reminds Grable she can't wed until she's at least twenty-one. Jackie has no such studio hassles and/or deals.

FEBRUARY 1936: Jackie and Grable, in Chicago for a joint stage appearance, are robbed by two men in what sounds like an early version of the carjack. The bad guys make off with $50 and Grable's five-carat engagement ring. Not that the police don't believe the couple or anything, but they ask the two to submit to lie-detector tests.

NOVEMBER 20, 1937: Jackie weds Grable at St. Brendan's Catholic Church in Los Angeles. Bob Hope is an usher; Jack Haley (*The Wizard of Oz*) is in attendance. The papers duly note the event as: Betty Grable (name-above-the-title star) weds Jackie Coogan (who was in *The Kid* eighteen years ago).

APRIL 4, 1938: All hell breaks loose.

On that April day in 1938, a lawsuit was filed in Los Angeles

Superior Court accusing one Lillian R. Coogan Bernstein and one Arthur L. Bernstein of cheating one Jackie Coogan out of an estimated $4 million in earnings and investments compiled during the heyday of the latter party's career. Lillian was Jackie's mom. Arthur was his manager and, since 1935, Lillian's husband.

The Coogan suit claimed that for all Jackie's years on the Hollywood A-list, he had netted the following (give or take a sock or two): food, clothing, housing, a college education (at the University of Southern California and Villanova), railroad transportation, $1,500 in gifts, a $50 offering on birthdays and Christmas, and $1,000 on the day before his twenty-first birthday.

Oh, and the $6.50 weekly allowance.

Oh, and the money pipeline (including the $6.50-a-week thing) was shut down on October 26, 1935 – the day Jackie turned twenty-one.

What about the "first portion of the million dollars . . . that he earned as a child movie star years ago?" What about the trust fund (est. 1922) where "his earnings [were] to be impounded?"

Well, what about them?

"I have waited patiently for some time for my mother and Bernstein to make an accounting to me of my property," Jackie said the day he filed suit. "I owe a duty to my wife and to myself not to wait longer."

"The Kid" absolved his late father – the force behind Jackie Coogan Productions – of any guilt ("If my father had lived, no controversy of this sort would have arisen"), and directed his ire at his living stepfather ("All I know is that I have earned millions of dollars and don't have anything now, while my stepfather is rolling in wealth").

By way of defense, Lillian and Arthur Bernstein maintained complete innocence. In the words of their lawyer Charles J. Katz, Jackie had "received everything that he is entitled to and more."

The way the Bernsteins saw it, Jackie's mother was entitled to everything Jackie had earned up until the day he became an adult because, well, that was the way existing California law saw it, too. Any argument by Jackie to the contrary was the result of "hallucination" on the young man's part. On a personal level, Mother Coogan was at a loss to explain her twenty-four-year-old son's agitated, suing-mad state. The two had always been so close, she said. And besides, the whole business about her refusing to give Jackie any part of the estate was nonsense. Said Lillian, "No promises were ever made to give him anything."

Actually, Jackie told the press his mother *had* made a promise: "It's all mine and Arthur's," he quoted Lillian as saying, "and so far as we are concerned you will never get a cent."

Well, then.

One could go on and on with sordid details ("If Betty thinks she is marrying a rich boy she is very much mistaken. He hasn't a cent. Jackie is a pauper." – Mother Coogan's reputed advice to Betty Grable, per Grable) and petty squabbles (Jackie charging Arthur Bernstein sat up in the clubhouse at the racetrack, placing $100 bets, while he toiled in the $1 seats, placing $2 bets) and devilish tales ("Don't ever teach him arithmetic, because someday he's going to wonder where all of his money has gone to." – Mother Coogan's reputed advice to a fellow mother, per columnist Walter Winchell) and salacious innuendo (Jackie accusing Arthur Bernstein of "stepping out" with an entertainer name of Miss Luana; Metro's L.B. Mayer reputedly offering Jackie a new movie deal if he dropped the lawsuit) until you had enough material for two season's worth of *Mysteries & Scandals*. But when all the dish was dished, you'd end up with the same sorry truth: Jackie Coogan never had a chance.

On April 20, 1939, the warring parties – perhaps spent of ammo, vitriol, or attorneys' fees – called a truce and told the court they'd agreed to agree. The lawsuit was duly removed from the docket. Then on August 16, 1939, it was all over. As part of the settlement entered into the Los Angeles Superior Court, Jackie – who'd asked for $4 million, who'd auctioned off the furnishings from his Beverly Hills house as the case dragged on – got $126,000. His mom got the other $126,000.

Subsequently in 1939, California lawmakers approved what was to be known as the Coogan Law, early (but not complete, it would be argued in the years to come) protections against parents and/or guardians gobbling up a child actor's paycheck. Behind the law, a novel idea: a child's earnings should belong to the child. The one child the law would never, ever protect: Jackie Coogan.

So this is what it came down to: After more than a dozen movies, after two decades in Hollywood, after being the sort of kid that Babe Ruth would visit – not once, but twice – Jackie Coogan was worth a grand sum of $252,000, of which he was entitled to half. Now, seeing as how Lillian Coogan figured she had the right to the whole (depleted) kitty anyway, Jackie making off with fifty percent wasn't all that bad, huh? Why, Jackie might have even gone off and celebrated the victory with his wife, except . . . Oh, wait. He didn't have a wife anymore. On New Year's Day 1939, Jackie and Betty Grable had separated, with the reserve clause that they "hoped to return to each other when his financial troubles were straightened out." Unfortunately, Jackie found that a tenth of a million dollars didn't go very far in the straightening-out department. Coogan and Grable divorced later that year.

So, to recap: in 1939, Jackie Coogan, formerly the No. 1 box-office attraction in Hollywood, formerly the most famous boy in the world, had: no wife, no career, and no money.

Welcome to the world, former child star.

THE SURFER

"No matter what I do now, I was the first," Jackie said in 1972. "Nobody can ever take that away from me."

He was right. How do you top an opening act like that?

Scandal, tragedy, familial strife, financial ruin . . . lawyers?

It's enough to make you think Jackie Coogan starred on *Diff'rent Strokes*.

But seriously: this is a no-brainer, right? This is how things had to turn out for the world's very first former child star, otherwise he wouldn't have been the world's very first former child star – he'd have been Ron Howard or something. If the first former child star turned out to be a happily married, well-adjusted, professionally and financially stable upstanding citizen, this whole former-child-star thing wouldn't be as much fun, would it? Not for us, anyway. We *need* this story. It makes our world safe for "the curse." It makes our every cliché fall into place. It makes Gary Coleman so much easier to explain.

Now, not to spoil the argument or anything, but Jackie Coogan pretty much *did* turn out to be a happily married, well-adjusted, professionally and financially stable upstanding citizen. Contrary to popular belief, his story, his life, did not end in 1939.

First, there was the Good War. Unlike kid actors who came of age in the 1950s and beyond, Jackie had an honest-to-God world war to lose himself in. Didn't matter if he'd once blubbered onscreen or modeled short pants or been known to a nation as "Peck's Bad Boy." In the end, and in uniform, he was a soldier – just like the other guys. Sure, Jackie got ribbed by recruits who held him personally responsible for the Dutch-boy haircut – a look their parents had forced on them in their youth. But in the end, and in uniform, Jackie and the guys all looked the same (and wore the same haircut). No longer a failed star or an ex-star, Jackie was a soldier. It was an identity he perfected through nearly five years in the army as a glider instructor. Most of his World War II tenure was spent amid the relative peace of California, but when the call came for a raid in the China-Burma-India theater, Jackie was there. And he won medals. How a Judy Garland (to name a screwed-up Coogan contemporary) or a Todd Bridges (to name a successor) could have benefited from a similar battle-tested breather is a tantalizing thought. But no matter. They didn't go to war; he did. Jackie survived WWII like he survived Hollywood – he dropped all pretense of being the movies' once-upon-a-time most famous kid actor and simply sought to make a living.

After the war, Jackie put together a club act, which was followed by TV work (*Playhouse 90*, *Perry Mason*, etc.), which was supplemented by film work (*The Joker Is Wild*, *High School Confidential*, etc.), which was followed by more TV work (*Alfred Hitchcock Presents*, *Mr. Lucky*, etc.). He wasn't a star – lights, camera, cover shots – anymore; he was an actor. Over the years, his eyes lost to the nose in the battle for most prominent facial feature. The adult Jackie Coogan had a look, too, but it wasn't a leading-man look. It was the look of a character actor. Seemingly waiting until he became finally and completely unrecognizable from his kiddie-star past, Coogan definitively reemerged in 1964 as the bald, lumpy Uncle Fester on TV's *The Addams Family*. It wasn't *Hamlet*. It wasn't glamour. It wasn't Chaplin. It was *work*. (And a bit of renewed fame, too.) Even after the sitcom's run, he stayed in the television pipeline for years. He went on to appear with the leading pint-size prime time titans of the day – Danny Bonaduce (*Partridge Family* episodes in 1970 and 1973), Butch Patrick (*The Munsters*, 1964), Ron Howard (*The Andy Griffith Show*, 1960), the Brady kids (*The Brady Bunch*, episodes in 1971 and 1972), and Anissa Jones and Johnny Whitaker (*Family Affair*, 1967).

In between the guest shots and supporting bits, Jackie dabbled as a businessman: a dance studio here, a used-car dealership there. Whatever it took.

No Hollywood pariah, the adult Jackie ran with the likes of Dean Martin, Jerry Lewis, Jackie Gleason, Abbott and Costello, Donald O'Connor, even the young Paul Newman. "It was a really great group they had," remembered Don Stroud. "And they were all really big stars." Stroud was Jackie's stepson by "The Kid"'s second marriage to singer Ann McCormick from 1947 to 1951. Later a durable character actor himself (*The Buddy Holly Story*, *Mickey Spillane's Mike Hammer*), Stroud said he never heard Jackie complain about anything. Never heard him go off on the lawsuit, Lillian Coogan, or the settlement. Said Stroud, "I don't think Jack was ever a complainer."

What Jackie was instead was a surfer. One of the first. As a young man, he rode waves from Baja, California, straight up to San Francisco. As an older man, he drove down to the beach at Malibu – his Rolls-Royce convertible toting a board.

Said Stroud: "Jack definitely had his ups and downs. [But] he reminds me of one of the beach guys – a surfer. I'm telling you, everybody should surf because you can live a certain way in life that's great. . . . I've had ups and downs and I've slept in my car and all that stuff, but I was a surfer, you know what I mean? And it was great; it's like, God, you ride in style."

Jackie rode in style. He settled down for keeps in Palm Springs with his fourth wife, the former Dorothea Lamphere, a dancer, and their two children. When a Hollywood job called, he drove into town. When it didn't, he played Scrabble. When Jackie thought regrets, he thought about stuff he'd done, not stuff others had done to him. In one interview, he said his big wish-I'd-done-that involved Chaplin. "I don't think I ever told that guy how much I thought of him," Jackie said. "I was like in the picture. I never really caught up."

In the late 1970s, he saw his grandchild, Keith Mitchell, born to his daughter Joan (from his marriage to McCormick), become something of a ubiquitous child actor himself. Keith wasn't a star, but he was a face, working steadily in prime time (including a season-long stint on *The Waltons*). As a child, Keith's face was Jackie's used-to-be face – same eyes, same smile, same hair. As of the early 1980s, he had the same name, billing himself as "Keith Coogan." And for a time there, Keith even had Jackie-esque troubles – not of the financial kind, but of the parental kind. In 1986, Keith, then sixteen, made minor headlines when his mother reported him to Los Angeles police as a runaway. (The two had argued over car repairs; Keith left in a huff, his bicycle in tow.) Keith turned up a week later, safe and sound, at Jackie's old Palm Springs place. After all the hand-wringing stories ("Oh, those poor child stars . . .") died down, Keith did what he had always done, what his granddad had always done – work, amassing some thirty film credits through the 1990s. (The most notable: a costarring role in the 1985 demi-classic, *Adventures in Babysitting*.)

Jackie didn't live to see Keith's trouble, or later successes. He died on March 1, 1984, at age sixty-nine. His last years were marked by declining health and dialysis. A heart attack finally got him. He died at Santa Monica Hospital in Santa Monica, California, two hours after being admitted to the emergency room.

To hear Don Stroud tell it, it was the not-so-funniest of timings.

Jackie's mother, with whom Jackie had maintained a relationship even after the lawsuit, had preceded him in death by some years. The estate Lillian left behind was indeed stately. She owned, per Stroud's recollection, a prized block of land near the Universal Studios theme park in California's San Fernando Valley. After Lillian died, there were the usual legal tangles to untangle before her heirs came into the property and money. Finally, the issues were resolved and Jackie got his share.

And then – give or take a few days, Stroud said – Jackie died.

Was it a tragedy? Was Jackie Coogan's life one cosmic joke?

Jackie was a surfer. He rolled with the waves – and all the high tides, low tides, and rip curls that came with them. It was a way of life that said you're cool if you've got fifty cents in your pocket or $50,000. You're king. You can handle it.

"Jack had that attitude going when he was young," Stroud said. "I always thought maybe because he was a surfer. Anyway, that's my little fantasy that I'll keep going."

Our little fantasy, of course, is that Jackie Coogan got screwed – by the courts, by California law, by the industry, by his own parents – and, in so doing, set the pace for all the Gary Colemans to come. And, yes, in a way he did set the pace. His story would become the outline for numerous child actors to follow. Professionally, he found it difficult to maintain star status as an adult; personally, his family life suffered for the attendant riches his career brought.

But you know what? That's not called being a former child star, cursed or otherwise. That's called being (a) an actor, (b) a person, and (c) a rich person. It ain't easy landing jobs in a ninety-percent unemployment industry. It ain't easy growing up. It ain't easy striking it rich or balancing a family life once you strike it rich.

That's the stuff of life.

And "The Kid" surfed it.

CHAPTER THREE

THE
FRIENDS

"They don't pay you enough for forever."

— PAUL PETERSEN (THE DONNA REED SHOW)

At his peak, Jackie Coogan was a movie star. At their peaks, Chip Douglas was your friend, Beaver your kid brother, Ricky Nelson your ideal.

The differences made all the difference.

Chip, Beaver, and Ricky were TV characters (except in the case of Ricky who, of course, also doubled as a real person). They were portrayed, respectively, by Stanley Livingston, Jerry Mathers, and, yes, Ricky Nelson. Those guys were TV stars.

But more than anything, they – Chip/Stanley, Beaver/Jerry, Ricky/Ricky, and their equally interchangeable peers of the 1950s and 1960s – were friends.

Our perfect, virtual, forever friends.

Forever.

THE PERFECT FIT

When Jackie Coogan hit TV in the late 1940s, the new medium – exciting or no – was less a destination and more a refuge. It was for vaudeville guys (Milton Berle) who needed breathing audiences, radio teams (Burns & Allen) who needed higher-visibility gigs, used-to-be film people (Ronald Reagan, Lucille Ball . . . and, yes, Coogan) who needed jobs. There was no real shame in TV, of course. Who did Ball need to apologize to for becoming the nation's most beloved comedienne? Why did any TV players need to hang their heads over being part of the most influential commercial movement of our lifetimes? But the truth was that if Lucille Ball had had the career, say, of a Clark Gable, she wouldn't have been doing TV in 1951. No self-respecting film stars worth their next pictures did (or do).

It's like the Woody Allen joke: those who can, do; those who can't, teach gym. In Hollywood, it is (and was): those who can, do film; those who can't, do TV (until they get famous enough and then they do film, too). You can get rich off TV like you can get rich off movies. You can get famous off TV like you can get famous off movies. Sometimes TV can even make you *more* rich and *more* famous than movies. But at the end of the day, everybody wants to be a movie star. You could name a dozen reasons why film's the dream and TV's the backup plan. And the reasons would be clichés – and they'd be true. Film's larger than life, TV's smaller than life; film's important, TV's schlock; film's art, TV's commerce; film's timeless, TV's disposable; film's chargeable, TV's free; film's film, TV's TV.

The bottom line: no Clark Gable was gonna do the tube.

But a Stanley Livingston? Or a Jerry Mathers? Or a Ricky Nelson? Sure, why not? See, if Gable was too big (literally, figuratively, and ego-wise) for television, then kids were just the right size (at just the right time). In the 1950s, the movie studios

– which once raided grade schools for talent (populating their properties with the likes of Coogan, Shirley Temple, Judy Garland, Jackie Cooper, and Freddie Bartholomew) – could no longer trust the bankability of bangs and scraped knees. TV, after all, might have been viewed as something less than film, but it still scared the bejeezus out of studio heads (in no small part because the blasted box was driving audiences out of theaters and onto their living-room couches).

Locked in a presumed do-or-die struggle with television, filmmakers turned to Cinerama-sized epics to tout their industry's distinguishing attribute: size. Movies were huge, remember? *The Greatest Show on Earth* – literally. TV was small, remember? The thing that fit in your den. To carry their wide-screen epics, directors needed broad-shouldered stars. Memo to Central Casting: Hold the Skippy (and the Johnny and the Sally and the . . .); get Charlton Heston on the set, pronto.

Oh, the kids could still work, and maybe they could even still work in movies (Stanley Livingston, Jerry Mathers, and Ricky Nelson certainly did), but television – *that* was where they *belonged*. They were the perfect fit – for the medium's budgets (ain't no kid gonna be demanding a star salary – at least for a couple of years), for its scope (little people for little stories), and, most of all, for its audience (kids watching kids). It always comes back to that last one, doesn't it? TV and baby boomers; baby boomers and TV. You know the drill. Lots of babies born post-World War II; lots of TV sets and corresponding TV shows introduced at the same time. A perfect match. (Insert falsely sentimental references to *Howdy Doody* and Maypo here.) Trite, overstated, boring. But there's no way around it: baby boomers *were* the first generation raised in front of the tube. And baby boomers, in turn, *did* help raise the first generation of TV stars.

And yet . . .

They were far from the medium's first die-hard fans. After all, it wasn't little Jimmy who shelled out a couple of paychecks to buy a four-inch screen to watch the fights. It wasn't little Janie who made *Fireside Theatre* a Top 10 show in 1952. Depression-era adults who'd been weaned on mass-media entertainment of their own (like, um, radio) were just as game for the new-fangled television as their new-era kids. And their tastes, even more than their kiddies', were reflected in the ratings. Baby boomers revolutionize television? Hardly. They didn't make it; they didn't even watch most of it. In fact, you could almost feel sorry for the little guys (and gals) if they didn't forever boast how they *did* change everything (TV, popular music, the aging process, coffee, station wagons, the world, etc.). Fact was, it took a while for both the kids on TV and the kids on the couch to make their impact felt. Their sensibilities (such as they were) were shoved aside as the 800-pound dinosaurs roamed prime time. Jimmy Durante, Bing Crosby, Milton Berle, Arthur Godfrey, etc. – these were the wrinkled and lined likes who enjoyed the TV-star thing in the late 1940s and early 1950s.

What about all the kids? Well, what about them? Where were they? After Lucille Ball's own newborn Desi Jr. appeared on *TV Guide*'s first cover back in 1951, there wasn't an under-eighteen type who rated that sort of coverage – that sort of popular, Nielsen seal of approval – for another two years. And when, in 1953, another kid (or kids: David and Ricky Nelson) finally did make the cover, they had to be chaperoned (by their mom and portrait costar, Harriet Nelson). Embarrassing. The kids were getting rolled by the grown-ups. They needed a leader. A breakout. Their own Lucille Ball. Somebody who could show that TV was rightfully a kids' medium – in front of the camera, and in front of the tube. Somebody who could prove that kids and TV *were* the perfect fit.

"BOY, I DON'T MESS AROUND"

Ricky Nelson did not look like Jackie Coogan. He did not act like Jackie Coogan. He just served the same purpose.

If Jackie Coogan was the world's first child star – movie division; Nelson was the world's first child star – TV division. Nelson did not create the immediate sensation of Coogan. It took him a good five years to work himself into frenzy status. But he did all right. He made up for lost time. And then some.

Eric Hilliard Nelson was born on May 8, 1940, to the band-leader, Ozzie Nelson, and the singer, the former Harriet Hilliard (who was the former-*former* Peggy Lou Snyder, Harriet's given name). In the pantheon of Hollywood child stars, Ricky was a relative slacker; he didn't work until he was eight. His career wasn't even his parents' idea. It was his. In late 1948, Ricky and older brother David (born 1936) heard from one of Bing Crosby's kids that he (the Crosby offspring) was going to be on their parents' radio show at Christmastime. If Lindsay Crosby could do it, Ricky figured, so could he and David. A family meeting was called.

Showbiz parents or no, Ozzie and Harriet hadn't enlisted their brood in the act. To hear them tell it, they'd shielded the boys, hiring actors to play their "sons" in the radio version of their lives, a program called *The Adventures of Ozzie & Harriet*. For more than four years, that was how the thing played – real parents, fake kids. Then Ricky and David held their huddle. Then they talked to their parents. Then the parents held auditions. Then Ricky got a laugh. Then the "sons" were fired and the sons were hired.

The real Ricky and David Nelson debuted as the radio Ricky and David Nelson in February 1949. A little more than a year later, they were all film stars. *Here Come the Nelsons* (1952) was something of a minor work with something of a minor story (about houseguests and a rodeo) with something of major consequences, for TV history, anyway. Before the dawn of pilots, *Here Comes the Nelsons* was it – a test to see if Ozzie, Harriet, David, and Ricky played in person like they played as voices on the radio. (Apparently to be sure the project didn't stray off course, the movie, in fact, played like nothing more than a filmed radio script.) And visionary storytellers or no, the gambit worked. The onscreen Nelsons were naturals (well, at least half of them were – master-stammerer Ozzie and Harriet had easy screen presences; David and Ricky had kinda stiff, but cute, ones). And visionary talents or no, the Nelsons got their TV deal. David would later compare the family act to a family grocery store: "We didn't think about whether we liked it or not; we just showed up for work."

The Adventures of Ozzie & Harriet (the TV show) debuted on ABC on October 3, 1952, even as *The Adventures of Ozzie & Harriet* (the radio show) continued its weekly broadcasts (through 1954). Despite its title, *The Adventures of Ozzie & Harriet* was notoriously short of "adventures." Something of the de-sexed *Seinfeld* of its day, *Ozzie & Harriet* was essentially about nothing. An entire episode could be (and was) devoted to the subject of, say, pancake mix. The show was as swashbuckling as its oh-so-deliberate opening, in which each and every blessed Nelson was introduced (in chronological order) to the camera – from Ozzie on down to "the little guy with the twinkle in his eye," or as they would be known in their latter-day *Seinfeld* incarnations: Jerry and Kramer. Like Kramer, Ricky had sky-high hair, a contrary disposition, and the best lines. In the pancake episode, for instance, it was Ricky who insisted the family pursue the double-your-money-back offer on the inferior mix and then schemed to make riches by buying (and returning) even more boxes. As his signature line stated, he "didn't mess around, boy." In a family of television stars, Ricky was the special one – the youngest, the cutest, the most popular. The kid didn't have the best acting chops. He didn't have the most engaging personality (unless you go for deadpan). He just had "it." As a thirteen-year-old Ricky put it, "My mother gave me some good advice some years ago when she said, 'Son, there is no such thing as a comedian. If you want to be funny, try to be funny by being natural rather than by trying to act like an adult.'"

In the beginning, Ricky not only stood apart from other Nelsons, but from the other TV stars, as well. Unlike Ball, Berle, Benny, Hope, Skelton, or even Ozzie and Harriet, Ricky actually looked (and sorta talked) like his pajama-clad audience. Sure, David was a kid, too. But he was more serious-looking, a three-quarter-size Ozzie clone. Ricky, on the other hand, was an out-and-out punk. That pancake-mix scheme? Why, that kind of behavior bordered on extortion by docile Nelson family standards. David would never pull something like that. Comparisons between Ricky and Jackie Coogan are also something of a stretch. Ricky was a wiry rascal who did little to evoke doe-eyed Jackie, except that his look, like Jackie's look, set the standard – if not the mandate – for TV kids to come.

THE TYPE

Adult, kid, or animal – if you're an actor, you've got to be a type. Leading man, bombshell, comic relief, bad guy, whatever. Post-Jackie Coogan, the casting sheet for a big-screen kid called for the outsized bangs, the larger-than-life personality, and the otherworldly talent for on-demand tears. Post-Ricky Nelson, the casting sheet for a little-screen kid called for a bike-riding, milk-drinking neighborhood type possessed of two (big) extras – a big smile and a big mouth (the better with which to rattle off punch lines).

So, to recap: you had to be average, but not.

You had to be an angel with a devilish streak.

Easy?

Well, from a producer's standpoint, the TV tyke was at least easier to find than a Lucille Ball.

From 1952 to 1957, when both shows were in production, *I Love Lucy* enjoyed far greater commercial success than *Ozzie & Harriet*. The former was TV's perennial No. 1; the latter was a perennial Top 20 no-show. But if you're a network executive, circa 1954, which format do you try to steal? The one dependent on the star performance? Or the one with the relatively cheap, unknown kid actors? Frankly, if you're a network executive, you try to steal both. But budgetary restrictions likely encourage you to exploit the cheaper option first. And so while *I Love Lucy* made significant contributions to the art of the sitcom (such as it is) – pioneering the use of the studio audience, championing the deployment of the three-camera production format, and literally adding the "situation" to the "situation comedy" – *Ozzie & Harriet* got the nod for perfecting the half-hour family comedy.

In the years following *Ozzie & Harriet*'s modest debut came *Make Room for Daddy* (premiered 1953), *Father Knows Best* (premiered 1954), *Leave It to Beaver* (premiered 1957), and *Dennis the Menace* (premiered 1959). Like its model, each show – even the nightclub-oriented *Make Room for Daddy* (later *The Danny Thomas Show*) and the comics-inspired *Dennis* – was built around a solidly middle-class, two-parent nuclear family. And like its model, each show was ultimately distinguished by its kid factor.

If Ricky Nelson was the reason to check out *Ozzie & Harriet*, then Rusty Hamer as the smart-mouthed Rusty Williams was a tune-in factor for *Make Room for Daddy*. On *Leave It to Beaver*, it was Jerry Mathers as the befuddled Beaver Cleaver. (Although the stalwart, David Nelsonesque Tony Dow had his following as Beaver's brother-protector Wally, as well.) On *Dennis*, it was precocious Jay North as the precocious prankster Dennis Mitchell. And on *Father Knows Best*, it was Billy Gray as cool kid Bud Anderson.

"When I was a teenager I used to watch reruns of *Father Knows Best*, and I used to think Bud Anderson was the coolest," said Billy Mumy, who became the "It" factor on his own TV show of a slightly later era (*Lost in Space*, 1965–68). "'Cause he was human, you know. He was just so great."

For Jerry Mathers, too, the secret to success was being natural. He got the *Beaver* job at age eight by fidgeting through the audition before finally announcing he had a Cub Scouts meeting to attend. For Billy Gray, the secret was *sounding* natural. "My mother's advice to me was to just be natural, not be 'read-ie' – that was the term at the time," Gray said. "She would say a line, I would hear her say it. Never read it – couldn't sound read-ie."

So, to recap: to be a successful kid star of TV's Golden Era, you had to look and sound natural.

Even if your lines were scripted.

Even if your days were produced.

Even if your lives were anything but.

You had to be natural.

Naturally.

THE GIG

It's not exactly coal-mine duty, but making a film ain't a breeze, either. There's the long hours. There's the ungodly 5 a.m. set calls. There's the boredom. There's the pressure. But, then again, if you're lucky, it's all over in two to three months.

In the 1950s, TV actors were lucky if it was all over before they dropped dead of exhaustion. The infant industry was quite simply a grind – a relatively well-paid, celebrated, glamorous grind. Even more than film, TV was a monster – a monster that demanded attention. You didn't wrap in time, the network went to a test pattern in a few weeks. And so serve the monster the TV actor did – to every man, woman, and child.

The assembly line was open.

"We went to work when it was dark, and we finished work after it was dark. The first two years we worked six days a week," said Elinor Donahue, an eighteen-year-old when she debuted as eldest daughter Betty Anderson on *Father Knows Best*.

Castmate Lauren Chapin – the little Anderson known as "Kitten"– remembered irregular work hours, irregular school hours, and just one regular, all-important mandate from the studio: learn your lines.

To Jon Provost, who as a towheaded seven-year-old stepped into the farmhouse on *Lassie* in 1957 as orphan Timmy Martin, the TV set was anything but disorderly. Or unregimented. Recalled Provost with exacting detail more than forty years later, "It would be a ten-hour day – one hour for transportation, one hour for lunch, three hours of schooling, four hours of filming, and then an hour of recreation."

"I guess that adds up to ten."

That it did.

The other important bit of arithmetic for stars of the era was thirty-nine.

Some series – including *Ozzie & Harriet*, *Lassie*, and *Father Knows Best* – cranked out as many as thirty-nine new episodes each season. Network stars a half-century later – an age where twenty-two-episode seasons were the norm – would earn millions upon millions producing nearly forty-five percent less product. To meet the product demand, the *Lassie* crew filmed parts of as many as three different episodes in a day – one scene here for Episode A, one scene there for Episode B, another scene over there for Episode C. To make the disjointed appear seamless to unwitting viewers at home, Provost said he was clad in the same checkered-shirt-and-jeans ensemble for virtually his entire series tenure. It didn't matter what page (or what day) Provost was on, Timmy must always look like Timmy.

Other productions met the thirty-nine-episode commitment the old-fashioned way: shooting one episode a week, for thirty-nine long weeks. That left exactly thirteen weeks of downtime for the prime-time performer. All right, so who was complaining about a thirteen-week vacation? Not the shoe salesman who got two. Not the school kid who got an eight- to nine-week summer hiatus. The bottom line: a thirteen-week break ain't bad.

If it's a thirteen-week break.

Said Provost, "The three months that we were off on a hiatus, we would do personal appearances, we would do all kinds of stuff, so [the show] was really a yearlong event."

For *Leave It to Beaver's* Tony Dow, it was a decade-long event. "I was asked to go to a high school and participate in a '50s week and they wanted me to get up and talk about what the '50s were like," Dow recalled of a latter-day speaking engagement. "And I kept sort of procrastinating – what I was gonna do? And I kept thinking, well, this should be easy, and I was on a plane going to an airport to the high school . . . and I realized I don't have anything to talk about.

"I didn't experience the '50s."

No, he didn't. He *worked* the '50s.

Said Paul Petersen, who worked the tail end of the '50s as good son Jeff Stone on *The Donna Reed Show*, "The world revolved around the show. [Costar] Shelley Fabares says it perfectly: it's like being in prison. Your life is completely dominated by this part you're playing."

As in any business, those who didn't get *with* the program got drummed *out* of the program. In 1955, a tousle-haired, gapped-tooth Petersen was one of sixteen children (culled from a five-thousand-strong cattle-call audition) cast for Disney's great virtual-peer contribution, *The Mickey Mouse Club*. Instead of becoming a household name like fellow club member Annette Funicello, the ten-year-old Petersen distinguished himself by becoming the "the world's first ex-Mouseketeer" – fired after seven weeks for "conduct unbecoming" one of Walt's charges.

"I was rambunctious and confrontational and undisciplined," said Petersen. "Heck, my third-grade teacher said that, 'While Paul was one of the smartest boys in his class his behavior is abominable.' And that pretty much explains why I was fired."

That, and he reportedly punched the casting director in the stomach after being called a "mouse" one too many annoying times. As Petersen would later sum it up: "I didn't know that kid actors aren't supposed to be children."

Though playing average onscreen was the gig, the working TV kid (as well as the working TV adult) was not the average working person, was not the average school kid. Average people didn't answer to a real family *and* a TV family *and* an agent *and* a producer *and* a director *and* a network.

To be a TV kid was to be a kid divided and subdivided.

"I was a quarter of a thing," David Nelson once said. "Whatever I did, I felt the burden of three other people and all the crew who worked on the show."

Recalled Provost: "It was tough. There were a lot of times when I did not want to be there. There's time, you know, when I may have been sick and possibly was working and breaking certain, you know, child labor laws. But there were times when you had to do that. And there were times when instead of my mother grabbing [me], saying, 'No, we're leaving right now,' they'd say, 'Look, please, we just need this last shot – this last shot.'"

None of these pressures were new to performers in Hollywood. None of these pressures were unique to players in any high-stakes, high-profile job. And none of these pressures were necessarily debilitating to the spirit.

They were just new, that's all.

Kids had performed on stage. Kids had performed in movies. Kids had performed on radio. But until Ricky and David and their freckled, cow-licked brethren landed in the 1950s, they'd never been on TV.

More key: they'd never been regularly beamed to living rooms – and then, in their off weeks, asked to attend gym class with their viewers/peers.

Yes, it was good to be Lucille Ball (or any fortysomething TV star). No state law required her to hang with real-life housewives during her hiatus. And no mandate sent her packing to school. Again, Hollywood kids had been balancing the school thing and the work thing for decades before the first TV generation was spawned. But unlike movieland contract players, who generally existed within the confines of the studio (and the studio school) year-round, the Ricky Nelsonites were thrown out to the real world every spring and winter break. With little precedent, little training, no warning. For TV kids, simply getting used to being around other kids, as opposed to the usual contingent of grown-ups, could be a trip. After all, on the *Lassie* set, Jon Provost laughed, "it was me and thirty-five adults and a couple of dogs."

From the adult perspective, there was nothing strange about this arrangement. In 1957, Ozzie Nelson conceded that while his TV show made "inroads on the boys' normal activities," those inroads were kept at a minimum; school (in the form of Hollywood High, for Ricky) was a breeze. "David and Ricky don't look upon themselves as celebrities," Ozzie said, "and they seem to be popular with other kids."

Popularity, of course, according to those who actually did the TV/school dance, was a tricky thing to gauge. Stanley Livingston, a kid actor who earned several guest spots as a neighbor tyke on

Ozzie & Harriet in the 1950s before going on to earn his prime-time stripes as Chip Douglas on *My Three Sons*, attended public school during production breaks. Whereas the studio school was run straight up ("We had really a good teacher. You know, [the production company] abided by whatever the rules were; there was no hanky panky. . . ."), real-world junior high was a little rough, he said, for all the reasons that junior high is a little rough for every eleven-year-old: you're a little kid amid a campus of raging-hormone types.

But the TV kid was never just any kid.

Said Livingston, "I had the added thing of [being] a guy from *My Three Sons*, and there were people that liked your show and wanted to be your friend. Other ones just wanted to, you know, beat you up 'cause you're too famous and people are coming up and being nice to you and you had celebrity."

At the end of the day (or semester), Livingston didn't have a horrific, scarring school experience – just a *different* one.

And that, arguably, was the in-a-nutshell experience of the pioneering TV kids: they were different. Their parents could keep them grounded, their on-set mentors could keep them protected, but no matter how all parties tried, they weren't the Johnson kid down the street. The best they could do was *play* regular in real life, just like they *played* regular in prime time. For better and not always for worse, they *were* different.

For one thing, their perks were a lot better.

TEEN IDOLS

In spring 1957, Ricky Nelson wasn't a kid anymore. He was nearly seventeen. And depending on which memory you're tapping, either (a) Ozzie asked him to sing on the show, or (b) Ricky asked Ozzie to sing on the show because (1) he'd wanted to for a couple of years, but was too shy to ask before, and/or

(2) he wanted to impress a pretty Hollywood High Elvis fan name of Arline.

The end result was the same. On the April 10, 1957, episode of *Ozzie & Harriet* (entitled "Little Drummer Boy"), Ricky as Ricky got up in front of a house band, strapped on a guitar, and pretended to strum the Fats Domino hit "I'm Walkin'." Two weeks later, Ricky's version – pressed and unexpectedly rushed into release as a single with the flipside "A Teenager's Romance" – had sold one million copies.

And so the TV-era teen idol was born.

Just as the smart-mouthed version of Ricky spawned its own cottage industry, so did the slick-haired crooning version of Ricky. The way Stanley Livingston remembered it, TV guys got split into two camps – the (almost) men and the boys. Said Livingston: "I think in the era I came out of the kid's look, they seemed to be these little blond-headed [kids] – Jay [North] kind of had that look, Jon Provost had sort of that look. And it seemed like the older ones, like Paul Petersen [and] Tim Considine, with the crew cuts, darker hair – kind of combed back – [had] more of a teen-idol look."

Paul Petersen, rejected Mouseketeer, had mounted his prime-time career in 1958 as the sole male spawn of Carl Betz and Donna Reed on *The Donna Reed Show.* Tim Considine, *Mickey Mouse Club* alum in good standing, was tall, dark, and nineteen when he debuted as eldest sibling Mike Douglas on *My Three Sons* in 1960. Neither was a true Ricky Nelson clone, but they fit the suit well enough – in a Johnny Bravo sort of way.

The TV teen idol expanded the scope and power of the TV kid star. The TV teen idol didn't need to be buried in TV family publicity stills. The TV teen could stand alone as a commodity – much like Jackie Coogan or Shirley Temple once could in film. As an added bonus, the TV teen idol could sell records with the TV show and sell the TV show with records. No film star had that kind of access. No pop star had that kind of access. Not Fabian, not Frankie Avalon, not Elvis (who didn't need it, thankyouverymuch).

It was good to be a TV teen idol.

Said Petersen: "You just can't miss when thirty million people a week are watching your show [and] a good chunk of them are teenyboppers and they'll buy your records."

Petersen sure didn't miss – not that he had much choice. In the early 1960s, the powers-that-be at *The Donna Reed Show* informed Petersen and TV sibling Shelley Fabares that, effective immediately, they'd be singing *Ozzie & Harriet*-style in the show's upcoming season. (Ricky's own musical numbers had become a staple in his parents' show since the 1957 break-through episode.) "Both Paul and I said it was a great idea," Fabares once recalled, "but we couldn't sing." To invoke the Johnny Bravo reference again, it simply didn't matter whether they could sing, hum, or tap their feet – *they fit the suit*. Or, more specifically, they fit the type. Clean-cut Petersen was to be cast as sort of a Paul Anka-ish Ricky Nelson; good-girl Fabares as a lighter shade of Annette (the fairest – and most bankable – Mouseketeer of them all). The teenyboppers didn't let them down. Demand for Petersen was sufficient that he was allowed to record six albums for Columbia Pictures' Colpix label through the mid-1960s. One of the cuts – 1962's "My Dad" – sold more than one million copies. As for the ever-reluctant Fabares? She made her way to the No. 1 position on the singles charts in 1962 with forever-oldies-radio staple "Johnny Angel."

Not every TV teen from the early 1960s on would fare as well in the record business as Petersen, Fabares, and Nelson, but nearly every TV teen from the early 1960s on would be asked to try – from the obvious suspects (David Cassidy, Shaun Cassidy) to the less obvious ones (Kristy McNichol, Patty Duke). Glenn Scarpelli was among those asked to give the teen-idol thing a shot. Scarpelli attracted the attention of the *Tiger Beat* press (and the attendant teenybopper record industry) when he joined the cast of top-rated CBS sitcom *One Day at a Time* in 1980. In short order, Scarpelli cut the requisite (overproduced) album, posed for the requisite (shirtless) photos, and made the requisite (tough) choices.

"I did the [magazine] shoots," Scarpelli said. "And they made me shave my chest, which was a very interesting thing because I was like, 'I'm Italian . . . it's me.' I couldn't believe it. I had just started to grow hair on my chest, I was thrilled. I'm like, 'Look at this, yeah! One right here!' I mean, I was like so thrilled when it started to happen. [But] I went there [to the photo sessions] and they were like, 'Well, you know, teenage girls get very intimidated by guys with hair on their chest and we got to keep you looking young and da-dah-da . . .' And I did it, I definitely did it." Just like, a generation before, his *One Day* costar Fabares had done it (the teen-idol thing, not shaving her chest or posing shirtless). Being the object of teen desire and adulation made for more work and hassles, sure, but few complained as the records sold and the fans swooned.

Said Petersen: "Believe me, it was fun because I was aware of how many babes Rick Nelson got. And, you know, when you're fifteen and sixteen, that was my world. All I cared about at sixteen was fast cars and faster women."

It was good to be a TV teen idol.

CANCELLED PEOPLE

It was not as good to be a TV teen idol after the Beatles disembarked from their Pan-Am jetliner in New York City in January 1964. It pretty much meant, in fact, that you weren't a TV teen idol anymore. Wasn't nobody much buying Paul Petersen records once the British Invasion hit. Ditto for Fabares. What chance did the kids from *The Donna Reed Show* have if even Elvis was bound for a dry spell? (Until 1969's "Suspicious Minds," in fact, Presley's last chart-topping song was "Good Luck Charm," released all the way back in 1962 when it bounced Fabares' "Johnny Angel" from the No. 1 spot.)

Ricky Nelson – or Rick, since his 1961 album *Rick Is 21* – got blindsided by the Beatles, too, of course. His music career might have had more solid roots than those of his TV peers, his records might have sold boatloads more copies than those of his TV peers, and his thirty-three Top 40 singles ("Poor Little Fool," "Lonesome Town," and "It's Late" among them) might have amounted to a fairly enviable greatest-hits package, but commercially it all counted for zip. Ricky Nelson was over. His last No. 1 single was 1961's "Travelin' Man" (with the flipside "Hello Mary Lou"); his last notable single of the go-go '60s was 1963's "Fools Rush In." And then, as if to seal his M.O. as an *ex*-idol, Nelson went off and got married. Granted, he was old enough. He was twenty-three (his bride was seventeen), but still – *married?!?* The Ozzies of the world get married, not the Rickys (unless – uh, oh – the Rickys *turn into* the Ozzies).

Ricky didn't really turn into Ozzie, of course. But he didn't exactly rebel at his father/boss, either. Through the red-hot music career and the promising movie career (*Rio Bravo*) to the cooling music career and the stalled movie career (the Ozzie-directed *Love and Kisses*), Ricky stayed the course on *Ozzie & Harriet*. Like the dutiful grocery-store-owner's son, he even introduced his bride to the family business. Starting in 1963, Ricky's wife, the former Kristin Harmon, joined the cast as Ricky's TV wife, name of, yes, Kristin. (David would say the show became its most confusing at this point – he, an aspiring director and accomplished circus performer, playing an attorney alongside real-life wife June Blair, with Ricky, a best-selling rock star and notoriously poor student, playing a diligent undergrad alongside *his* real-life wife.)

Even as David prepped for a life after *Ozzie & Harriet* by handling some of Ozzie's behind-the-scenes production chores, Ricky didn't seem to be looking for an out. He just phoned it in, year after year after year. As an actor on *Ozzie & Harriet*, Ricky peaked during his spiky-haired, wiseacre stage. The older Ricky got, the stiffer (and quieter) Ricky got. He was not his father's stammerer. No matter. The laconic idol, who at the height of his draw in 1958 remarked that he "sort of fell into [a music career] more or less," apparently recognized a good gig when he saw it. Teen-idol popdom – as the likes of Fabian had proved, was fleeting, but a TV show – at least, *his* TV show – went on and on. From the Eisenhower administration (both terms) to the Kennedy administration to the Johnson administration, *Ozzie & Harriet* was there. Being there apparently was its job. It just went on.

Right?

It was rarely that easy. Said Stanley Livingston: "Every year, it was the network's option to renew us. So, we were kind of stuck there at their mercy. You know, you got a good indicator. I mean [our] show was in the Top 10, so it's sort of, 'Who's gonna cancel a Top 10 show?'"

The same people who could cancel a Top 10 kid. Tommy Rettig was the first TV child star to learn that lesson. When *Lassie* came to television in 1954, courtesy the good folks at Campbell Soup, twelve-year-old Rettig became the most famous dog master in the country as Lassie's faithful owner Jeff Miller. By 1957, the laws of addition tell us, Rettig had become fifteen – too old, the soup people deigned, to be tussling about the countryside with a collie. It was nothing personal against Rettig – a kid who after landing the *Lassie* gig, endeared himself to the powers-that-be by announcing, "With Lassie, I'd gladly work for free" – but he had to go. So as to not draw (much) attention to Rettig's absence, it was decided that the two adults on the show (Jan Clayton as Jeff's widowed mom and George Cleveland as the boy's grandfather) had to go as well. Or, as *Lassie* producer Robert Maxwell delicately put it to the *New York Times* in 1957, "We decided on a clean sweep, but a very gradual clean sweep."

In practice, the "gradual clean sweep" consisted of Rettig, Clayton, and Cleveland hanging on to their jobs until the new cast (headed by seven-year-old Jon Provost) could be transitioned into Lassie's farmhouse. (It was also a way to hedge their bets and go back to Plan A in case the Provost team bombed.) As it turned out, George "Gramps" Cleveland died before the start of the 1957–58 season, so at least one part of the "sweep" was destined to be eternal, not "gradual." In the end, the Provost team didn't bomb (even if its newly installed TV mom – one Cloris Leachman – hightailed it out of the series after just one season, to be replaced by June Lockhart). To hear Provost tell it, Tommy Rettig wasn't bent out of shape about giving over his show (well, the dog's show) to a second-grader who, at the time, knew how to write only four words. "You know, he seemed to be fine with it," said Provost.

And to hear Rettig tell it, he *was* fine with it. Said an adult Rettig years later, "I didn't enjoy the wide recognition [the role brought]. I couldn't go to dinner. I couldn't stand in line for a show without attracting a crowd."

Tommy Rettig's situation was unique – he was a cancelled person. His old show, on the other hand, was fine. Like *Ozzie & Harriet*, *Lassie* went on and on (and on). But if members of the first generation of TV kid stars were hoping for some sort of flyer on Hollywood unemployment, were hoping everything could be *Lassie*, they were out of luck. *The Mickey Mouse Club* ended production in 1959; *Father Knows Best*, in 1960; *Leave It to Beaver* and *Dennis the Menace* in 1963; *Make Room for Daddy* in 1964; and *The Donna Reed Show*, in 1966. In the

Ozzie & Harriet endurance department, *My Three Sons* lasted until 1972 (although Considine checked out in 1965). *Lassie*, in various forms, outlasted all his/her owners, running around the countryside until 1974. Provost had departed in 1964. Like Rettig, he, too, became a canceled person – except that it was Provost who wrote his pink slip. Said Provost: "I had a seven-year contract with a three-year option and it was getting up to the seven years. I was fourteen years old and obviously they wanted to continue the series. I told my parents, 'Look, I can't see myself being Timmy till I was seventeen or eighteen years old.'"

And so he wasn't. Provost left.

In 1966, the ax fell on the Nelsons.

The final prime time *Ozzie & Harriet* aired on September 3, 1966. For the first time since 1944 (dating back to the Nelsons' radio show), the titular parents were just plain old parents, not actors who also *played* parents. For the first time since 1949, the boys (turned men) were just regular old sons, not actors who also *played* sons.

"After the series ended, I didn't know what I wanted to do," Ricky said. "I didn't have to worry about money or a job, but I didn't have any real interest in a career."

He was lost.

But he was not gone.

THE RERUN

It was not changing times that killed *Ozzie & Harriet*. It was not the arguably incongruous sight of the still-wholesome Nelson clan in the supposedly revolutionary 1960s. (Revolution? What revolution? Not in prime time. How else to explain puffball stuff like *The Beverly Hillbillies* and *Gomer Pyle* – shows every bit as non-threatening as *Ozzie & Harriet* – dominating the Nielsen rankings in the Age of Aquarius?) What did in *Ozzie &*

Harriet was old age. It ran fourteen seasons. It produced a beyond-prodigious 435 episodes. It was the longest-running family sitcom of its day. It was *old*. The fall after its demise, its time slot was taken over by *Batman* which briefly perked up ratings for ABC because it was *new*.

But if prime time was about the new, then the afternoon (and the weekend) was about comfort.

Hence, the rerun.

And not just any rerun – not the it's-summer-so-here's-that-episode-of-*Beaver*-you-missed-last-February prime-time rerun. The comfort rerun was the off-network, syndicated rerun – the one that showed up on local stations (and later cable networks) day in, day out, day in, day out. Forever.

Paul Petersen noticed the first *Donna Reed* comfort rerun in 1962, while the show was still in production. It bothered him ("I was closing in on six feet, I was a bubblegum star with hit records, and yet the shows they were showing were of me at twelve. And anybody who has been subjected to the endless family home movies on a Saturday afternoon that your parents insist on watching can understand that that's crazy-making."), but he didn't think much about it. Most of his peers didn't think much about it. Why would they? For one thing, they were in the middle of it – some of them still working, even.

And for another thing, what was a rerun?

"As kids, you don't have any sense of anything. Except you've got to get up at seven-thirty and go to work," said Tony Dow. "I probably never thought of the word *rerun* once until I started getting checks, and then I thought very little of them until they stopped coming, which was shortly thereafter."

By the mid-1960s, Petersen, for one, figured the *Donna Reed Show* episodes and their ilk would soon fall out of favor with stations because they were black-and-white throwbacks in a suddenly color-TV world. When Columbia Pictures offered a onetime buyout of his residual rights in 1966, he figured it a good business deal to take the cash in hand. "I came to the conclusion that there would be no life left in this show," he says. The concept of Nick at Nite didn't cross his mind, obviously. And for good reason: tele-nostalgia simply didn't exist in the 1950s and 1960s. None of the stars of the era had been brought up to believe, much less comprehend, that their week at work in, say, November 1959 would be beamed across the world *ad infinitum* from that point forward.

In the pre-television age, movies went into theaters and went out of theaters. They lived on in memories, in still pictures, and occasional revivals. That was it. In the pre-home-video age, the work of a Jackie Coogan or (more likely) a Shirley Temple made its way to TV as fodder for the occasional Saturday-afternoon movie showcase. And that was it. In the comfort-rerun age, the work of a Paul Petersen, of a Tony Dow, of a Jerry Mathers, of a Ricky Nelson, of an anybody/anything ever captured on a once-semi-popular or sorta-notable TV show *never went away*. Once a ten-year-old Beaver Cleaver, always a ten-year-old Beaver Cleaver.

TV kid stars of the era would later talk about the phenomenon as the job that never went away, the photo-album snapshots that never got filed, the home movies that never burned. Was virtual immortality one of the perks of being a TV kid star? Or was it its "curse"?
Paul Petersen had his theory: "They don't pay you enough for forever."

THE "HAPPY MEDIUM"

Paul Petersen, of course, didn't espouse that theory for a good thirty years. And, again, for good reason. In 1995, Paul Petersen was looking back on 1965 with thirty years' worth of perspective.

With thirty years' worth of Jeff Stone baggage.

But in 1965? There were no glitches in 1965. The pioneering TV kid stars were either still too busy on the set, in the recording studio, catching up on kicking-back time, catching up on studies, or lining up their next glorious projects to be bothered with problems.

Oh, sure, there were a couple of things. A couple of bothersome things.

There was the nasty story going around about how little Lauren Chapin showed up for work on the *Father Knows Best* set in 1960, only to be turned away at the studio gate with an "I'm sorry, Miss Chapin, you don't work here anymore." (And that she didn't. Chapin and her TV family had been replaced – by their own reruns. In the recycling move of the decade, CBS shut down the tiring *Father Knows Best*, opting to run old episodes on its prime-time schedule through 1963.)

Then there was the Billy Gray incident – or scandal, really. Dear Bud Anderson had been arrested on March 25, 1962, in West Hollywood, California, on suspicion of drunken driving. But that wasn't the half of it. Police said that after they pulled his car over (for erratic driving, it was noted), they found a plastic bag containing "marijuana seed and residue" under the front seat. Let the cracks begin: Bud busted for bud?!? Actually, he was worse than busted. Gray was convicted on the marijuana rap, sent to jail (more than a month behind bars), and subjected to a court-ordered screening program for morphine. Morphine?!? "That was the fallout from Bobby," Gray said, referring to Bobby Driscoll, a movie-star kid (*Treasure Island*) gone wrong by drugs. "Kid actor/heroine addict was the connection."

All right, so those things were troubling, but they weren't fatal or anything. After all, Lauren Chapin would find other work, right? Hollywood wouldn't turn its back on Billy Gray for one scrape with the law, right?

And besides, new, bright kids were being added to the prime-time roster every year: Ron Howard (*The Andy Griffith Show*), Patty Duke (*The Patty Duke Show*), Butch Patrick (*The Munsters*), Billy Mumy (*Lost in Space*), Anissa Jones and Johnny Whitaker (*Family Affair*), Brandon Cruz (*The Courtship of Eddie's Father*), the *Brady Bunch* kids, the *Partridge Family* kids.

The fallout from their workloads? Their symbiotic connection with the audience? Their messed-up home lives? Those were eons away.

The immediate picture looked great: they were wholesome, clean-cut, Wonder Bread kids who were living the American dream as much as they were creating it, week in and week out, on their beyond-reproach TV series. Everything else was just hindsight.

> "I mean, it would have been great, and it didn't happen until 1969, if somebody like a Jackie Cooper in 1961 had sat me down when he was directing *Donna Reed* shows and said, 'Paul, when this show is over, your career is over.' Because he knew it was going to happen. But how do you share that with a youngster who's so full of himself? At that time I really did scrape my ears off when I walked through a door." (Paul Petersen)

They were young. They were rich. They were famous.

They weren't even *former* child stars yet.

"TV is a happy medium when you get into the swing of things," Petersen's TV mom, Donna Reed, observed in 1958. "It's a furious business."

She meant that as a compliment.

CHAPTER FOUR

BUFFY

"Child TV Star Found Dead"

— ANISSA JONES OBIT IN *NEW YORK DAILY NEWS*

There it is. The headline we've been waiting for. Forget all the set-up stuff about Jackie Coogan, Ricky Nelson, and other people who lived a million years ago. Where were the goods in those tales? Where was the *E! True Hollywood Story*? Coogan dying of natural causes in a hospital? Oh, that's choice. Where was the dirt on Nelson? (It's coming – later.) Truth is, if you skimmed, skipped, or blew through the first three chapters and opened the book to this page, you'd be in business. This is what it's about, isn't it? "Child TV Star Found Dead."

Cut, print.

Perfect.

It's a headline, it's a punchline, it's a way of life (theirs, thank God).

And the beauty of the line is that it was the first. (And we use the word *beauty* with all due sensitivity and respect, just like they would on *E! True Hollywood Story*, because, of course, there is absolutely nothing beautiful about anybody, much less Anissa Jones, passing on in an untimely manner – however cool it may be.) In any case, the beauty of the "Child TV Star Found Dead" thing is that the *Daily News* came up with it on its very own. There was no precedent – get it? It was 1976. The only ex-kid stars who'd been "found dead" at that point were burnouts from the old Hollywood studio system – Judy Garland (d. 1969), Bobby Driscoll (d. 1969), people like that. And, the truth was, that stuff was getting old. Were we supposed to feel guilty the rest of our lives for enjoying *The Wizard of Oz* just because some doctor had Garland on the Hunter S. Thompson nutrition program? Enough with the guilt. Enough with those dead old-time movie stars.

Now, dead TV stars. *That* was interesting. And new.

See, we'd begun to suspect that something was up with TV kid stars. Make that *former* TV kid stars. (Forgive the *Daily News* for its oversight in leaving out that key word: *former*. Might have been space considerations. There is only so much headline space, after all, that five-line obits can be allotted.)

So, back to the formers: did you hear about the interview Billy Gray gave to that weekly in '74? He dissed *Father Knows Best*, claimed the Andersons set unrealistic standards for viewers, *and* he used the "F" word. (Sayeth Gray, "People got fucked over because they weren't as even, as Pollyanna-ish.")

And that *Esquire* article on the Nelsons – did you see that one? Came out in '71. Had all kinds of cool stuff – said Ozzie (Ozzie!) was an atheist, said Harriet (Harriet!) couldn't cook, said David (David!) was kinda bitter, said Ricky (Ricky!) did it for the first time with a hooker in London when he was fourteen. Now, how 'bout *them* adventures!

Yeah, this was good stuff. Can you imagine – Bud Anderson

dropping the "F" bomb? An underage Ricky Nelson – that "skinny sex fiend," in the words of his brother – bagging a wanton woman of the night? Why, they weren't like that on their sitcoms. Not at all. Yeah, all right, maybe we could have – should have – been more sophisticated. Maybe we could have – should have – seen this coming. After all, no one ever said *Father Knows Best* was a documentary, right? Billy Gray wasn't *really* Bud Anderson, icon. He was always just Billy Gray, human.

But you know what? It was more fun to play dumb. It was more fun to be shocked that the Nelsons had sex. 'Cause, honestly, if Billy Gray and Ricky Nelson had been as squeaky-clean perfect as their TV selves, that'd be kinda annoying. No, it was more fun to be outraged and disillusioned and disabused of our childhood notions. It also meant that if we were very good, one day somebody would invent *E! True Hollywood Story* and outrage and disillusion and disabuse us of our childhood notions every blessed night.

But back to Buffy. Er, Anissa Jones.

So as to not get ahead of our story, let's remember that in the early 1970s, about the only things that shocked us about former TV child stars were a couple of quotes in a couple of magazines.

Then came Anissa Jones.

Or, actually, there *went* Anissa Jones.

She was "found dead," you know.

And, let's be honest: being "found dead" is so much richer than "succumbing to a long illness" or "dying in a freak mishap." For melodramatic purposes, "killed" is pretty good, too. But "found dead" is the best.

It indicates one was lost.

Anissa Jones, formerly the cherubic Buffy Davis on the supremely congenial *Family Affair*, was "found dead" of a drug overdose in the Oceanside, California, home of a friend on August 28, 1976. She was eighteen.

The *Daily News* summed up her life and career in a photo caption; *Variety* in seven lines.

Sound like the worthy subject of an entire book chapter?

Well, yeah.

Anissa Jones didn't have the rap sheet of an Adam Rich. Or the rep of a Gary Coleman. She didn't get the in-memoriam press of a Jackie Coogan.

But she was also a first.

The first official, honest-to-God former TV child star statistic.

And Enquiring minds need/want to know: why?

The evidence please. . . .

1. THE GIRL

Mary Anissa Jones was born on March 11, 1958, in West Lafayette, Indiana. Her father, John, and mother, Paula, were academics. (John, in fact, was a graduate assistant instructor of chemistry at Indiana's own Purdue University.) The family unit was rounded out by son Paul (full name: John Paul), born in 1959. Following a stint in Paula's hometown of Charleston, West Virginia, the Joneses headed to the Los Angeles area when Anissa was five. By 1965, the family unit – as it was – was over. Paula and John divorced – a nasty split that also essentially divorced John from the lives of his children. Anissa and Paul, along with Paula, formed a new, more streamlined family unit – "the three musketeers," their mother called it.

After the split, Paula, a onetime junior-high teacher, went into real estate; Anissa, whose prior performance experience outside of dance class had consisted of neighborhood puppet shows, went on auditions. She landed her first agent, and subsequently her first commercial, in February 1964 when she was six. As a nine-year-old, Anissa remembered her big break this way: "My mother has a girlfriend, and this girlfriend has a little girl. She [had] been doing commercials. . . . Anyhow, this girl's mother told my mother that her agent was looking for a child who was six years old but who looked younger than that."

Anissa looked younger than that.

Professionally, Mary Anissa was known as Anissa, seemingly if only so deadline-saddled feature writers could be sure to note when pressed for time and creativity that her name was pronounced "A-nees-ah" and meant "little friend" in Lebanese. Actually, according to her future network bio, not only did her name *mean* "little friend," she *was* little (or "tiny for her age," as the copy would note). It was all part of her charm (and employability). Anissa was tiny, not even four feet tall by the time of her prime-time debut. She was blonde. She was blue-eyed. She was freckled. She was cute. She got work. More commercials – as many as twenty – followed.

When she wasn't a little girl at work, she was a little girl – collected troll dolls, did the Brownies, went to school, played with her brother. Little-girl stuff.

When she was eight, she was the first child cast in a proposed Brian Keith series for CBS about a trio of orphans and the bachelor uncle who reluctantly agrees to care for them. Anissa's appeal? Producer Don Fedderson (*My Three Sons*) needed an eight-year-old who looked six.

Anissa looked like that.

She was not a master thespian, nor was she expected to be. Anissa said she believed she aced her screen test because "I just did what I was told." That was all well and good, as the show wasn't supposed to be about its kids. It was to be an adult-oriented series about the adults – chiefly, Keith's uncle character. The kids were to be eye candy – huggable, lovable eye candy. That Anissa could do.

Her mother once said she had no qualms about allowing or encouraging Anissa to go showbiz as a grade-schooler. Said single-mom Paula, "We'd starve otherwise."

2. THE SHOW

Family Affair – the Brian Keith series – premiered on CBS on September 12, 1966. The first episode was called "Buffy." That was the name of Anissa's character. She was Buffy Davis, youngest niece of well-to-do building designer Bill Davis of Manhattan's Fifth Avenue (a neighborhood that would play host to the Drummonds of *Diff'rent Strokes* a decade later). The cast was rounded out by Keith (natch) as the designer (better known as Uncle Bill) and rotund, bearded British actor Sebastian Cabot as Mr. French, Bill's "gentleman's gentleman" (and the show's resident master thespian), with Johnny Whitaker (or "Johnnie," as he was listed in the credits) and Kathy Garver as Jody and Cissy Davis, respectively, the remaining two-thirds of Uncle Bill's poor, parentless trio. (According to series backstory, the kids, who hailed from Terre Haute, Indiana, acquired their orphan status when their parents – Bill's brother and sister-in-law – were killed in a car accident.)

The completed pilot reflected a couple of drawing-board revisions. First, the designer thing. Reportedly in the early drafts, Keith's character was to be a retired judge. Presumably it was decided that (a) no honorable judge would be able to afford Uncle Bill's swank, Central Park-fronting apartment (not to mention the manservant that came with it); and/or (b) a construction executive was a more manly profession for the ladies' man that Keith was to portray. (All those tall, erect skyscrapers, you know.)

Second was the kid thing. As originally sketched out, Cissy was supposed to be a sixteen-year-old; Jody, a ten-year-old (either boy or girl – producers couldn't decide); and Buffy, a six-year-old. Per the Great Law of Sitcom Plotting, it is written that three children, representing three different age groups, is the most desirable character makeup for a family series. The result is a supposedly diverse canvas with which the writer can tell supposedly diverse stories – for teens, for little kids, and for the in-betweeners. Displaying a rare backbone and innovative touch arguably never to be seen again on the series, the *Family Affair* producers ended up willingly and willfully violating the Great Law of Sitcom Plotting, making two of the kids – Buffy and Jody – the same age. During casting, Brian Keith suggested that Anissa and Johnny Whitaker, the six-year-old who was the leading male candidate to play Jody, looked like twins – and so they were to be.

Remembered Whitaker: "As soon as they saw Anissa and me together it was magic."

If the whole our-parents-were-killed-wontcha-please-take-us-in premise (augmented with a dash of custody squabble) doesn't sound like the most light-hearted way to launch a comedy series, then it wasn't. And *Family Affair*, while classified as a sitcom and laugh-tracked like a sitcom, wasn't all that funny. Buffy and Jody were cute to look at (a matched set of chubby cheeks, freckles, and curls), but other than that the show was as serious as the bleeding ulcers that Cabot suffered in season No. 1 or the heart attack that struck him in season No. 4. A 1968 episode about Jody getting a crush on a substitute teacher was handled with all the lightness of spirit of *Schindler's List*. Week in, week out, the Davis household, though ostensibly sporting a dating-age teen and two first-graders, had an eerie, mausoleum quiet. Perhaps Mr. French kept house too well. Or perhaps it was no coincidence that the end-credit sequence, with its titles on a bejeweled, velvety blue background, looked as if it were framed on the inside of a coffin. Was that the laugh-track laughing . . . or wailing? If *TV Guide* had been asked to supply a blurb review for the series, "appalling" would have worked as well as any of the barbs directed at it by writer Cleveland Amory.

Clearly, somebody – lots of somebodies – watched. *Family Affair* finished the 1966–67 season ranked fifteenth. For that, Uncle Bill and his young charges could thank the CBS executives who nestled the baby in a sweepstakes-winning time slot after *The Andy Griffith Show*, at the time the nation's most popular half-hour comedy series. What did *Andy Griffith* fans get out of *Family Affair*? Well, for one thing, a change of pace. *Family Affair* wasn't Mayberry. It wasn't *Green Acres*, either. It was big city. (At least, in the stock-footage location shots.) And how about that Uncle Bill fellow? He was a bit of a different bird. Seemed to have something of an inner life going on there. He was no Andy Taylor or Steve Douglas (*My Three Sons*); a viewer reasonably might have surmised that Uncle Bill got more than quick goodnight kisses from his various lady friends. Or then again, maybe he didn't. (Most of Bill's dates played – and looked – like variations on Eleanor Parker's chilly would-be stepmother character from *The Sound of Music*.)

But by far the main selling point of *Family Affair* was its made-for-TV twins. Ron Howard getting a bit too big (i.e., un-cute) over on *Andy Griffith*? Well, then stay tuned and check out the "larceny artists," as a (presumably) bemused Sebastian Cabot described his two scene-stealing costars. ("Now those kids, bless 'em, they don't use any tricks," Cabot said in 1967. "But they grin that big empty-toothed grin and you're in trouble!")

The series that was supposed to be about adults for adults became a show for adults primarily about two cute little kids, Brian Keith's comforting, quietly domineering performance notwithstanding. There was the episode about (gasp!) Jody getting beat up by a girl bully. There was the episode about (uh-oh!) Buffy wanting to join the Brownies. For good measure, there was the episode (a couple of them, actually) about a suitor asking for the hand of the fair Cissy.

At the center, in popularity, if not the story-line department, was Anissa's Buffy. (Or was it Buffy's Anissa?) Her/their secret? Well, it certainly wasn't her/their acting ability. And it certainly wasn't her/their ability to sell a laugh line. (Indeed, the stone-faced Buffy Davis might have been the most joyless moppet in the history of the family comedy.) So, what was it?

She/they were tiny, blonde, blue-eyed, freckled, and cute.

It worked.

3. THE SET

The little kids called Brian Keith "Brian" and regarded him as a true uncle, if not a father figure. Anissa named one of her cats "Sabby" after the imposing Sebastian "Sabby" Cabot (whom the kids nonetheless addressed as "Mr. Cabot").

Said Kathy Garver, "We were really a family when we were on the *Family Affair* set."

Disclosed an insider to *TV Guide*, "The warmth between Brian and the kids isn't a put-on."

Hmm. Well, *that* was exciting.

Next.

4. THE TWOSOME

Did we mention the curls? The curls were key to the magic of Anissa. Or Buffy.

Whoever.

There were two of them. (The curls, that is.) They hung (or

seemed sprung, like wings) from her head at the sides. They bounced when she walked. They were a perfect complement to school wear or jammie wear. They were more sophisticated than pigtails. They were more little-girly than plain, straight hair.

And they were attainable if you had rubber-band-tying talent – or practiced the art of Buffy on your very own plastic Buffy head.

Anissa/Buffy wasn't just a person, see; she was an industry.

In addition to the assorted *Family Affair* paraphernalia that come with any successful series (the lunch boxes, coloring books, tie-in novels, etc.), Anissa/Buffy had her own toy deal with Mattel (home of Barbie), allowing her likeness to be featured on paper dolls, talking dolls, and the ever-popular, aforementioned plastic doll heads (the better with which to test your makeup/hairdressing skills on). If owning Anissa/Buffy's cranium wasn't enough, you could take the jumper off her back. Or at least buy it, via Anissa/Buffy's personally endorsed clothing line. (Which Anissa/Buffy personally wore herself.)

In other tie-in news, she was also a Halloween costume.

Her reach only expanded as the show's audience expanded – from seasons No. 2 to 4, *Family Affair* was television's fifth most popular show. Assuming dolls eventually break and kiddie clothes eventually wear out their welcome (and usefulness), then Anissa/Buffy's most lasting fashion legacy came in the guise of Cindy Brady. Cindy Brady, as TV history tells us, was a denizen of rival family sitcom *The Brady Bunch*, which premiered at the height of Anissa/Buffy mania in 1969. In the show's theme song, Cindy – as played by appropriately tiny, blonde, and cute Susan Olsen – was referred to as "the youngest one in curls." Presumably because "the youngest one with the Buffy rip-off do" was deigned too wordy – and honest – a lyric.

Olsen, who came to curse the curls as the years wore on, grew out of them ever so slightly in the *Bunch*'s final season in

1974. On *Family Affair*, Anissa/Buffy never outgrew the curls because, well, Anissa/Buffy *was* her curls. (She wasn't the master thespian, remember?) Besides, *could* Anissa be Buffy without the curls? Or vice versa?

The identity thing was tricky. Forget Jody and Buffy. The real twins on the *Family Affair* set were Anissa and Buffy. Which one was she/they really? Not even her cast mates seemed to know for sure. "Good ol' Buffy here . . . or Anissa. I always call her Buffy," a genial, oblivious Mr. Cabot remarked on a 1969 installment of *The Mike Douglas Show*. "I always forget her real name." (Mike's celebrity cohost that day? One Anissa Jones – introduced by Mike, of course, as "Little Buffy." To be fair, Douglas did tag on the clarifier: "Little Buffy . . . who is Anissa Jones.")

Buffy probably wouldn't be bothered by such slip-ups or confusions, but Anissa could be. When she did promotional appearances (and she did lots of those), she'd get the predictable (and numerous) "Hiya, Buffys" from fans. That bugged her.

"I hate it when they call me that," she complained to her mother during a magazine interview in 1970. "Don't they care about me?"

Well, they did, in their own way. The character locks in audiences first, then the actor. If they like your character, then they like you. They may not remember your name, but they like you. And you know what? They like you even better when they're convinced you are the character.

In the case of Anissa/Buffy, empirical evidence told the audience that the two were fairly interchangeable. (Just the way we liked it.) They looked alike (obviously). They dressed alike on the show and off. Personality-wise, they seemed like a good match, too. On *Family Affair*, Buffy was sullen, somber, and seemingly forever on the verge of boredom. (But, oh, she *was* cute!) In interviews, Anissa was portrayed as distracted, bothered, and seemingly forever on the verge of boredom.

Anissa on acting: "I don't know. I just do it. I don't think about it."

Anissa on her job: "Shooting is work. I like going to my own school better, I see my friends there."

Anissa on Santa Claus: "Do you believe in Santa Claus? There really isn't a Santa Claus."

Anissa on her career aspirations: "I want to be a sign painter."

On that last one, Anissa's mother assured the *Citizen News Family Weekly* writer that her daughter wasn't serious. Said Paula Jones, "I knew she would say that because last night she played with a little girl whose father is a sign painter." But, oh, that Anissa *was* cute!

And when she (Anissa, not Buffy) had an audience with President Lyndon B. Johnson in 1968? Oh, she was cute then, too. Read her lines (something about kicking off the annual Christmas Seals program), gave the Commander in Cheek the perfunctory handshake and kiss, and then, bereft of a script, had, um, nothing else to say or do.

"Well, bye," she finally concluded.

Couldn't you just see Uncle Bill rolling his eyes at that one?

As Sabby himself once said, "She's the greatest putter-on."

He meant Buffy.

Er, Anissa.

5. THE DOLL

One of the quirks – perhaps the only one – of Anissa's dead-eyed TV self was the bespectacled, schoolmarm rag doll name of Mrs. Beasley to whom Buffy was very much attached. The young orphan babied it, spoke to it, listened to it. (Note: Beasley didn't actually speak. Like Buffy, she was the short, silent type.) For her part, Anissa brought her along for personal appearances.

In 1967, Mattel issued its first line of Mrs. Beasley dolls. Popular as Anissa/Buffy was, Mrs. Beasley arguably was more popular. Anissa/Buffy, after all, might have been a Halloween costume; but Mrs. Beasley, in addition to being a best-selling doll, was a board game called Where's Mrs. Beasley?.

And unlike Anissa/Buffy, whose viability as a celebrity was very much tied to the TV show, Beasley did not live or die by the Nielsens. In 1973, two years after *Family Affair* had ended production, Mattel was *still* making Mrs. Beasley dolls.

She was, as some collectors put it, "the biggest star of the show" and "the program's most desirable and valuable artifact."

6. THE QUOTE FULL OF PORTENT AND A GREAT DEAL OF FORESHADOWING

Anissa loved to swim. Mostly in the pool, her mother said, but sometimes in the ocean. Once, she broke her leg while playing in the Pacific. When she got her cast off, she dove right back in. Broke the leg again in the same place.

Explained a nine-year-old Anissa on matters of water: "You know at the ocean there's a little wave, then a medium wave, then a great big wave? You never know how deep it is. But in a pool it's marked two feet, three feet, so you know.

"That's the trouble with the ocean. It doesn't say how deep it is."

7. THE OTHER TWIN

Johnny Whitaker was something of the control experiment to Anissa. He was a lot like her and a lot *not* like her. Where she hailed from a single-parent home, he came from a two-parent home. Where she did little else than be Buffy during *Family Affair*, he regularly freelanced (including guest work on *Green*

Acres and *Bewitched*, and a starring role in the 1971 TV movie, *The Littlest Angel*). While she was a relative novice when the series started, he'd been offered his first regular TV work at age four. Where she seemed nonplussed by acting, he seemed in love with it. Where she didn't believe in Santa Claus, his six-year-old heart very much did. ("I heard him laugh and go, 'Ho, ho, ho!' as his sleigh passed over our house.")

Born on December 13, 1959, in Van Nuys, California, Johnny sang his way to his first showbiz contact, discovered by an agent as he sang a solo ("I Am a Child of God") in church. Said his mother Thelma, "It's that face of his." Like Anissa, Johnny was a catch for a casting agent. Everybody wanted him, his mother said. His hair was red and curly. His speaking voice was just a touch froggy and terribly earnest. His face was freckled (with precisely 3,251 freckles, by Johnny's count) and it crinkled up nicely when in full-smile mode.

Johnny's parents were wary about Hollywood angling in for *that face*. Like Anissa's parents, Johnny's mother and father were civilians, not industry sharks. Father John Orson Whitaker Sr. was a shop teacher at Pacoima Junior High in Pacoima, California; Thelma was a homemaker. When Johnny got that TV series offer at age four, the Whitakers rejected it on the grounds they thought their preschooler too young for a steady job. But commercials were okay, as were occasional film and television gigs.

Johnny made his first series appearance in 1965 on the ABC daytime soap opera *General Hospital*. A part in the 1966 big-screen comedy *The Russians Are Coming! The Russians Are Coming!*, in which he played the nephew of star Brian Keith, followed. Later, Keith put in a good word for Johnny to the *Family Affair* staff. The role of Jody would come down to Johnny and a girl, with Johnny (obviously) winning out. A cute story went that Johnny actually was troubled by his victory ("Will I have to work all my life?"), until informed he'd be reunited with Keith. From there on, *Family Affair* was fine by him. He got along famously with Keith and heard *Winnie the Pooh* read at the foot of Sebastian Cabot. As for his relationship with Anissa? He both looked up to and harbored a not-so-secret crush on his TV sibling. Being a sophisticated eight-year-old, nearly two years older than Johnny, Anissa did not return the crush.

8. THE MOTHER

It would be disingenuous to suggest that during *Family Affair* Paula Jones received as much attention as her daughter. But for a junior-high teacher turned real-estate agent she did get an awful lot of ink.

As did Johnny's mom.

Paula Jones and Thelma Whitaker were played off each other – the entertainment-news media made much of their respective child stars' contrasting home lives. Johnny, fans were told over and again, was the fifth of eight children – the product of a devout Mormon clan that gathered for Monday family nights. Anissa, by contrast, was the broken-home kid with the fiercely independent single mom who refused to talk about her ex. If it was a battle of old, nuclear-family America vs. new, broken-family America, it wasn't close. Thelma Whitaker always won. She was the one, dispatches from Hollywood informed us, who stressed that Johnny was only doing what he wanted to do, when he wanted to do it. She was the one who said the best thing about Johnny's career was that it helped provide for the education of all her children. She was the one who said her life didn't revolve around Johnny's career. She was the one who said she didn't feel comfortable with the residual, bleed-over attention that came her way.

The implications, of course, were that Paula Jones *wasn't*

the one. One magazine article said it straight up, referring to Paula Jones as "the one who enjoys the attention, prestige, and limelight." Elsewhere, writers of the day made sure to note any minor mother-daughter squabbles heard within earshot. One scene, recounted in a 1970 *Coronet* magazine, played like a mild *Mommie Dearest* bit, with Paula Jones goading Anissa into a who-do-you-love-the-most, how-much-do-you-love routine. (Paula Jones: "Who do you love?" Anissa: "You." Paula Jones: "How much?" Anissa: "Oh, Mom." Paula Jones: "Okay!") By some miracle of vocabulary, the term "stage mother" was never used.

Paula Jones couldn't win. If the knock on some Hollywood parents was that they didn't stick up for their kids on the set, entrusting others to guard their welfare, then Paula Jones was dinged for *always* being on the set. If the knock on some Hollywood parents was that they favored their star kids over their non-star kids, then Paula Jones was dinged for bringing her son into the fold and encouraging him to do extra work on the series. (Paul's TV career, such as it was, was big sister Anissa's idea, Paula said.) Thelma Whitaker, it was noted, sometimes couldn't even be with Johnny because she had sick kids back at home, or because she had, you know, a husband to tend to (and therefore a life).

To hear Paula Jones tell it, she ran a loving, tight-knit household. When she purchased a duplex near the beach in Playa Del Rey, California, she even consulted a psychologist to see if it was a good thing to allow the children such easy access to the ocean on their own. She was assured they'd be okay.

Said Paula Jones: "I let the children come and go in the neighborhood without me, but I insist they leave notes for me saying exactly where they've gone and when they'll be back."

9. THE DAVY JONES CONNECTION

In 1967, Anissa/Buffy attended the Emmy Awards. She handed out the Outstanding Comedy Series trophy to Bert Schneider and Bob Rafelson, producers of The Monkees. Anissa liked to brag to friends that she might be related to her Monkees namesake, Davy Jones. (Buffy would never engage in any conversation that referenced pop culture and/or the real world.)

Anyway, no bloodline link between Anissa Jones and Davy Jones was ever established.

That would seem to suggest that at least one person is off the hook in the blame department in this story.

[Dramatic pause.]

Or does it?

10. THE BEGINNING OF THE END

Maybe it was Flip Wilson's fault.

In the fall of 1970, the comic launched an hourlong variety series on NBC, introduced a couple of catchphrases ("The devil made me do it" and "Here comes da judge"), and picked up where *Laugh-In* left off (palatable mainstream entertainment in the guise of underground comedy), finishing the season as the No. 2 show on television. Nothing that aired opposite Flip on Thursday nights that season survived another year. Not *Matt Lincoln*. Not *The Jim Nabors Show*. Not *Family Affair*. A Top 5 show before Flip, post-Flip *Family Affair* couldn't crack the Top 25. As bad luck would have it, *Family Affair* drooped just as CBS was cleaning house. In the spring of 1971, the network ran *Mayberry R.F.D.* and *Hee Haw*, and those shows finished No. 15 and No. 16, respectively.

Two factors were behind the pink-slip blizzard. For one thing, CBS was in the midst of its great suburban cleansing movement, ridding itself of shows that appealed to the hinter-lands (e.g., *Hee Haw*) and repositioning itself with shows that appealed to big-city folks (e.g., *The Mary Tyler Moore Show*). And while the Manhattan-set *Family Affair* theoretically fit the network's new mandate, there was no convincing anybody that the square Davises weren't as hick as the *Hee Haw Honeys*.

Demographic merit aside, the second factor that doomed *Family Affair* and other series was a simple space crunch. Since 1949, networks had programmed their prime-time fare to run from 7:30 p.m. to 11 p.m. on weeknights and Saturdays. (On Sundays, the schedules spanned 7 p.m. to 11 p.m.). But starting in the fall of 1971, per a federal government ruling, the 7:30-8 p.m. Monday-Saturday half-hour was to be returned to local stations. And on Sundays, the 7-7:30 half-hour was cut (not to be restored until 1975). For each network, that meant three-and-a-half hours less airtime a week. Shows had to be reshuffled and pushed back. And some had to go. At CBS, *The Ed Sullivan Show* was evicted after twenty-three years, *Lassie* after seventeen years (although new episodes would continue to be produced for syndication), *The Beverly Hillbillies*, after nine, and on down the line.

Family Affair was only five when it got the hook, and while it might appear that it was young enough to be forgiven a rat-ings stumble and young enough to milk more stories (and more money) out of its setup, it wasn't. *Family Affair* was an *old* show. If it aged faster than, says, *Ozzie & Harriet*, that's because its chief distinguishing assets dried up faster. The Ricky factor aside, *Ozzie & Harriet* largely was about the family unit; *Family Affair* was about its cute little kids. By 1971, Anissa was thir-teen, Johnnie twelve. Anissa/Buffy was just about as small as ever and the TV character was just about as young as ever, but the gig was up. *Family Affair* was not a show built to see the twins through puberty. It was a show built to make people go,

"Awww," when a walking, talking version of a Cabbage Patch kid hugged Uncle Bill.

It was over. The show knew it, too. The second-to-last episode – No. 136 of 138 – was called "Goodbye, Mrs. Beasley" and concerned Anissa/Buffy being convinced to put away her childish things.

Unfortunately, one of Anissa/Buffy's childish things was a TV show.

Said Johnny nearly thirty years later, "It's not easy when you've been at the pinnacle of your career at eleven."

Johnny himself didn't come close to peaking at eleven. After *Family Affair*, the kid who loved acting did what he'd been doing on *Family Affair* – TV guest spots (*Gunsmoke*) and film (1972's *The Biscuit Eater*). As a teen, he wasn't as cute as he'd been at six, but he had a look – his red hair approaching Afro-esque heights; his easy, wide grin as contagious as ever – and warranted minor mentions in the teen bibles (e.g., *Tiger Beat*) of the early 1970s. By 1973, he was starring in a big-screen musical version of *Tom Sawyer* (alongside his Becky Thatcher, one Jodie Foster), returning to weekly TV on the Saturday morning Krofft Brothers concoction *Sigmund and the Sea Monsters*, dabbling in a pop-music career ("Friends"), playing the Hollywood Bowl on the same bill as the Brady Kids, and, in Anissa/Buffy style, continuing to endorse his own clothing line.

"And I'm hoping to maybe go on working in the movie industry," he told the *Los Angeles Times* in 1973.

As for Anissa/Buffy? She (Anissa) did a movie. Once. With Elvis in *The Trouble with Girls*. It came out in 1969.

And, um . . .

Well . . .

Mrs. Beasley was still in production.

11. THE CHRISTMAS CARD
(OR, ANOTHER QUOTE FULL OF PORTENT AND A GREAT DEAL OF FORESHADOWING)

Seasonal greetings from Anissa Jones, circa 1975:

"May love surround you at Christmas and always."

That was the card's printed text.

The handwritten message from the seventeen-year-old former child star went like this:

"Thanks for remembering me."

12. THE END

She was found on the floor. An empty envelope for the prescription barbiturate Seconal by her side.

"Child TV Star Found Dead."

It was the bicentennial summer of 1976. In the five years since *Family Affair* ended, Anissa had warred with her mom, moved in with the dad that her mom had insisted was out of the lives of "the three musketeers," lost her dad to heart failure (in 1974), grown out her Buffy curls until she looked like Caroline Kennedy (except not as tall), turned eighteen, and came into her *Family Affair* earnings (about $70,000). Above all, she'd become a private citizen. And in the summer of '76, the private citizen was doing what private citizens are wont to do – hanging with friends. Anissa did a lot of her hanging in Oceanside, California, near San Diego. In mid-August, she spent a week at the Oceanside home of a friend – one Helen Hennessy. On August 27, a Friday, she returned to the neighborhood with three pals in tow. That night, Anissa returned to the Hennessy house to crash in an upstairs bedroom. At about noon on the following Saturday, police said, another friend, Carla Machado, found Anissa still asleep, still in her nightclothes. Machado tried to rouse her. Couldn't. Paramedics were called; the empty

Seconal package noted; Anissa declared dead (after being "found" as such) at 12:27 p.m.

"Her death could possibly have been an accidental overdose," Oceanside police detective John Wagner told reporters. "There was no indication of suicide."

Initial autopsy results had been inconclusive. Toxicology tests, returned about two weeks later, were not. Present in her system at the time of death were: Seconal, cocaine, angel dust, and Quaalude. It was, said County Coroner Robert L. Creason, "one of the most severe cases of drug overdose ever seen in San Diego County."

It was also, Creason's office ruled, self-administered and accidental.

On her death certificate, Anissa Jones was an actress again. It said right there on the line "Last Occupation." The name of her "Last Employer": Columbia Broadcasting Co.

There was no mention of Buffy.

13. THE REAL, TRUE HOLLYWOOD STORY

So many questions.

Based on the incidents presented above, which of the following persons and/or situations contributed to Anissa Jones being "found dead"?

(a) Hollywood;
(b) *Family Affair*;
(c) *The Mike Douglas Show*;
(d) Mommie Dearest;
(e) her career as a working child actor;
(f) her life as a formerly working child actor;
(g) Flip Wilson;
(h) LBJ;

(i) a broken family;

(j) a self-destructive streak;

(k) people who called her "Buffy," when they really meant "Anissa";

(l) Mrs. Beasley;

(m) all of the above, but mostly (a).

While we ponder that, let's not forget the whole, weird first-name/middle-name thing. "Anissa," as we have learned, was actually Anissa Jones' middle name. In a startling coincidence, Anissa's true name was Mary – like her mother, who went by Paula. And her brother? He was John – except everybody called him Paul.

What was that about? Was the family denying their true selves? Did they lose their souls (and not just their given names) in Hollywood? Were they sad, unwitting victims of the dream factory?

You know what?

Sometimes a middle name is just a middle name used as a first name.

Sometimes things just are. Sometimes they don't mean anything.

Sometimes they don't mean anything until we – the fans, the writers, the observers, the outsiders – pick over the bones (literally) and assign Motive A to End Result B. It's nice and tidy for us. We like resolution. We like things to make sense. We like to find *meaning* – all in the name, of course, of HELPING SAVE JUST ONE LIFE.

You know what?

There is no big picture where Anissa Jones was concerned.

There is no use in asking if her death was a tragedy. There is no use in asking if she was a lost soul. If we can assume that anyone who dies – consciously or unconsciously by their own hand – well before their body would be expected to give out is something of a tragic figure, then so be it. Anissa Jones was a tragic figure.

But beyond that?

We don't know, never will know, and, if Anissa Jones unexpectedly placed a phone call to Larry King tonight, *still* wouldn't know how she ended up where she ended up. (Would she tell us stuff to make us feel better? Would she tell us stuff to make us feel worse? Would she herself even know?)

Here's all we really have to go on: Anissa Jones lived. Worked on a TV show. Died. Young.

"Child TV Star Found Dead."

The significance of her story lies in that headline – why it stopped us cold, why it made us expect more of the same.

Cue the smoke machine. Punch up the sad piano music. Round up the talking heads. (And, please, would you ask the talking heads to shake said heads occasionally while they talk? Looks more tragic that way.)

Let the circus begin.

CHAPTER FIVE

EEK, A FORMER CHILD STAR!

*"I spent four hours in jail and was bailed out by the
National Enquirer."*

— DANNY BONADUCE, ON A 1985 COCAINE BUST

So, whatever happened to Mrs. Beasley?

"Mrs. Beasley is currently a hooker on Sunset and Gower,"
wrote Danny Bonaduce in *Esquire* magazine in 1991. "For fifty
dollars, she's the best piece of plastic you ever had."

Ba-du-dum-bum.

Bonaduce, the once-upon-a-time "red-haired wisecracking
kid" or (depending on which shorthand cliché you preferred)
"redheaded, freckle-faced kid" from *The Partridge Family*
(1970–74), wrote the essay after he was arrested for busting a
transvestite in the chops (after he was arrested in a crack house
. . . after he was arrested for coke possession).

Ba-du-dum-bum.

These are the jokes, folks. We got a million of 'em. What do you want to hear? The one about Adam (*Eight Is Enough*) Rich stealing socks? Darlene (*The Mickey Mouse Club*) Gillespie being accused of shoplifting four on-sale shirts? Mackenzie (*One Day at a Time*) Phillips getting canned from her sitcom? Lauren (*Father Knows Best*) Chapin trying to chop off her own hand with a meat cleaver? Anything work for you here? You like true crime? Sordid drug tales? Tell-all confessions? Suicides? Take your pick. Like we said, we got a million of 'em. (Did we mention the one about the girl from *The Addams Family* and the porn star?)

Yes, lock the doors, hide the children, say your prayers. Here comes *Dennis the Menace*:

> "I still go into a batting cage and pretend that the baseballs are the heads of my aunt and uncle and the studio people who exploited me as 'Dennis the Menace.' And I always hit the ball well." (Jay North)

All right, all together now: what the hell . . . ?

What the hell happened to these people? How did we go from squeaky-clean *Leave It to Beaver* tykes in the 1950s and 1960s to *Village of the Damned* spawn in the 1970s and beyond? Did every blinkin' kid who used to be on a blinkin' TV show lose it? What the hell happened?

Perhaps the better question again is: what didn't happen?

It's not for nothing that "former child star" became confused as a synonym for "screw-up." This part of the saga is no myth: as of the 1970s, lots of ex-TV tykes made lots of headlines for lots of not-so-stellar things. So what happened? Life, Hollywood, the world, Phil Donahue.

Like we said, what didn't happen?

ANISSA JONES HAPPENED . . .

Suicide is a non-inherited inherited disease. For example, Dr. Clarence Hemingway kills himself; son Ernest Hemingway kills *himself*; great-granddaughter Margaux kills *herself*. There is no genetic factor, doctors say, that sets a bloodline on a self-destructive course. There's actually no disease involved at all. It's just a really bad habit. The first suicide in a family tree is the schoolyard equivalent of the bad kid who turns the other kids onto cigarettes. Suddenly, the forbidden seems possible. The awful is thinkable. There is no turning back.

Before Jones' death in 1976, the TV generation of kid actors largely avoided the sort of horror stories that plagued the golden era of the movie kid actor. After her death, the forbidden seemed possible, etc., etc. The numbers are staggering. Do you know how many TV kids made nasty headlines for passing out on a public street (and subsequently getting busted for coke possession) *before* Anissa Jones died? None. Do you know how long it took for the first famed passer-outer to hit the ground *after* she died? Fifteen months. (A record established in November 1977 by the aforementioned Mackenzie Phillips.)

Whether or not Anissa Jones intentionally took her life (and she did not) is immaterial. The point here isn't suicide, it's this: before Anissa Jones, next to nothing in the TV former child star scandal department. After Anissa Jones, everything including the kitchen sink, the bathroom tile, Adam Rich's purloined hosiery, and Danny Bonaduce's misadventures in dating. One way or another, the dam broke.

AND DRUGS HAPPENED . . .

Jon Provost remembered the Hollywood drug scene of the 1950s – he remembers he didn't know there was one. "When I was working, I think the only drugs that were really there

[were] alcohol and cigarettes," the *Lassie* star said. "I mean, I don't even think people smoked pot back then."

People did, of course. None other than Bud Anderson, er, Billy Gray, later revealed he started smoking when he was fourteen and didn't stop during the entire *Father Knows Best* run. So, forgive Timmy Martin his sheltered life. He did, after all, grow up on a farm. And truth was, lots of Americans essentially grew up on the same bucolic farm. When the first TV kids were being produced back in the 1950s, the U.S. drug culture wasn't all that. Same with the early 1960s. A 1962 study showed that a grand total of four million red-white-and-blue types (out of about 179.3 million) had copped to "trying" an illegal drug. While that statistical finding likely was a shock to the system of a people who still lived in a black-and-white TV world, it was nothing compared with the Electric Kool-Aid Acid Test that followed. By 1998, 78.1 million people (out of more than 248 million) claimed they'd done some sort of illicit drug at least once.

Summed up Provost: "When you got into the '60s and '70s, you know, everything hit the fan."

Headline-wise, Gray's 1962 marijuana conviction ("for a handful of seeds and stems") was the first TV kid drug rap. His saga wasn't exactly *Midnight Express* material, but for the era of Camelot, it was close enough. "I couldn't get a job after that," Gray said, adding that he didn't really want one anyway. "I was ready to take a hiatus." If the pot bust didn't weigh on Gray's mind, it apparently weighed (heavily) on the minds of others, both in and out of Hollywood. As a 1974 profile on Gray noted, "Drugs are sometimes mentioned in the 'Whatever became of . . .' rumors trailing him." More than mentioned, they got plopped right in a noted reference book – critic Leonard Maltin's annual movie guide. From 1974 to 1997, editions featured a capsule review of the 1971 film *Dusty and Sweets McGee* that referred to Gray as one of the "real-life addicts and pushers shown" in the docudrama-style flick about heroin users in Los Angeles. Oh, Gray *did* appear in the film. Thing was, he only *played* a heroin addict; he didn't *become* one – a discrepancy Maltin corrected and apologized for in 1998 (after Gray, who didn't learn about the listing himself until the late 1990s, filed a libel suit). In his mandated public *mea culpa*, Maltin maintained he meant no harm, after all: "I grew up watching and enjoying Billy Gray on the television series *Father Knows Best* . . ."

Drug rumors also trailed Tommy Rettig – except they weren't really rumors. In the pre-Anissa Jones era, Jon Provost's *Lassie* forerunner was a genuine wild card, something of the Timothy Leary of ex-kid stars. Not only did Rettig get arrested for pot (a 1972 charge he shared with his wife for growing the stuff in their backyard), he unabashedly liked the stuff and went on to fight for its legalization. And it wasn't just marijuana he promoted. He would tell *Rolling Stone* about how "LSD saved my life." And to the *Los Angeles Times*, he would tout how drugs were "natural substances [that] have been around long before man. . . . I think no one can achieve a certain growth without [them]."

Then, in 1975, the then-most-scandalous thing that ever happened to a former child star happened to Tommy Rettig: he was taken into custody at his Morro Bay, California, home by federal drug agents on charges of smuggling Peruvian cocaine into the States via liqueur bottles. Said the *Village Voice*, "Lassie's First Master Accused of Cocaine Karma." Rettig's claims that he and a friend, who was also tried in the case, were framed by real-deal coke dealers because they were at work on a book about pushers went unheeded and he was convicted – sentenced to five and a half years in prison. In 1979, the conviction was overturned. (The feds were dinged for botching the search on Rettig's home. Oh, and one more thing: none of the reputedly smuggled-in coke was ever found.) Another scrape followed in 1980 – this one coming at a reputed drug lab near California's Lake Arrowhead, where 600 to 800 grams of coke allegedly were uncovered. Rettig and three others were arrested. (The case eventually was dropped; he was never charged.) All told, Rettig compiled one career marijuana bust, two didn't-stand-up coke charges, and a thick wad of newspaper clippings along the lines of "Tommy Rettig, Ex-Child Star of *Lassie*, Arrested in Cocaine Raid." It was a tad more exciting than Gray's C-list pot rap, yes, but not exactly a passage from the John Belushi biography, either.

Fact was, if Rettig and Gray had represented the extent of the nation's drug problem, it wouldn't have been much of a problem. And if Rettig and Gray had represented the extent of kid actors' troubles with drugs, they wouldn't have been very big troubles. But Rettig and Gray did *not* represent. They were pioneers, not prime examples. They were highly functional individuals, not screwups. And they were merely the opening act. The kids who followed – the stars of the 1960s, 1970s, and beyond – were the stars of this story. By virtue of inflation-sized paychecks, they had more access to cash and (if they so desired) more drugs. Growing pot in your backyard was supremely old school compared with what youth, money, and fame (or residual fame) could buy you at the height of the drug revolution (which, according to studies, peaked among teens and adults in 1979–80). They had the means, the opportunity, and the right environment. It was there for the taking.

DANNY BONADUCE (*The Partridge Family*): Arrested in September 1985, after Los Angeles police find 50 grams of coke in his sports car; arrested in March 1990 at a Daytona Beach, Florida, crack house after police find coke on his person in the form of wadded-up twenty-dollar bills. "Why does anybody get into drugs?"

he later said. "I had a lot of time on my hands. I started recreationally, and next thing I know it was the focus of my life."

RICK NELSON (*Ozzie & Harriet*): Toxicology tests following a fatal New Year's Eve 1985 plane crash that killed him, his fiancée, four band members, and a soundman in DeKalb, Texas, showed Rick, forty-five, had traces of cocaine, marijuana, and the painkiller Darvon in his system at the time of the accident. It was merely post-mortem evidence for what we had grown to suspect of this teen idol turned career rock performer: Ricky Nelson (gasp!) was not nearly as wooden or squeaky clean or boring as he appeared on TV. Recalled ex-wife Kristin of their relationship in 1987: "We were hippie rock 'n' rollers. We did what everyone else was doing all those years. . . . After a while we were totally messed up."

MACKENZIE PHILLIPS (*One Day at a Time*): Booked on felony cocaine possession after the found-in-the-street incident on November 23, 1977; released from *One Day at a Time* in 1980 due to her drug habit; released from *One Day at a Time* (again) in 1983; nearly died twice from overdoses (Mackenzie's own estimate); financed a $1,000-a-week habit (Mackenzie's own estimate). Said the actress, "You can really spend a lot of money on cocaine."

This is not meant to be an exhaustive list of TV notables' on-the-public-record encounters with drugs. And it's not even close to a thorough compendium of TV notables who got messed up on drugs but never earned the found-on-a-street-

corner headlines to go with their troubles. After Anissa Jones'
toxicological record-setting performance, former child star drug
tales became as common as McDonald's drive-thrus, as quickly
dispensed as lunchtime Big Macs. Seemingly everybody had a
story – from "A" (for Willie Aames – teen hearthrob Tommy
Bradford on *Eight Is Enough* from 1977 to 1981 – who once
put a finger to his nose and sniffed when asked how he blew a
million dollars) to "P" (for Paul Petersen, who spent his twenties making "terrible choices" – "drugs, alcohol, bad people" –
and recalled "the only thing I didn't do is stick a needle in my
arm") and back again. It got to the point where the supermarket
tabloids could be picky about which misfortune they spot-
lighted. When Brandon Cruz got arrested on a drunk-driving
charge in his twenties, he rang up the *National Enquirer* himself – "I wanted them to pay for the lawyer" – and planted the
story. But if Cruz was expecting the editors to jump at the
chance for a "*Courtship of Eddie's Father* Tyke Runs Afoul of
Law (in a Rather Ordinary Way)" headline, he was mistaken.
"They said, 'No, sorry, we're not interested.'"

So, clearly, drugs happened – for whatever that's worth, for
whatever that says about the child-of-Hollywood experience.
Drugs also happened to children of plumbers, children of
lawyers, and children of schoolteachers. The TV kids just happened to be more famous than the others. Did drugs happen to
every former child star? No. To enough of them to justify semi-
annual "After the Laugh Track Fades: Why Do So Many Kids
Who Make It Big in Hollywood Become Troubled Young
Adults?" trend stories? What do you think?

AND SUICIDES HAPPENED . . .

Trent Lehman hanged himself; Rusty Hamer shot himself. For
most of the history of TV former child stars, that was the extent

of suicides involving the peer groups' members – two. Not enough to top the druggies with sheer volume; just enough to qualify for the plural "suicides"; and, arguably, more than enough to cement the whole "screw-up" reputation. A drug habit, after all, is one thing – a dime-a-dozen, ho-hum thing, really. But if you really wanted to tell the world you're lost? Well, nothing like a suicide to impress us with your dedication to the cause.

Trent Lehman was the second- to third-banana kid on a minor TV sitcom (*Nanny and the Professor*) that ran all of a season and a half on ABC from 1970 to 1971. You've got to have a long memory to know anything about *Nanny and the Professor*, a cut-rate *Bewitched* with Juliet Mills' magical housekeeper in place of Elizabeth Montgomery's magical housewife. *TV Guide* once called the show a "half-hour bit of fluff," and, indeed, it flitted away like one – its short-lived network run followed by a relatively short-lived syndication run. Nothing much about *Nanny and the Professor* seemed to leave a dent – it wasn't memorably terrible, it wasn't memorably great. When it was over, Mills continued her TV/film career; Kim Richards, who played the youngest of Nanny Phoebe's three charges, became a Disney film star (*Escape to Witch Mountain*); *The Big Valley* alum Richard Long, who played Nanny's employer Professor Howard Everett, died of a heart attack in 1974; David Doremus, who costarred as Howard's eldest son, Hal, scored a recurring role on *The Waltons* from 1972 to 1977; and Trent Lehman, as the middle boy, Butch, never did prime time again.

Up until *Nanny*, the blond-haired Trent was a working cute, kid actor. Following his sister in the business, he booked his first commercial at age six and went on to guest-starring roles on *Gunsmoke* and the like. In other words, it was a typical existence for a working, cute kid actor. His home life appeared equally typical: during the *Nanny* run, he was a fourth-grader at Vena Avenue Elementary School in Arleta, California; his stepdad was a plant foreman at a local aircraft company; his mom was a mom; his sister a sister. Said *Nanny* producer Charles FitzSimmons of Trent, "He was 100 percent real boy." After the series ended, the "real boy" found acting gigs hard to come by. "He was getting older and bigger," Trent's onetime agent Don Schwartz said. "Sometimes the older kids have trouble finding work. The little kids are cuter."

In 1977, the Lehman family left California for Colorado — the line was Trent's mom "wanted peace" for her kids. In the summer of 1981, Trent moved back to Planet Hollywood (or North Hollywood, as was the case) on his own. His friends said he came looking for a girl. In early 1982, the love affair ended and his apartment got robbed. On January 19, he went to a buddy's house and asked to borrow a gun. Trent told the friend he wanted to kill himself. The friend did not give Trent a gun. Instead, he offered to put him up for the night. Trent accepted. Later that night, Trent visited his old Vena Avenue stomping grounds, roped a leather belt around his neck, and hanged himself from a chain-link fence. Quoth the newspaper, "Former Child Star, 20 'Depressed,' Hangs Himself."

While the lesser-known Trent Lehman was more accurately a "former child actor," Rusty Hamer was an outright former child star, who at one point, according to a newspaper column, was "the newest smash on television." The smash won the role of Danny Thomas' TV son on *Make Room for Daddy* in 1953. He was seven. During the audition, he endeared himself to the powers-that-be by sitting on his head and eating cookies (presumably not at the same time). Said Thomas, whose secretary had first spotted Rusty in a local play, "He was the best boy actor I ever saw in my life. . . . He had great memory . . . great timing." The childhood Rusty proclaimed no ambitions to be an actor when he grew up, insisting that he'd much rather fly through clouds and "make rain." Rusty nonetheless remained a working actor.

In December 1953, Rusty's father, Arthur, died and the newly employed TV star became the sole means of support for his family, which included his mother and two brothers. (Said Mother Hamer, "We had just bought a house and we would have given it up if Rusty hadn't been working.") At least Rusty's TV life was free of tragedy. The set was "very much a large family"; the TV parents (Danny Thomas and Marjorie Lord, who replaced the show's original mother figure, Jean Hagen), "always kind," fellow child actor Angela Cartwright would say. (Cartwright, later of *Lost in Space*, joined the cast of the retitled *The Danny Thomas Show* in 1957 as Rusty's stepsister, Patty.) Rusty stayed on as Rusty (as in wise-cracking Rusty Williams) until Thomas' show ended production in 1964.

After the sitcom, Rusty, in Thomas' words, "seemed like a fish out of water." On December 27, 1966, at age nineteen, he nearly died after shooting himself in the stomach with his own .22 caliber pistol. It was, police said, a "freak accident" – the result of an inadvertent discharge as Rusty unpacked guns from his car following a hunting trip. Rusty recovered and returned, briefly, to prime time in 1970 as, again, Rusty Williams in the revival sitcom *Make Room for Granddaddy*, also starring Thomas, Lord, and Cartwright. The show lasted a season, ending production in 1971. Later, Rusty worked for Exxon Oil, worked as a messenger, and worked at a restaurant owned by one of his brothers.

In January 1990, at age forty-two, he shot himself to death with a .357 Magnum. It was not a freak accident. Said brother John Hamer: "No one does something like that if they aren't confused."

AND ASSORTED SCANDALS HAPPENED . . .

This section should actually be entitled "And Assorted Scandals (Not Inclusive of Anissa Jones or the Aforementioned Drug and

Suicide Stories) Happened . . ." because, clearly, those were scandals, too. But here's a run-down of some of the garden-variety former child star scandals. Like the time when:

Danny Bonaduce punched the transvestite.

On March 31, 1991, Bonaduce, then a radio deejay in Phoenix, met up with one Darius Lee Barney. According to police, Bonaduce handed a twenty-dollar bill to Mr. Barney – who apparently wasn't really looking like a "mister" – and asked for sex. When Mr. Barney declined Bonaduce's offer, police said, Bonaduce (1) punched Mr. Barney in the nose; and (2) took back his twenty. Bonaduce ran away, but didn't get away. He was arrested for assault, robbery, and, well, running away. Making the bust all the more special in the annals of former child stardom was the fact that it hit the papers the same day as Adam (*Eight Is Enough*) Rich was accused of breaking into a pharmacy. (More – much more – on Rich later.) In the end, Bonaduce worked a plea bargain and agreed to pay Mr. Barney $3,000 to cover plastic surgery costs on his nose.

A federal court found ex-*Mickey Mouse Club* member Darlene Gillespie guilty of securities fraud. Or, as one headline put it, "Jury Says Mouseketeer Is Racketeer."

On the *Mouse Club*, Darlene was one of Mr. Disney's original do-gooders. She was also one of the show's original standouts. No mere Karen or Cubby back-grounder, Darlene starred on her own *Mouse Club* serial, "Corky and White Shadow," and appeared in its signature franchise, "The Adventures of Spin and Marty." Ultimately, though, she was no match for Annette Funicello in the battle for the hearts and minds of Mouseketeer fans. Annette was the one who had the teenybopper following, the teenybopper pop career, and her own *Mouse Club* series, "Annette." Suffice to note, there was no corresponding "Darlene." After the *Club* closed in 1959, Darlene went on to build a career in hospital nursing, and while that was a good thing, it still was not an Annette thing (i.e., a movie-star, recording-artist thing). In 1990, "Mouse Nurse," as she was called in the O.R., sued the Disney studio, mounting, perhaps, the ultimate former child star lawsuit challenge – claiming the Magic Kingdom had reneged on a promise to make her "a well-known artist." (She also claimed she was cheated out of royalties for Mouse Club reruns.) If biting the Mouse hand that made her (briefly) famous – justified or no – was not what the public expected of its Eared Ones, then neither was getting busted for lifting a quartet of shirts from a sales rack at a Ventura County, California, Macy's department store. In August 1997, Darlene's sentencing judge called her and her then-fiancé (and later, husband) Jerry Fraschilla "professional thieves" and slapped them both with three years' probation. The best/worst was yet to come.

In December 1998, Darlene Gillespie was convicted in federal court of twelve conspiracy, fraud, and perjury counts for what prosecutors called a seven-figure stock swindle. (Old friend Fraschilla preceded her in court, pleading guilty to twenty-one counts of fraud and earning an eighteen-month prison sentence.) Darlene, then fifty-seven, faced up to ninety years behind bars. On March 11, 1999, she got a (relative) break: she was sentenced to two years in prison. Darlene vowed to appeal: "I believe with all my heart that at the end of the day I will be vindicated."

Ricky Nelson's plane crashed.

What's scandalous about a plane crash? Why are toxicological tests being ordered on a man who wasn't anywhere near the controls when his band's doomed DC-3 went down? Because word after the crash had it that Ricky had helped spark the crash-inducing fire by freebasing in the cabin. After the lab tests came back positive for drugs, the rumors only got bigger. Then, fifteen months later, investigators, with much less fanfare, noted that – oh, by the way – Ricky Nelson and his band were *not* responsible for the fire and smoke that sealed their fates. What ignited the flames? A faulty cabin heater, the feds ruled in May 1987. In reality, no, not much of a scandal. But facts rarely get in the way of something that *should* be a scandal.

Tommy Rettig died.

Another non-scandal that got treated like one. In February 1996, Tommy Rettig died . . . of natural causes. (A suspected heart attack.) He was fifty-four. Every obit rehashed the drug arrests and noted that he never duplicated his Lassie success (in Hollywood, at least.) After *Lassie*, the *Los Angeles Times* said, "came a troubled life filled with failure to land adult roles" and a "string of jobs" (photographer, tool salesman, computer programmer, health-club manager), making it sound as if Rettig's life was somehow the equivalent of the Rusty Hamer story, or as if Rettig wasn't a noted software entrepreneur who once made the cover of *PC World* magazine on the strength of his company (dBase) and not his TV past, or as if Rettig was unhappy with how things turned out even if he himself called his life "a wonderful adventure." ". . . The adventures I have had in my life, both bad and good, I treasure them all," Rettig said in 1990. "None of them have been horrible." Right. We knew better. How could a TV former child star die content?

Kristy McNichol becomes a "physical, mental wreck." Kristy McNichol was the eerily adult, unfailingly reliable teen star of the suburban domestic-unit drama *Family* (1976–80). Jane Fonda called her "brilliant"; Emmy voters called her Outstanding Supporting Actress in a Drama Series, twice (1977, 1979). When the series ended, McNichol was eighteen and ready for more work. Feature films followed: *Little Darlings* (1980), *The Night the Lights Went Out in Georgia* (1981), *Only When I Laugh* (1981), etc. During Christmastime 1982, McNichol was doing even more work – her sixth film since *Little Darlings* – when she just couldn't do the work anymore. McNichol refused to return from a holiday break to the French set of her in-the-works romantic drama, *I Won't Dance*. There were rumors of drugs. Rumors of booze. Rumors of manic depression. Her brother, Jimmy, also an actor, described her as being a "physical, mental wreck." McNichol had her own diagnosis: she was having a reaction – a delayed reaction – to her childhood, or lack thereof. "From the time I was very young, I was a professional, making money and assuming responsibilities," McNichol said in 1989. ". . . I was living the life of a thirty-year-old." Ever the professional, McNichol eventually did return to the movie set. And the movie was eventually released, retitled: *Just the Way You Are.*

Wednesday Addams married a porn star.

Wednesday was the goth-looking daughter of Gomez and Morticia Addams, as played by Lisa Loring on TV's *The Addams Family* (1964–66). At fifteen, she wed. By sixteen, she divorced (and mourned the death of her mother). In the 1980s, she tried marriage for the third time, exchanging vows with actor Paul Siederman, better known to triple-X connoisseurs as porn star Jerry (*Raw Talent*) Butler. He said he tried to go legit for her. She told a supportive Jenny Jones audience that the doomed marriage "took me to one of the darkest places in my life," including heroin addiction. The scandal? Did you miss the part about little Wednesday Addams marrying a porn star? Like, you need any more than that?

Eddie Munster vs. the limo driver.

It was Halloween 1990. Butch Patrick (real name: Patrick Allan Lilley), who costarred as fanged wolfboy Eddie Munster on *The Munsters* (1964–66), was doing Chicago in a limo for a spook-season personal-appearances tour. Two days later, on November 2, Patrick and another man were charged with robbery – accused by their old acquaintance, the Chicago limo driver, of pinching $130 from the guy's wallet at a gas station. Patrick, through his public defender, said: Bogus. The thing was, the driver kept on getting lost, Patrick's camp explained. "A fight began and Munster, er, Mr. Lilley," said the attorney, "apparently took the wallet, claiming that the driver shouldn't have been paid in the first place." Summed up Patrick of his life years later, "My first twenty years were spent working in an adult world. I made up for it by being a hell-raiser for the next ten years."

Beaver Cleaver got killed in Vietnam; Danny Partridge got killed in Vietnam; Dennis the Menace died in the doctor's office; Cindy Brady OD'd; Jan Brady did porn; Eddie Haskell morphed into pioneer shock-rocker Alice Cooper and, later, into porn star John Holmes; That Kid with the Glasses Who Played Paul on *The Wonder Years* morphed into latter-day shock-rocker Marilyn Manson; and Mikey From Those Life Cereal Commercials in the 1970s swallowed Pop Rocks and Coke and then exploded.

Not to spoil the fun or anything, but none of this stuff happened. Like we said, facts rarely get in the way of a good scandal – or urban legend. Some of these stories had roots in genuine misunderstandings, like the time in the 1970s when actress Shelley Winters read that a Gerald Mathers had been killed in action in Vietnam combat and went on Johnny Carson's *Tonight Show* to tell America that the war was killing our children, including Jerry Mathers, the dear, ex-star of *Leave It to Beaver*. The Cindy Brady/Susan Olsen one appeared to have been started by people who never did figure out that Cindy was not Buffy from *Family Affair* – she only looked like her on TV. The Eddie Haskell rumors were beyond explanation – all the while Ken Osmond was rumored to be wearing eyeliner on the concert stage or working his member for the enjoyment of filmgoers everywhere, he was doing his sworn duty as a member of the Los Angeles Police Department. What was up with all these stories? Call us guilty – we're hooked on scandal. If it's a slow week, we'll just make something up. We make up stuff about lots of people, sure – you ever hear the one about Richard Gere and a certain rodent? – but former child stars are such easy targets. Honestly, if Mikey didn't really explode, what happened to him? It's not like he's on TV anymore or anything. (The boring truth: John Gilchrist went on to become a radio ad exec.)

You'll note the absence of any mention here of any former child star connected with the sitcom *Diff'rent Strokes*. The tales of those actors could be cataloged in their own book. For this book's purposes, they'll be cataloged in the following chapter.

AND ADAM RICH HAPPENED . . .

Adam Rich could also get his own chapter, but for space and time considerations, and due to the fact that, all things considered, he's just not terribly notorious, he won't. So as not to diminish his significance in the former-child-star saga, it should be noted that for an extraordinary twenty-month stretch in the early 1990s, no one outside of the *Diff'rent Strokes* crew did more to feed our suspicions of the stability and general well-being of Those People.

By way of a cursory biography, from 1977 to 1981, Rich was Nicholas Bradford, the pint-sized, floppy-haired, member of the zero-population-growth-defying Bradford family on ABC's *Eight Is Enough*. In a cast of nearly a dozen regulars, Rich was a standout. Even if an episode didn't revolve around his character, it usually opened and closed on him – Nicholas put fannies in the seats. Rich was a true child star. After *Eight Is Enough* went off the air, he segued into a short-lived firefighter series (*Code Red*, 1981–82) and a short-lived sitcom (*Gun Shy*, 1983). Then it was off to the occasional reunion TV movie (1987's *Eight Is Enough: A Family Reunion* and 1989's *An Eight Is Enough Wedding*), which served to show us how much he'd grown (or at least how much deeper his voice was). No subsequent role measured up, in our eyes, to the original (little) Nicholas Bradford. And then Rich became, in our eyes, a true former child star. A sampling of his work:

October 6, 1990: Arrested in West Hollywood, California, on a driving-under-the-influence charge.

November 29, 1990: Pleads guilty to drunken driving; gets five years' probation.

April 6, 1991: Arrested on suspicion of felony commercial burglary and reckless driving after Los Angeles area police say Adam broke two windows at a West Hills, California, pharmacy and sped away. In court, prosecutors charge that the ex-kid star had been on the prowl for morphine, resorting to the drugstore after a nearby hospital declined his request.

April 17, 1991: Arrested for allegedly shoplifting sunglasses and a pair of socks from a Northridge, California, department store.

April 22, 1991: *The Los Angeles Times* reports that Adam is "embarrassed" by his string of run-ins with the law. "I don't know why this happened, but I know I am sick," Adam says. "I have a disease. Some people are saying it was a cry for help, and I guess that's right. I am very remorseful, very embarrassed."

September 12, 1991: A Van Nuys Municipal Court hearing on the burglary case is stopped when prosecutors say they think defendant Rich is on drugs.

October 2, 1991: Ordered to stand trial on the pharmacy break-in case.

October 3, 1991: Closes out the stolen socks case by entering a no-contest plea to a lesser trespassing charge.

October 6, 1991: Arrested for allegedly stealing a drug-filled syringe from Daniel Freeman Marina Hospital in Marina Del Rey, California. Adam, at the hospital for a dislocated shoulder, tells authorities he wanted the syringe to service his injury; authorities say he wanted the syringe to service himself with Demerol.

October 31, 1991: Ordered to a live-in drug rehab facility; placed on two years' probation.

January 6, 1992: Ordered to Los Angeles County Jail for thirty days after getting booted from drug rehab facility for throwing himself down a flight of stairs in an alleged bid to earn himself some painkillers.

August 3, 1992: Pleads no contest to drugstore break-in case. Ordered to complete a new residential rehab facility, slapped with a four-year suspended sentence.

Think that kind of run didn't keep the stand-up circuit flush with killer material? Unfortunately for the quipmeisters, after the summer of 1992, Adam played spoilsport, steering clear of our nation's criminal justice system. For the public's purposes, he resurfaced only briefly in 1996 to help the humor magazine *Might* spoof our fallen-star fascination by cooperating in (and playing dead for) the cover story: "Adam Rich, 1968–1996: Fare Thee Well, Gentle Friend. His Final Days. His Last Interview. The Legacy He Leaves." The pitch-perfect parody confirmed what some had guessed as truth: if a former child star wasn't in trouble anymore, he must be dead.

AND THE MONEY HAPPENED . . .

There are other ways to destroy yourself. You can, for instance, earn a bunch of money, spend a bunch of money as if you are always going to earn a bunch of money, then learn that, no, you aren't always going earn that much money. There's nothing in the Coogan Law to protect you against that one.

If every (but not *really* every) former child star had a drug drama, then every (but not *really* every) former child star had a lost-fortune saga, too. And very few of the everybodys who aren't named Gary Coleman could claim that their parents and/or guardians had anything to do with the depleted funds. Said Jon Provost (of whom newspapers bragged in 1971, upon the occasion of his twenty-first birthday, "Jon Provost Becomes a Millionaire Today"), "I pretty much partied my money away."

> Question: "Do you remember the first thing you bought?"
> Jon Provost: "Cars, of course, cars."
> Q: "What kind of car?"
> JP: "A car, motorcycle, you know, that kind of stuff. The first car I bought was a Lotus. It's like I turned twenty-one, I retired, and I started to play."

Paul Petersen also looked at the age of twenty-one as a financial turning point. "I had set up my life to [the point where] after age twenty-one, I needed to work thirteen weeks every year to keep everything I had," he said. Everything he had, at one point, included twenty cars, five homes, thirty television sets. "The reality for me was that in the first year [after *The Donna Reed Show*] I worked sixteen weeks. . . . Then eight weeks, then four weeks, then not at all. And, you know, without the cash flow, everything came apart."

Got about a hundred years? There's more. Ricky Nelson supposedly didn't know the first thing about a checkbook – he died in debt. Tommy Rettig filed for bankruptcy in 1979 amid his drug trials and retrials. Patty Duke earned (she thought) up to $1 million from her TV show and other acting gigs – she picked up an $84,000 savings bond when she turned eighteen.

On one hand, TV kid stars who weren't mega-kid stars, who weren't bagging their own movie deals, who weren't earning solo *TV Guide* covers, never drew *Friends*-sized, seven-figure paychecks to begin with – a financial fact especially true of 1950s-era actors. Regardless of what the newspapers said, Jon Provost remembered getting paid $350 an episode (over a 30- to 35-episode season) during his best earning years on *Lassie*. For their decade-plus on prime time, David and Ricky Nelson each received $250,000 when they came of age at twenty-one. And they weren't complaining – a quarter of a million ain't a bad lump sum, and in the mid-20th century it was worth a lot more than not-so-bad. Fact was, even if TV kids were more likely to be thousandaires than millionaires, they were still making more than their burger-flipping peers. It was all good – provided you had a clue. (An eighteen-year-old Ricky on his investments, circa 1958: "I think David and I own part of a place called Santa Claus Village – near San Francisco. Then I think there's an apartment house. I actually don't know – they didn't explain it all to me.")

Glenn Scarpelli was a New York stage veteran wise to the ways of Al Pacino (with whom he worked on Broadway in *Richard III*) and former adult pinup statistic Dorothy Stratten (with whom he worked on the film *They All Laughed*) when he was hired to come West and join *One Day at a Time* in 1980 as single-parented teen Alex Handris. His take on the former-child-stars-and-money thing is as good as any to explain the concept of "they didn't explain it all to me." What they didn't explain, according to Scarpelli, was the value of a dollar: "My parents [would] say to me, 'What kind of car do you want?' And I'm like, 'I want a red Trans Am.' The next day I got a red

Trans Am, it was that simple. And I didn't know how hard it is to make money, you know? It came easy. And I needed to know that and I'm grateful for the times when I was broke – I needed to be broke for my own personal makeup for the person I am now. . . . I took it all for granted as a kid and when that money came in I took it all for granted. I had no idea that was a lot of money 'cause the people I hung out with had eighteen times more. I mean, I hung out with [Van Halen rocker] Eddie Van Halen and [his future wife *One Day* costar] Valerie Bertinelli. Hello? They're buying a Lamborghini every Monday – I mean, literally."

And supplying more fodder, literally.

AND TYPECASTING HAPPENED . . .

The guy who played Chekov on the original *Star Trek* was not a child star, is not a former child star. And yet he spent as much time trying (unsuccessfully) to be more to the public than the Guy Who Played Chekov on *Star Trek* as any former child star spent trying (with mixed results) to be more than That Kid on That Show.

Typecasting happens. It is the devil's deal of television. You know the drill: a TV series can make you rich and famous; a TV series character can make you virtually unhirable as anyone but that character. This much was apparent from the first season-long cycle. It was like Carol Burnett said all the way back in the 1950s: on a TV series, once you become a Mabel, you stay a Mabel. The then-*Garry Moore Show* variety performer saw danger in the weekly, character-based series. Burnett vowed to *TV Guide* that she'd never do one. And true to her word, Burnett stayed in variety and never did become a Mabel. But Paul Petersen became a Jeff Stone, Stanley Livingston a Chip Douglas, Billy Gray a Bud Anderson, and so on. Typecasting happened.

"Well, it was down to the last two [actors for the lead in the 1971 anti-war film, *Johnny Got His Gun*] and the reason I didn't get it — [writer/director] Dalton Trumbo was very honest about this — was because of my image. People will not forget Jeff Stone, he told me. And that, I think, was the signal to me that everything I thought, and that I was proud of — my previous achievements — meant nothing. I was so confused. You know, what had I done wrong?" (Paul Petersen)

"When the show was over, I went out and I realized how it was — meaning, I'm either wanted because of who I am or not wanted. You know what I realized? [That] if I wanted to be an actor, I'm back to square one." (Stanley Livingston)

"I was doing very good before I got that part [on *Father Knows Best*]. I had a movie career going [*The Day the Earth Stood Still*, *On Moonlight Bay*, etc.] before I got that part. I think it hurt me after the show was over 'cause the only thing people thought I was capable of doing was Bud Anderson. And those were the parts that were offered to me. And I had really tired of that." (Billy Gray)

Got a few hours? They got a million of these ones, too. Typecasting woes aren't as sexy as the-night-I-overdosed sob stories, but they're just as plentiful and arguably as painful. Again, former child stars do not own the patent on them, but give them this – their collective experience as That Kid on That Show is unique. For one thing, they start out in the business as kids, not cigar-chomping, middle-aged moguls. How were they supposed to know about the Mabel thing? Said Petersen, ". . . An adult has, well, hopefully a rather more mature understanding of the fleeting nature of work in this industry. [An understanding that] actors are mostly out of work. But for a kid, you don't get those messages. What you get is not preparation for the future, but an intense focus on the now."

For another thing, TV kids get typecast as something they're not, or, rather, something they're not going to be for long – namely, kids. It's the old Jackie Coogan story: cute little kid hits puberty becomes less cute teen becomes even less cute adult. A Tom Cruise comes to our attention as a fully formed being; he is what he is, a cute guy. But was he even cuter when he was seven? Would we think him less cute in *Risky Business* if we'd seen him flash a gap-toothed grin as a second-grader on, say, *The Courtship of Eddie's Father*? Don't know, can't say. We never saw Tom Cruise until he was about twenty; until he was the full package. Sure, TV kids get the paychecks to grow up on prime time, but then they get the bill. Their looks morph, their voices change – even as their skills often stay the same. It's the *other* old story: kid actors act by instinct, not as pupils of the Lee Strasberg method. They do what comes naturally, what worked for their shows. If you got laughs as a kid hamming up a ba-duh-dum-bum punchline before an easy studio audience, then you better get the phone numbers of the people in the bleachers, because you're going to need their support – they may well be your biggest (last) fans. ". . . TV has very little to do I think with mainstream acting," Livingston said. "In fact, I finally learned [that] what I learned [on *My Three Sons*] was almost useless except for that type of show. One of the first things I did afterward, the directors are, like, going, 'Do left. Do left,' and I'm going, what does that mean, 'Do left'?"

More trouble: TV kids – particularly those who grow up on wholesome, family series playing wholesome, family characters – get typecast as such: wholesome, family people. And unless you're going to forge a career as the next Michael Landon or as a good-hearted neighbor on, say, *7th Heaven*, you are, in a word, screwed. Disney cartoons aside, there ain't a lot of Holly-wood work for wholesome, family types. Prime time is about lawyer, doctor, and cop shows; the meat-and-potatoes of movies is action flicks. Where does a non-edge fellow like Jeff Stone – a dead ringer for a future insurance salesman – fit into all this? Well, pretty much nowhere. The gap between what a Jeff Stone could do (or be allowed to do) was no more apparent than after the series' demise in the late 1960s. "I had no idea how estranged I had become from not only my peer group but the people in Hollywood as well," Petersen said. ". . . I wasn't able then, because I was enmeshed in my culture, to understand that this prototypical American boy that I had portrayed, Jeff Stone, just didn't fit in a world that was falling all over itself for drugs, sex, and rock 'n' roll."

So, that's the big, bad rap on typecasting. As far as we, the fans, are concerned, it's a non-issue. No one's thinking former child stars are messed up because of typecasting; no one's run-ning off at the mouth, or running down the street scared because That Kid on That Show got typecast out of showbiz. It's the end results (the drugs, the suicides, etc.) that get our atten-tion (conjure up our pity, unleash our scorn, etc.). If an ex-kid star is branded as unusable by Hollywood as a teen or adult, then the ex-kid star disappears. And then we go, "So, whatever happened to That Kid on That Show?"

And then we check the tabs to see if anything cool hap-pened to him.

AND TELL-ALLS HAPPENED . . .

Drugs? Arrests? Suicides? More arrests? Bankruptcy? More arrests? Unemployment? Even *more* arrests? Now we're in business. In fact, you could go into business if you had the right (bad) story.

Christina Crawford's 1978 rendering of her life growing up

under the tyrannical regime of film legend Joan Crawford did more than inspire a camp-classic movie – *Mommie Dearest* virtually invented the *Mommie Dearest* industry. What's your excuse to stay silent about your problems when Crawford's laying it bare about an esteemed Hollywood leading lady going bonkers with a hatchet in the family rose garden? Other than discretion, valor, etc., there is no excuse – particularly when Crawford's book sold a lot and got turned into a movie (albeit, a bad one). The lesson was clear: Don't have an inspirational life story? Not to worry. There was gold in your lousy life if you were willing to tell all about the drugs, the suicides, the arrests, the bankruptcies, the whatevers (provided the whatevers were appropriately compelling to warrant a booking on *Donahue*). And so, from former child stars to former wives of Burt Reynolds, people typed and confessed and published. Not that Loni Anderson's memoirs aren't worthy of discussion, but for our purposes we're more concerned with tomes by the likes of:

PATTY DUKE: In 1987, the Oscar-winning child star produced *Call Me Anna: The Autobiography of Patty Duke*, in which Duke said she was a wannabe nun who was: forced into acting by a pair of cold, calculating Svengali manager-guardians who changed her name and ruled her life; never allowed to watch her own TV show by said manager-guardians because they didn't want her to get a big head; "in a constant haze of anger and depression" during the run of *Patty Duke* (1963–66); once married for all of thirteen days; and a diagnosed manic-depressive.

BARRY WILLIAMS (*The Brady Bunch*): The erstwhile Greg Brady turned his literary eye on the behind-the-scenes doings on the 1969–74 set of America's most-rerun family sitcom in *Growing Up Brady: I Was* *a Teenage Greg.* Among the most talked-about disclosures in the 1992 book: Barry had a thing for his TV sibling, Maureen McCormick; and Barry had a thing for his TV mom, Florence Henderson.

LAUREN CHAPIN: Chapter one of the curiously entitled *Father Knows Best* (published 1989) opened thusly: "The first eight days of my life must have been a frantic time for my parents. I spent them in the hospital suffering from a unique condition called 'piloridc stinosis.'" To hear prime time's onetime Princess tell it, it was all downhill from there. Way downhill. Through the course of the book, we learn that: (1) Lauren was molested by her father; (2) Lauren was molested by her father's friend; (3) Lauren was severely physically injured when she accidentally ran through a plate-glass window and severely psychically wounded when her mother didn't rush to comfort her; (4) Lauren witnessed her father hit her mother; (5) Lauren's mother wanted her to be perfect like her TV self; (6) Lauren couldn't be perfect like her TV self and, out of frustration, picked up a neighborhood cat and tossed it; (7) Lauren attempted suicide at age ten by downing two dozen aspirins, then hanging herself from a rope in her bedroom; (8) after the rope broke, Lauren banged her head against a wall for five minutes and then smoked a cigarette; (9) Lauren was beaten by her brother, who, on her mother's command, punched her in the stomach; (10) Lauren was treated for swollen ovaries, the result of her brother's blows; (11) as *Father Knows Best* wound down, Lauren watched her TV dad (Robert Young) cope with depression and her TV sister (Elinor Donahue) cope with a troubled marriage; (12) after cancellation, Lauren married at age sixteen; (13) Lauren divorced; (14) Lauren worked as a prostitute; (15) Lauren drove a car into a cliff in a suicide/murder attempt; (16) Lauren was high on acid during her second wedding; (17) Lauren OD'd on "China White"; (18) Lauren was busted in a border drug incident; (19) Lauren was arrested for check kiting; (20) Lauren tried to chop off her hand at the wrist with a meat cleaver; and (21) Lauren passed out on the street after buying heroin (to help her come down from coke-induced seizures). To be completist about it, Lauren also battled a three-pack-a-day cigarette habit, endured viral encephalitis and, in 1979, let Jesus become her Lord and Savior.

Well, then.

Those who didn't have the patience to put their travails to paper didn't need to. There were always reporters, tape recorders in hand, ready to pitch the latest version of "Star-Crossed Kids: Child Actors Can Face Pain After Fame" to their readers. All they needed were quotes. They got 'em.

LANCE KERWIN (*James at 15*): "I was an idiot who made some bad choices. Now I want to be a good dad and a good example." (Headline: "Remember 'James at 15'? Well, Now He's 38 and Helping People Like Him Kick Drugs")

PAUL PETERSEN: "I got started in show business because my mother was bigger than me. These little kids lie to you reporters and tell you they are the ones pursuing a career." (Headline: "Catch a Falling Star")

JAY NORTH: "I had reached the point where I said, 'I'm

either going to kill myself or I'm going to go out and commit horrible, violent acts against other people.'" (Headline: "Help Sought for Child Actors")

Jay North, in particular, was a king of the troubled-child-star soundbite. His *Dennis the Menace* gripes were well-documented by the press – he hated the show, hated the character, hated the aunt and uncle who tormented him on the set, wished he were one of those kids from *Village of the Damned* so he could exact revenge on those who made him miserable. Perhaps the inevitable *E! True Hollywood Story*, featuring all-new Jay North quotes, best summed up the Jay North experience: "And if his childhood was miserable," the narrator intoned, "the years that followed were an absolute nightmare."

So, who needs the tabloids to tattle when you're more than willing to handle that job yourself? Who needs to dispel the kids-of-Hollywood-are-messed-up legend when you're more than willing to add to its lore yourself? It's not exactly stoic, but it's no crime either. Why shouldn't a Patty Duke and a Lauren Chapin write down all the good/bad/awful stuff that happened to them? Why shouldn't a Jay North sit down with a reporter and tell about all the good/bad/awful stuff that happened to him? It's their lives; it's their stories; their absolute right to tell if they wish and/or dare. And it's their funeral. For what it's worth, tell-alls didn't exactly serve to upgrade the overall former child star image. Uplifting ending or no, Lauren Chapin's story is nobody's idea of a feel-good read. And it's beyond being a mere feel-bad one, too. Rather, it's the kind of tale that skews our perspective, gets us digging for scandal and tragedy every-where – even in places where we shouldn't even bother.

Consider Barry Williams' book for a moment. It hardly belongs in the company of Duke's and Chapin's – even as a tell-all, *Growing Up Brady* is thoroughly mild and cheerfully

Bradyesque. He had *a thing* for his TV sister? Had a *thing* for his TV mom? Gee, that's cute. Except, when the book was published, it was as if Barry had slipped the shooting script from *Caligula* in between the covers. *Brady* tabloid stories were hatched; seeds were planted for stuff like the Nixonian-sounding *The Bradys: The Last Days* (a latter-day Fox-TV "reenactment" of events depicted in the book and elsewhere). But most of all, tongues were sent a-wagging. (Did you hear that Greg Brady bagged his mom? Did you hear Greg Brady bagged his sister? Well, yeah, all right, he didn't *really* do either one, and, no, they weren't *really* his blood relatives to begin with, but still . . .)

The fun in celebrity autobiographies is getting carried away, reveling in the gory details about how unlike private person so-and-so is from his or her public person. Since former child stars, by virtue of their generally squeaky-clean TV character selves, are likeliest to have the least in common with their public personas, then, reason follows, former child star tell-alls are the most fun of all.

Kitten Anderson . . . a heroine-addict hooker?!? Patty Lane . . . a manic-depressive?!? Dennis Mitchell . . . a wannabe demon child? With all due respect to Loni Anderson, that sort of stuff just can't be topped.

AND TALK SHOWS HAPPENED . . .

So, you're a former child star who's not the literary sort? Don't trust people to get your gist in print? Would you rather talk out your experiences from the comfort of a TV studio? No problem. Have we got a talk show for you.

The first time Brandon Cruz was asked to appear on a TV show to talk about his past life as a former child star was 1981. The occasion was a prime time, Dick Clark-hosted, where-are-they-now special. He — and his green, punk-rock hair — appeared with his *Courtship of Eddie's Father* TV dad, Bill Bixby. Following the Clark gig, Cruz would recall doing upwards of fifty talk-show appearances over the next two decades, riding the *Donahue/Sally Jessy* 1980s, into the *Leeza/Maury* 1990s. (Note: It pays to have green hair. Seems to really captivate talk-show producer types. Said Cruz: "I did various other [shows] with purple hair, no hair, and they'd say, 'You know, why are you wearing a hat? What color is your hair today?' And they made a joke out of it every so often.")

At first, the panels Cruz was asked to take part in were not unlike the Dick Clark specials; they were shows devoted to genial, whatever-happened-to-those-old-TV-stars topics. In his *Esquire* article, Danny Bonaduce referred to the gigs – in which he participated – as "the has-been circuit." And, indeed, as Cruz described it, there was something of a repertory-company feel to the appearances. "It would usually consist of one member of *The Partridge Family*, *The Brady Bunch*, somebody older – not necessarily from a kids' show – but from *Gilligan's Island* or *Batman*. Paul Petersen was always there," he said. (Bonaduce's usual-suspect list included Cruz, the interchangeable *Brady Bunch* kid, Jon Provost, Butch Patrick, and, of course, himself.) Cruz, for one, had no problem with the shows: "If people were really needing to know where I was, I didn't mind telling them."

If where-are-they-now was the order of the day in the mid-1980s, then *why*-are-they-screwed-up-now became *the* topic of the 1990s. Said Cruz: "As soon as some of us started getting in trouble with the law and stuff, then they wanted to know, 'What is it behind kid actors? Why are all these kids who supposedly did well and had, by all standards of America, a lot of money, a lot of fame, cars, girls, whatever – why are they going bad? What's gone wrong here?'"

As (bad?) luck would have it, the arrests (of Adam Rich, the

Diff'rent Strokes gang, Bonaduce, etc.) dovetailed with the *Geraldo* effect. Just as Phil Donahue pioneered the afternoon talk show in the 1970s, bringing the issues of the day (and, occasionally, the Chippendale's dancers) to housewives, shut-ins, and other after-school viewers, Geraldo Rivera revolutionized the form in 1987, bringing chair-throwing skinheads, prostitutes, and women-who-cheat-on-their-husbands-with-other-men-who-cheat-on-their-pets wonders to the same unsuspecting audience. Rather than run away from what *Geraldo* was, the other, ever-expanding slate of shows (*Oprah, Rolanda, Rikki Lake, Joan Rivers,* etc.) picked up a couple of tricks, so to speak, and booked a couple of screamers.

The TV former child star was a perfect fit for the new format. Who better to titillate an audience than the ex-kid actor going on about how miserable his life as a youth was and how felonious his life as an adult had become? Former child stars might have been nonentities as far as movieland casting directors and producers were concerned, but on afternoon talk shows they were in demand. It got to the point where it didn't seem to matter *why* you were booking a former child star, as long as you *were* booking one. Cruz recalled a 1996 invite to *The Jim J. and Tammy Faye Show,* a short-lived cable effort hosted by ex-*Too Close for Comfort* comic Jim J. Bullock and ex-*PTL Club* crier Tammy Faye Bakker. They wanted him for a segment on how to cook chocolate fondue with sourdough bread. (Said Cruz: "Didn't sound very appealing, but I thought, what the heck, I'll be a good sport. Well, as it unfolds, Jim J. Bullock is just throwing chocolate and stuff's flying everywhere; Tammy Faye takes a piece of chocolate and sticks it down her top. A minute later, or even less, she pulls it out of her cleavage and shoves it in my mouth.") Make no mistake, though, the ultimate former-child-star talk show was about *messed-up* former child stars. Bonaduce called this era the "Hollywood Kids . . . in Trouble" tour. Cruz

joked he was booked on the new-look former child star panels as
a counterbalance – "I was the one who was never convicted."
Wanna hear something even funnier? Bonaduce even ended up
hosting one – 1995's *Danny!* (The exclamation point was his.)

None other than tell-all author Patty Duke passed judgment
on those who told-all to television viewers: "When I see other
former child stars on talk shows, I want to say to them, 'Oh,
God, stop hurting already, let it go.'"

Let it go? Let it go? You let it go.

We were transfixed.

AND THE, UH, CURSE HAPPENED . . . ?

The combined effect is staggering, no? Anissa Jones? Rusty
Hamer? Trent Lehman? Danny Bonaduce? Adam Rich?
Mackenzie Phillips? Patty Duke? Lauren Chapin? Jay North?
Paul Petersen? Every blinkin' kid from every blinkin' TV show.
(Well, not the Patron Saints of TV former child stars – Jodie
Foster and Ron Howard – but you get the point.)

If all the pain, troubles, and traumas these people endured
(or brought on themselves) weren't the result of an out-and-out,
black-cats-and-witches curse (brought on by the untimely
demise of Anissa Jones, no doubt), then what *were* they the
result of?

Would you believe, nothing in particular?

AND THEN NOTHING HAPPENED IN
PARTICULAR HAPPENED . . .

Bad things have always happened to child stars (and adult
actors and garbagemen and architects and . . .); always will. If
there was a difference, post-Anissa Jones as opposed to pre-
Anissa Jones, it was that TV kid stars (openly) aired their gripes

and (openly) talked about their problems. The juicy stuff was news to us, not to them.

> Question: "It didn't come [out until] later, what was going on [on the set of, for example] *Father Knows Best*?"
> Paul Petersen: "We all knew about them."
> Q: "Did you all know?"
> PP: "Absolutely, Hollywood is filled with secrets, and when you're a young kid, believe it or not, you hear even more of those secrets because people think you're not listening."

Bad things have always happened to former child stars; always will. Sometimes bad things have even happened to them regardless of whether or not they were former child stars. Take the Mackenzie Phillips story. Was she in and out of rehab because she made her film debut at age twelve (in *American Graffiti*), or because she was cast in *One Day at a Time* when she was fifteen? Or was it because she grew up with a rock 'n' roll father (John Phillips of the Mamas and the Papas) who taught her how to roll joints at age ten and whose own autobiographical tome (*Papa John*) was more John Belushi than just about anything lived (or written) by any former child star anywhere? "If she wasn't the one on *One Day at a Time* or didn't get *American Graffiti*, this shit probably would've still happened," said *One Day* costar Glenn Scarpelli. "It might be worse, who knows?" Take the Rusty Hamer story. Was he depressed because he wasn't on TV anymore, because he'd been set up for a career that was never meant to be long-term? Or was he down a strike at the beginning – forced to step into a breadwinner role as a grade-schooler because of the death of his father? Take the Danny Bonaduce line. When he did time in rehab, he would say, he was the only former child star among forty-eight patients – nine of whom, he added, were dentists.

Screwed-up people are screwed-up people. (How else to explain Bonaduce's dentists?) The fame and the money that a TV show bring alter the picture, sure. Is Paul Petersen going out and splurging on five homes if he doesn't have the paycheck to back at least a couple of them up? Is Patty Duke getting ripped off by her caretakers if she has nothing to rip off? Is Billy Gray not getting hired to run a four-star restaurant because potential employers can't see past the fact that he worked at a McDonald's as a kid? But the fame and the money can only alter the picture so much. Screwed-up people are screwed-up people.

Reminded Stanley Livingston: "You know, these guys that work with the post office go bananas, [too]."

. . . EXCEPT FOR MAYBE THE JOKES

Postal workers, clearly, are no stranger to the punchline. Neither are dentists. The world does not single out the former child star for, as the Beaver would put it, "the business." The only difference lies in the inciting incidents; the moments when somebody goes from being a benign presence to Grade A comedy material. For the postal worker, it was a spate of postal-worker shootings and a clever person turning the phrase "going postal." For the former child star, it was Anissa Jones. From her death onward, it was open season on former child stars.

Jones was the excuse we were looking for – the excuse to pity, to fear, and to mock the kids who lived inside the television while we mere mortals watched from the outside. She was the horror story we were waiting for – the horror story to prove that the perfect TV worlds in which their images were disseminated were lies. And she was the out we were hoping for – the out to smooth over any feelings of our own inadequacies. (Happy?!? How can we be expected to be happy when some kid who made a mint on a TV show – who gave the freakin' Monkees an Emmy – is zonking out on angel dust?)

And we, her public, happened to think the dichotomy hilarious.

Hilarious? A young woman setting something of a toxicology record in a major California jurisdiction, hilarious? Well, look, they don't write punk-rock songs about Mother Teresa slipping off the mortal coil. They write punk songs about Anissa Jones overdosing. It's not right, it's not admirable, but it's what we do – we think former child stars are fair game for hijinks and hilarity, and besides, we figure, we're bigger than they are (in physical and/or social stature, take your pick). Maybe if Anissa Jones had been the only police-blotter entry. Maybe then we would have kept our distance, held our fire, stifled the giggles.

But they just kept coming and coming and coming . . .

A million of 'em.

"Knock, knock."
"Who is it?"
"A former child star."
"AAAAGGGGGHHHHH!"

Put simply, the notion of former child star as joke was born. And the show that would virtually corner the market on related punch lines was hatched.

Ba-du-dum-bum.

CHAPTER SIX

DIFF'RENT
STROKES

"The following program is based on events
in the lives of the cast of *Diff'rent Strokes*."

— *AFTER DIFF'RENT STROKES: WHEN THE LAUGHTER STOPPED*

Arguably, this is the most superfluous chapter in the book. If there was a topic, or a people, you're likely already versed in, it's this topic (*Diff'rent Strokes*) and these people (Gary Coleman, Todd Bridges, Dana Plato). What's this book going to say that two *E! True Hollywood Stories*, dozens of *Leezas, Sally Jessys* and *Extras!*, a telephone book's worth of *People* magazine articles, an encyclopedia's worth of *National Enquirer* articles, a key Howard Stern radio interview, and a Very Special hourlong Fox docudrama (*After Diff'rent Strokes: When the Laughter Stopped*) haven't blabbed about already? The Fox thing even gave us the money shot that Dana Plato's last boyfriend was said to have wanted (but was denied): dead

Dana, in her coffin. All right, it wasn't really her (it was an actress playing her), but it was close enough.

We know this story from beginning to end and back again, and, frankly, we think sometimes, if we never again heard Gary Coleman prattle on about his life or his career or his parents, then that'd be more than fine. What could this lone chapter possibly do to convince you it's different from all the other entries in the extensive *Diff'rent Strokes* canon? Find Gary Coleman's lost millions? Inspire the resurrection of Todd Bridges' prime-time career? Provide an interview with a beyond-the-grave Dana Plato?

Well, here's warning you right here, this chapter doesn't – can't – do any of that.

Arguably, this might be the most key and most compelling, chapter in the book. It's got every experience of the TV former child star – the good times, the bad times, the found riches, the lost riches, the fame, the notoriety – encapsulated in the lives of three actors who worked together on the same show for eight years. In truth, only one of them – Gary Coleman – was a true child star; the other two were child costars. In truth, only one of them – Gary Coleman – amassed a fortune; the other two were merely handsomely paid. In truth, only one of them – Gary Coleman – is the quintessential former child star; the other two are sidebars. But put all three together and they're funny as hell.

Did you hear the Jay Leno one about how the *Diff'rent Strokes* kids were getting together for a reunion? On *America's Most Wanted*?

Did you hear the Billy Crystal one about how "the FBI says it will not rest until every member of the *Diff'rent Strokes* cast is behind bars?"

The Kid (1921): Charlie Chaplin made the movie; Jackie Coogan stole it. A child star was born
THE EVERETT COLLECTION

Critics predicted Jackie would be exploited for his box-office value. They didn't know the half of it
PHOTOFEST

Jackie with future wife Betty Grable in 1935. Her star was rising even as his fortunes were dwindling   AP PHOTO

Doing time as Uncle Fester on TV's
The Addams Family (circa 1964)
ARCHIVE PHOTOS

"Jack definitely had his ups and downs," stepson Don Stroud said, but he rode them out — like the surfer he was   NATE CUTLER/GLOBE PHOTOS

"Boy, I don't mess around." TV's first true child star — Ricky Nelson   ARCHIVE PHOTOS

The Adventures of Ozzie & Harriet was the *Seinfeld* of its day — a show about absolutely nothing   KOBAL COLLECTION

"Believe me," said fellow teen-idol type Paul Petersen, "I was aware of how many babes Ricky Nelson got"   AP PHOTO

Post-Beatles, the hits stopped coming, but Ricky kept playing   PHOTOFEST

On *My Three Sons,* Stanley Livingston (far left) was a star. When the show ended, he was "back to square one" as an actor   GLOBE PHOTOS

Defrocked Mouseketeer Paul Petersen (front left) as good son Paul Stone on *The Donna Reed Show* in 1958   PHOTOFEST

Writer Dalton Trumbo warned Paul (with TV mom Donna Reed) that audiences would not soon forget his sitcom self. Then Trumbo vetoed him for a film role   GLOBE PHOTOS

Lassie's original TV master: Tommy Rettig as Jeff Miller   PHOTOFEST

A "gradual clean sweep" eliminated Rettig and costars George Cleveland (left) and Jan Clayton (right) from *Lassie* in 1957   GLOBE PHOTOS

Lassie's new TV master: Second-grader Jon Provost as orphan Timmy Martin
ARCHIVE PHOTOS

Counting public appearances, Provost said the TV show "was really a year-long event"
KOBAL COLLECTION

A *Family Affair* family portrait (clockwise from left): Sebastian Cabot, Johnny Whitaker, Anissa Jones, Brian Keith, Kathy Garver
GLOBE PHOTOS

Anissa with Mrs. Beasley, "the program's most desirable and valuable artifact"

Johnny joins the "three musketeers" (Paula Jones, son Paul, and daughter Anissa) at the Ice Follies in 1967

The six-year-old Johnny believed in Santa Claus; the elder Anissa did not

Johnny, Anissa, and Mrs. Beasley hold court with President Johnson in 1968

After *Nanny and the Professor* ended its brief run in 1971, Trent Lehman (far right) stayed out of the public eye — until he was found hanged at a schoolyard in 1982

Brandon Cruz with TV dad Bill Bixby in *The Courtship of Eddie's Father*   SHOOTING STAR

The adult Brandon worked the talk-show circuit in the 1990s: "I was the one who was never convicted"
SPIKE MANNARELLO/SHOOTING STAR

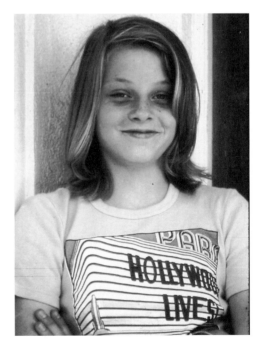

Danny Bonaduce riding high on *The Partridge Family*
YORAM KAHANA/SHOOTING STAR

With no hit series to call her own, hired gun Jodie Foster, circa 1975, stood apart from her TV child star peers   YORAM KAHANA/SHOOTING STAR

Even if Mackenzie Phillips hadn't starred on *One Day at a Time,* her well-documented struggle with sobriety probably still would have happened, costar Glenn Scarpelli said. "It might be worse, who knows?"
PHOTOFEST

Adam Rich as Nicholas — the youngest member of *Eight Is Enough*'s zero-population-growth-defying Bradford family STEVE SCHATZBERG/GLOBE PHOTOS

Adam Rich as defendant — arrested four times during a twelve-month stretch from 1990-91
AP PHOTO

Gary Coleman, in the beginning: With parents Sue and W.G. Coleman
GENE TRINDEL/GLOBE PHOTOS

Gary was hailed as a genius and rewarded like a king. At his peak, he reportedly made as much as $3 million a year
RALPH DOMINGUEZ/
GLOBE PHOTOS

The *Diff'rent Strokes* three: Dana Plato, Gary and Todd Bridges. Their misfortunes were more dazzling to us than their once-upon-a-time successes   NBC/GLOBE PHOTOS

"I long for days where I'm not recognized," said Gary, shown here in his familiar Arnold Jackson pout
KOBAL COLLECTION

The summit: First Lady Nancy Reagan (with *Strokes* costar Mary Jo Catlett, left) used Gary to help spread her anti-drug message in 1983
AP PHOTO

Gary en route to court in 1999

REED SAXON/CP PICTURE ARCHIVE

Dana in court in 1992

LEE ZAICHICK/CP PICTURE ARCHIVE

Todd in court in 1989

NICK UT/AP PHOTO

The Indomitable One (and date) at the 72nd Annual
Academy Awards in 2000

CHRIS PIZZELLO/CP PICTURE ARCHIVE

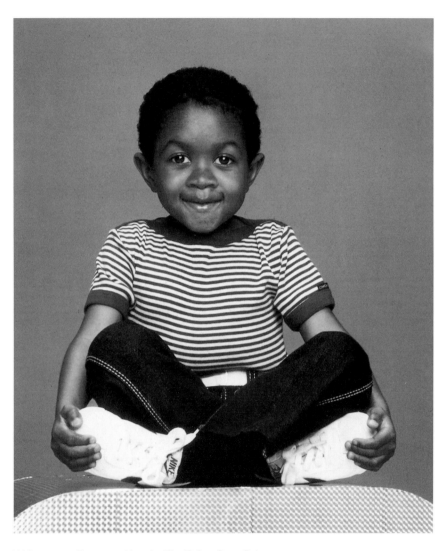

Webster star Emmanuel Lewis: The Teflon Gary Coleman

Ricky Schroder doing cute
during his *Silver Spoons*
heyday

Rick Schroder drinking in his
NYPD Blue comeback

Did you hear the Dana Plato one about how, considering all the *Strokes* kids' problems, that Mr. Drummond sure must have been a terrible father?

Did you hear the one about the medically challenged kid who claimed his parents ripped him off, or the promising actor who got sucked in by drugs, or the young mother who died at age thirty-four with the face of a fifty-four-year old?

No, you're not going anywhere. Face it, even the old stuff is good stuff. The story of *Diff'rent Strokes* is no less than a modern-day fairy tale. It's oft-told, it's crowd-pleasin', it's wildly unreal, and it's always a lot darker than you figure it for going in.

Why do we like to hear it? Why do we slow to a crawl on the freeway to check out the crumpled car on the shoulder? Given a choice between the morally uplifting and the incredibly, awesomely shocking, we go with the latter nine out of ten times. It's not a good trait, it's not a bad trait, it's a hard-wired gene that enables the *National Enquirer* to scale heights as "the largest selling paper in America."

And so we can't help it. This book can't help it. For the nine-billionth time, what follows is the story of *Diff'rent Strokes*. We will pretend this is all for the greater sociological good – that to know *Diff'rent Strokes* is to know ourselves. We will pretend it all goes back to our thesis – about how it's *our* perceptions and obsessions that are responsible for the former child star "curse." We will pretend it's a key period in the history of the species – that it defined and refined the former child star as joke. But most of all, we will recount the story of *Diff'rent Strokes* for the nine-billionth time because the video-story robbery thing never gets old.

Once upon a time . . .

THERE WAS A BOY NAMED GARY COLEMAN . . .

Gary Wayne Coleman was born, it is said, on February 8, 1968, in Zion, Illinois, outside Chicago. It is also said, in Gary Coleman's 1981 family-penned autobiography, *Gary Coleman: Medical Miracle*, that Gary was a "fairly easy delivery" to the mother who believed herself to be infertile. "I never thought it would happen," the former Edmonia Sue Lovelace said in the book. Only later was it reported that Gary Wayne Coleman was adopted by Sue (as she was known) and husband W.G. (Willie) Coleman at four days old. Gary knew from an early age that he was adopted. In a 1999 online chat, he talked about hiring a private investigator "about twenty years ago" to find his biological mother. The P.I. turned up a lady in Michigan who claimed to be the real deal, but Gary didn't buy it and dropped the issue. At one time, Gary said he believed he was "at least" his father's son "because I do look like a lot of his family, and him" – a point argued in *Medical Miracle*, wherein Gary is described as a "miniature replica" of W.G. At another time, Gary said he just didn't care. "[In the book,] I guess, they were trying to hide [the adoption] – I don't know why. I guess there's an issue with that that I don't know of and frankly don't really want to know."

Gary Coleman has every right to downplay the matter of his birthright – it is *his* birthright. But it's not a minor point if you subscribe to the popular notion that Gary Coleman was a child star who had everything and lost everything. If we can be misled about the circumstances surrounding his very birth, then how can we be sure his life was ever all that? Maybe – is it possible? – he never *really* had everything. (Yeah, we know, it's less tragic that way, but just go with it for a bit.)

Certainly, Gary Coleman never really had much in the health department. Physically, Gary was a normal human being for approximately twenty-two months – the first twenty-two

months of his life. This, before he came down with a fever, and his worried mother, herself a nurse, took him to the hospital, and Gary got worse and came down with pneumonia, and the doctors finally told the Colemans that Gary had messed-up kidneys, or, more accurately, he had a messed-up ureter that, in turn, had messed up his kidneys. The ureter is the duct that funnels urine from the kidneys to the bladder. Gary's was all "twisted up," causing backup (and failure) in the kidneys. The right one wasn't working at all; the left one was at forty percent. Gary subsequently was treated to his first surgery – with his doctors working like traffic engineers, they rerouted the bladder-bound tubes to a pair of holes that were cut in his stomach. This was the nitty-gritty of it: when it was time for Gary to relieve himself, he would relieve himself through the holes. And so until another surgery, when he was about four, Gary depended on diapers and depended on his parents to change and clean the diapers. W.G. insisted that Gary "never had a Pamper on his body," and made sure that cloth – never disposable – diapers were used. During the second procedure that allowed the boy a smidgen more independence, Gary was fitted with a single outlet through which urine would flow into an outside pouch. As Gary approached and entered school age, he became adept at monitoring – and emptying – the pouch (he didn't have the benefit of a full bladder to tell him when it was time to "go," or if, indeed, he had already "gone"). In case any classmates eye-spied him in the restroom, Gary said he could manipulate the valve on the pouch to "make it look like I was peeing with my penis."

Then, as an eleven-year-old Gary would later put it, he "got a Greek kidney donated from a kid who was hit by a car." On December 3, 1973, a six-year-old boy in Indiana was run over by a hit-and-run driver. He was dead but for the machines. Five days later, the boy's family decided to remove him from life support and agreed to donate his organs – including the kidneys. And so on December 18, at Children's Memorial Hospital in Chicago, Gary, age five, received a transplant, complementing his sorta-working left kidney with a slightly used, healthy right one. There was one catch: in order to prevent the new kidney from being rejected, Gary, who had been developing normally up to that point, was placed on a steroid regimen – a regimen that doctors told the Colemans straight up would retard his growth, would prevent him from ever seeing the other side of five feet. No one was happy about it, but there wasn't exactly a choice. Gary, who was never one to play along with the media and indulge its angle-happy ways, once allowed that, yes, he did suffer from a curse – the curse of height, or lack thereof.

If his size was an issue to Gary, then, all things considered, 1974 was a good year. Gary was six, he was out of the hospital, and he was still about eye-to-eye with his peers. Anticipating the days ahead when Gary would be left behind physically, Sue Coleman encouraged her son to pursue the arts, or Montgomery Ward fashion shows, whichever the case might be. The Ward store in Waukegan, Illinois, represented the Coleman's sole semi-showbiz "in": Sue had a cousin who had a young daughter who did modeling at the Waukegan store. In the summer of 1974, Gary wrote the store and informed them that many people thought he looked like Rodney Allen Rippy, then the hot, young, burger-pusher of Jack-in-the-Box commercial fame. By the fall, Gary had done his first Ward show (donning a three-piece corduroy suit). Within a year, he had done several more. By the end of 1975, he had hooked up with a talent agent and booked his first commercial, for Jack-in-the-Box rival McDonald's. (Apparently, the ad folks thought Gary looked very much like Rodney Allen Rippy, too.)

In his autobiography, Gary noted that the idea of the

McDonald's shoot was very exciting, but the business of doing the shoot was very boring. Nonetheless, he did more commercials. And he was still doing them when, in 1976, Norman Lear's Tandem Productions targeted him during a nationwide kid-actor search for a new *Little Rascals* series. By way of quick background, Norman Lear was a Really Famous Producer. If you watched prime time in the 1970s, you watched a Lear/Tandem-spawned show: *All in the Family, Maude, Good Times, One Day at a Time, Mary Hartman, Mary Hartman, Fernwood 2-Night, Hot L Baltimore* – and that was just through the mid-1970s. In 1976, one of Lear's minions caught Coleman's act in a local Chicago bank commercial (a commercial in which Gary stressed to viewers, "You can never save too much money"). While he was in Los Angeles on yet another commercial shoot (for Bisquick), Gary was summoned to a meeting at Tandem. Lear liked him, signed him to a contract, and cast him as Stymie in the *Rascals* pilot. The show didn't go, but Lear had plenty of other up-and-running shows to let Gary play in, including *Good Times* and *The Jeffersons*.

Gary's historic first prime-time appearance came in a 1978 episode of the non-historic *The Jeffersons*. Gary was cast as Raymond, the wise-cracking nephew of George Jefferson (Sherman Hemsley), the show's resident verbally abusive dry-cleaning mogul. Raymond was supposed to be eight; Gary was ten. The best (most employable) kid actors always play just a little young, so Gary was in business. Onscreen, he was quite a sight – clad in a burnt-orange suit and turtleneck sweater, looking like the Montgomery Ward runway from whence he came. He also was really, really cute. Big, chubby cheeks. A couple of missing front teeth. A high-pitched squeal of a voice (his first onscreen dialogue: "Hi!") that belied the sassy stuff coming out of his mouth ("Hey, I'm eight years old. I don't kiss unless it's serious."). In short, it was quintessential Gary Coleman. A smart kid/mini-adult with a smart mouth who outsmarted the real adults around him. Gary Coleman Inc. was in business.

... AND A BOY NAMED TODD BRIDGES ...

Todd Bridges was born on May 27, 1965, in San Francisco. He was the youngest of three children in a working showbiz clan. His father, James, was an actor who later branched out as an agent; mother Betty was an actor, too, and sometimes an acting teacher. Unlike Gary, Todd was not afflicted with a congenital medical disorder. But his life was not all that, either. For the purposes of an *E! True Hollywood Story* some decades later, Bridges would remember his home life as thus: "My father was a raging alcoholic. He was out of control. He abused my mother. He abused me. He abused my sister. . . ." For the purposes of a *Jenny Jones* also some decades later, Bridges would remember being molested at age twelve by "a friend of the family."

On the upside, he was a regular on ABC's *Barney Miller* spinoff *Fish* (1977–78). The preteen Bridges played Loomis, a juvenile delinquent taken in by retired New York Police Detective Phil Fish (Abe Vigoda). Bridges did not like his character's name ("Who ever heard of a 'Loomis'?"), but he did seem to enjoy acting. He was good at it, too – had a husky voice, good looks, and moody disposition that gave him an edge over the standard kid actor. Bridges wouldn't be what you hired if you needed a regular ol' cute kid, but if you needed a counterbalance, a semi-tough kid who could pass for, you know, urban, he was the one.

Todd once said he joined the family business at age six at his mother's urging. The first commercial he did was a Jell-O spot featuring the entire Bridges clan – brother James and sister Vida included. Like his elder siblings, Todd soon began securing prime-time guest spots — starting at age eight, he did a bit on *Barney Miller* here, a bit on the miniseries *Roots* there, a bit on *Little House on the Prairie*. Then came *Fish*.

Off a set, Todd liked bicycles and girls and tinkering with stuff. "The crew on *Fish* used to give me batteries and wires and old bookshelves and all kinds of stuff to build with," Todd said in 1980. He also liked that he was the baby on the *Fish* set — the youngest juvenile delinquent of them all — just like he was at home (the youngest child, not the youngest juvenile delinquent). There was nothing unusual in any of this, really. And that was the key to Todd Bridges, it seemed. Above all, he maintained, he was a regular kid.

"I think that people like me because of the fact that I'm not stuck-up or anything like that," Todd also said in 1980. "I work in television and films. That's my business, it's never going to go to my head."

. . . AND A GIRL NAMED DANA PLATO

By most accounts, Dana Plato was born on November 7, 1964, in Maywood, California; by her death certificate, she was born on November 1, 1963. Discrepancies were part of the life that was Dana Plato. She would say she was clean and sober for a decade, even as others would say they saw coke — literally — dribbling out of her nose. She would say she didn't want to change her image, even as she would pose minus her pants for an adult magazine. She would say she'd never been happier one day, take a lethal drug overdose the next day.

Some facts can be agreed upon: Dana was born to a teenager, name of Linda, who put her up for adoption. In short order, she became the welcome newborn addition to the household of Dean and Kay Plato, who jointly ran a trucking company. Dean and Kay split when Dana was little more than two. From that point forward, it was a twosome against the world – Dana and Kay. Dana was encouraged to put her bubbly persona to use on the stage – any stage. Figure skating, tap dancing, ballet. It was during a ballet recital at age six, Dana would say, that she was discovered by Hollywood. Mortified that she'd botched a routine, Dana began to cry. An agent sitting in the audience thought her pain cute. Said Dana: "And that was that." The blond-haired, All-American-girl type got busy in commercials. Her first was shot when she was seven. Dana said she went on to do (a) more than one hundred; and/or (b) more than two hundred and fifty. Her favorite was a spot for Arco ("I got to talk about saving energy."); her most memorable, an ad for Dole in which retakes necessitated that she eat eighty-two bananas ("Or maybe it just seemed like eighty-two").

Dana Plato lore tells us that her next career milestone came in 1972, when she was eight (or nine), and she won the coveted role of Regan MacNeil in the feature film adaptation of *The Exorcist*. As the story also goes, Dana was forced to turned down the role because Kay thought it would typecast her daughter. (As what, it was not clear.) The source of the story appears to have been Dana herself – it apparently first turned up in print alongside her 1989 *Playboy* pictorial. As far as *The Exorcist* was concerned, though, there was no mention of a Dana Plato in that production's much-fabled, much-chronicled lore. Author William Peter Blatty, who published *The Exorcist* in 1971 and, later, drafted its Oscar-winning screenplay, worked closely with director William Friedkin during the casting stage. He once termed the movie's three leads – Ellen Burstyn as mother Chris MacNeil, Jason Miller as Father Karras, and Linda Blair as the vomit-spewing Regan – as Friedkin's "first choices," although other names of stars (including Jane Fonda and Gene Hackman) had been batted about early on for the adult parts. Asked specifically about Dana Plato being tendered

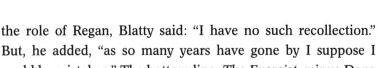

the role of Regan, Blatty said: "I have no such recollection." But, he added, "as so many years have gone by I suppose I could be mistaken." The bottom line: *The Exorcist*, minus Dana Plato, opened in theaters in December 1973, en route to grossing a still-strong (and a then-staggering) $165 million, and earning Linda Blair an Oscar nomination (not to mention forever employment in the knockoff horror spoof of her choice).

According to Dana, she did not regret *not* doing *The Exorcist*, nor *not* doing *Pretty Baby*, the 1978 Louis Malle film about a twelve-year-old prostitute that made Brooke Shields an international hot-button topic (and which, Dana said, was another movie that she got – and that her mother nixed). Either project, Dana explained, would have made her too famous, would have made her too much of a child star – like, say, Brooke Shields. ("If Brooke Shields didn't have Bob Hope, I don't know where she'd be," Dana said in 1999.) Dana did not consider herself a child star, even as she went on to score roles that her mother apparently did not block – the 1975 TV movie *Beyond the Bermuda Triangle*, the G-rated exploitation flick *Return to Boggy Creek* (1977), and the 1978 comedy *California Suite* (as Jane Fonda's onscreen daughter). Given her history, perhaps her strangest gig came in 1977, when she appeared in the sequel to a movie she was supposedly barred from the first time around, *The Exorcist II: The Heretic*. Dana's part, as a child healed by the formerly demonic Linda Blair, was brief and wordless and non-star-making. (Whew.)

As it turned out, if Dana had wanted to avoid child stardom all together, she should have avoided *The Gong Show*. In 1978, according to Dana, she auditioned for the cheeseball TV talent show with the football cheerleader squad of which she was a member. The award-winning squad wasn't sufficiently cheeseball for *The Gong Show*, and the gang was rejected for a slot. But all was not lost. Producer Al Burton, who'd remembered Dana from some test readings she'd done for the in-development Tandem sitcom *Hello, Larry*, spotted her at the *Gong Show* set. Burton thought Dana might be right for another in-development Tandem sitcom.

THE THREE MET ON A SHOW CALLED DIFF'RENT STROKES

The project was originally called *45 Minutes from Harlem*. Like other Norman Lear productions of the day, it was a nominally button-pushing premise – a comedy about a rich, white Manhattanite (name of Phillip Drummond), his sexy housekeeper, and the orphaned, inner-city black kid he takes into his home. The sitcom was designed to pair off two of Tandem's under-contract actors: Conrad Bain and Gary Coleman. ABC, which had a deal with Lear's production company, passed. The script was reworked (deleting the sexy part from the housekeeper's role, giving the inner-city black kid an older brother, and bolstering the rich, white guy with a teen daughter), retitled (to *Diff'rent Strokes*), and repitched to NBC, where programming honcho Fred Silverman was known to be a Gary Coleman fan dating back to the days of the never-was *Little Rascals* series. For the role of the older brother, Willis Jackson, Tandem hired Todd Bridges, then just a little shy of thirteen. Gary, Todd, and Bain met for the first time in the spring of 1978 on the occasion of a script reading for NBC executives. The meeting produced a season-long commitment from NBC to do the series. A November 1978 launch date was ordered. The Burton-scouted Dana subsequently was hired to fill in the role (such as it was) of the daughter, Kimberly Drummond; comic actress Charlotte Rae was ordered into the housekeeping duds as Mrs. Edna Garrett.

Silverman, whose promotional ways helped make stars of Henry (*Happy Days*) Winkler, Farrah (*Charlie's Angels*) Fawcett, and John (*Welcome Back, Kotter*) Travolta during his days at ABC, had the same in mind for ten-year-old Gary (*Diff'rent Strokes*) Coleman. Gary was dispatched to *The Tonight Show*, where he cracked up Johnny Carson by dropping three-syllable words like "designate," and professing not to know (or care) what the "birds and bees" were. He was airlifted into the World Series (as broadcast on NBC), via a series of network promos deigned "The Wit and Wisdom of Mr. Gary Coleman." He was, simply, the star of *Diff'rent Strokes* before the show even aired.

And when the show *did* air – on November 3, 1978 – Gary Coleman *was* the star. Oh, he shared second billing with Todd Bridges (Conrad Bain got first; Dana Plato didn't rate the opening credits at all), but he was the forty-three-inch-tall Chosen One upon whom all doted. In the pilot alone, Gary – in the guise as streetwise, sassy, but entirely non-threatening Arnold Jackson – was picked up three times (by Bain, Todd, and Rae), pinched on the cheeks (by Dana), tickled, and, for good measure, paraded around on a pony. *Diff'rent Strokes* was nothing if not unsubtle. Gary's Arnold was the cute kid who sold the zingers, Todd's Willis was the angry kid who created the conflict, Dana's Kimberly was the token white girl. Those were their roles at the beginning, and with the exception of Arnold growing a little more angry and Willis growing a little *less* angry as the years wore on, those were their roles at the end. The only element missing in the pilot was "Whatchu talkin' 'bout, Willis?" (or, as it appeared on the printed page, "What are you talking about?"). The catchphrase that would become Gary Coleman's meal ticket and albatross presumably was somewhere in the drawing-board stages when the show premiered. Instead, Gary had to make do with stuff like "What's she smoking?" (as delivered to Kimberly). He delivered it just fine. The laughtrack loved him.

The critics, meanwhile, did not. To be fair, it wasn't so much

Gary they didn't love – how could you give that face a bad review? – it was his show. To low-tolerance, grown-up media types, *Diff'rent Strokes* was just so much more *CPO Sharkey* crap from NBC – except, maybe worse, it was treacly and had little kids in it. So, let 'em complain. Plenty of hit shows debuted with worse notices. They called *Family Affair* "appalling," didn't they? *Diff'rent Strokes* could do worse than be put in the same company as *Family Affair*. And when you thought about it, the two shows – *Diff'rent Strokes* and *Family Affair* – *were* almost soul mates. Both boasted Park Avenue zip codes. Both featured the three-kid, bachelor-father, live-in-housekeeper formula. And both minted bona-fide child stars. In the case of *Diff'rent Strokes*, its child star was the biggest in prime time (discounting the *Brady Bunch* and *Partridge Family* kids of the early 1970s whose fame worked on a unit, rather than individual, basis) since, well, *Family Affair*. At the center of *Family Affair* was Anissa/Buffy; at the center of *Diff'rent Strokes*, Gary/Arnold. Who was more adorable: Anissa/Buffy or Gary/Arnold? If that was too close to call, this wasn't: Gary/Arnold was no pushover who would share a storyline with a twin, much less a doll. Gary/Arnold demanded attention. And he got it.

THE SHOW MADE GARY COLEMAN RICH

Diff'rent Strokes hit fast and Gary Coleman learned fast. He could tell you – and did – that the show pulled down thirty-five shares, meaning that more than a third of all televisions in use during the show's time slot were tuned to *his* show. Get any-body associated with the sitcom near a tape recorder and they'd tell you (and probably still would) that Gary was a genius – albeit a very specific one. Gary's genius did not involve rocket-fuel formulas or international diplomacy or interpersonal relations. It involved being able to get laughs out of gag lines cranked out by teams of (largely) middle-aged white guys. For that, he was lauded by the likes of Bob Hope and Lucille Ball. For that, he was a magazine cover boy. For that, he was the most famous child star on television.

Team Gary Coleman, which included his parents and agent Vic Perillo, moved quickly to get the boy his proper financial due. By the spring of 1979, toward the end of the first *Diff'rent Strokes* season, they were letting it be known that NBC's antidote to *Supertrain* was getting a "shockingly low" (in the words of a 1979 *People* magazine) $1,600 an episode (or $41,200 for the full, twenty-six-week season). Come July 1979, Gary Coleman Inc. was in full salary-dispute mode. When production began on the new season, Gary did not return to the set. One week passed. Two weeks passed. Then NBC blinked. It gave Gary Coleman Inc. a seven-year pact, upping the kid's salary to a reported $16,000 a week for season No. 2. The network balked at the camp's request for a bodyguard (Team Gary Coleman ended up funding that one on its own) and consigned its leading kid to helping the network launch the long-awaited (and, ultimately, short-lived) *Hello, Larry,* now, technically, a *Diff'rent Strokes* spinoff, by making Gary put in a couple of appearances on the fledgling show. (He was also asked to lend his presence to *The Facts of Life,* another *Strokes* spinoff, this one featuring the Mrs. Garrett character in an all-girls-school setting.) When Gary returned to the *Diff'rent Strokes* set at the end of July 1979, a guest star befitting his A-list stature was set for the first episode: Muhammad Ali.

But much as Gary bored of commercials even as he shot his first one, the *Diff'rent Strokes* fame game seemed to wear on him quickly, as well. For one thing, being a network star meant he had to talk to the press. Gary Coleman neither liked nor tolerated the press. Of articles written about him, he said, "I throw them away like old rags." Gary was eleven. *Eleven.* In October

1979, also at age eleven, he threatened to sue Geraldo Rivera for bringing a camera crew from ABC's 20/20 to his *Diff'rent Strokes* dressing room. At twelve, he railed about being repeatedly asked about his health: "Everyone has my record, but they want to ask about it again and again. That's a bother and a bore." At age thirteen, he told the *New York Daily News* he was "not in interview mode" and proceeded to watch a cartoon during the scheduled chat (in the company of his bodyguard, natch). Wrote reporter Ann Guarino: "He sounds arrogant and self-important. He gets away with it because he is so cute and amusing." It was Gary's prerogative not to embrace the press – reporter types certainly did not endear themselves to him early on. At a press conference in Atlanta to promote *Diff'rent Strokes'* first season, Gary was asked if he was a midget. "Are you addressing someone else in the room that I don't see here?" he shot back.

It wasn't just the media that bored him, though. It was the show, as well. And not just the do-we-have-to-do-this-bleep-again sixth (or seventh or eighth . . .) season. Gary Coleman's honeymoon with Hollywood never really happened. In his autobiography, he was quoted as saying he found *Diff'rent Strokes* hard work from the get-go and "only once in a while, was it fun." In 1980, he copped to being "impatient during rehearsals" and as grouchy as *Sesame Street*'s Oscar the Grouch. By way of a compliment, Conrad Bain once said, "I sometimes have the feeling he's so far ahead of us we're boring to him."

Boring, boring, boring – that was Gary's theme. Everything was boring, or in lieu of that, not very good. Gary didn't like his show's scripts, in particular; he didn't like television, in general (found it too imperfect a medium). Gary, frankly, didn't like much of anything. He didn't like girls ("If Mom wants grandchildren, I'll adopt one, because I'm never getting married," he announced in 1981, at age thirteen. "I'm not going to step into something I'm going to regret. Women like money. Look at Burt Reynolds. He had four women and they all left him"), he didn't like being called cute ("That bugs me like a bee bugs me"), he didn't even cut *Star Wars* slack ("You could tell Darth Vader's ships were glued together," the eleven-year-old critic said).

And fans? Not high on his list. Said costar Shavar Ross, who appeared on nearly fifty *Diff'rent Strokes* episodes from 1980 to 1986 as Arnold's school chum Dudley, "I remember he just did not like to be around people and his father would pass out these autographed little pictures – about three-by-five – to people, and they'd just try to get rid of them so he [could] really enjoy his life." Steven Mond, who guested on twentysomething *Diff'rent Strokes* episodes, also from 1980 to 1986, as Arnold's *other* school chum Robbie, experienced Gary's wariness first-hand. Said Mond: "On the last day after we taped [Mond's first show in 1980] – 'cause I didn't know I was coming back – I wanted to get an autograph, get a picture taken with [Gary], hang out a little bit with him in his dressing room – and he wouldn't come out. And part of [that] was that there were also about twelve or thirteen extras who were about my age, too, who were running around wanting the same thing."

So, all right, Gary was a preternatural curmudgeon. Maybe he had a right, or at least a couple very good excuses. "Looking back on it, I can really understand [Gary's attitude] and really feel for the guy," Mond said. "He was playing a character who was about four to five years younger than who he really was. He was about twelve years old playing seven and a lot of the people around the set started to treat him like he was seven, and it's pretty easy to start acting like you're seven when that sort of thing starts happening." The other half of it was, if Gary distrusted his fan base, it was because the fans, like reporters, gave him reason to distrust them. Said Todd Bridges in 1980, "People try to pick him up and everything."

It wasn't easy being Gary or being around Gary. He lived with pressure and he applied pressure. He was given power and he exacted power. Said Shavar Ross: "He used to like to play-fight a lot. And when he would get rough with me – [and] me being the kid from New York, you know – I'd get rough back with him. And I remember one time he hit me and I hit him back. And I hit him hard. And then I remember all the producers, they sat me around, and it was like a really big deal. They told me, 'You can't play that rough with him because he's a very sick child, he has a kidney problem and so if he ever hits you or plays around just play lightly back with him.' Ever since then, I knew that it was very important that he didn't get hurt. You know, he was like the star in the show."

And, like Shavar Ross said, Gary Coleman was a sick kid – quite possibly the sickest man, woman, or child working as a regular on a weekly television series in America. It could be argued that the chronic kidney disorder made Gary Coleman everything that he was – it made him mature beyond his years, it made him short, it made him impatient. Two out of the three qualities, in turn, made him rich and famous; the other made him, at times, insufferable. But most of all, the kidney disorder made him sick. In 1982, the miracle transplant's magic began to fade; the donated organ began to fail. Gary was put on self-administered dialysis – every four hours he filled his stomach with solution, every four hours he drained it, and so on. "It's a terribly complicated process involving scrubbing up and wearing a mask," Conrad Bain said. But Gary did it – during his lunch hour, before rehearsal, etc. – never missing a beat, never missing a show. The rest of his work and/or life schedule was equally regimented. Every fall through spring, he carried *Diff'rent Strokes*; every summer, he carried a movie – typically produced through his own company, Zephyr Productions (named after

Gary's favorite trains and presided over by his father, W.G.). In the summer of 1979, it was *The Kid from Left Field*. In 1980, *Scout's Honor*. In 1981, *On the Right Track*. In 1982, *The Kid with the Broken Halo*. In 1983, *Jimmy the Kid*. In 1984, *The Kid with the 200 I.Q.* and *The Fantastic World of D.C. Collins*. To hear the press releases, tell it, making a movie "was like a vacation for Gary Coleman." Of course, it was only "like" a vacation, because it wasn't *really* one. Nonetheless, Gary actually allowed that doing, say, *On the Right Track* (his first theatrical release), was easier and better than doing TV. At least, he allowed that in the press release for, say, *On the Right Track*: "You have more time doing it, more time, more fun," Gary was quoted as raving in the publicity materials. "Hey, man, it's been fun." Later, to a real-live reporter, during an interview hyping the film, he said of Hollywood: "It's all hard work." Hard, profitable work. His *Diff'rent Strokes* salary alone rose from $20,000 an episode, to $25,000, to $40,000, to a reported top weekly paycheck of $70,000. According to Team Gary Coleman, there was no pressure on its star to soldier the workload for the sake of that paycheck. Sue Coleman maintained time and again, it was all Gary's to walk away from. "He just likes to do his own thing," Sue said in 1981. "So far, he still enjoys acting – except for the crowds and all those autographs. He has fun doing the rest of it."

Thanks to "the rest of it," Gary Coleman of Zion, Illinois, hit a peak haul, by some estimates, of $3 million a year.

THE SHOW MADE TODD AND DANA INVISIBLE

During the run of *Diff'rent Strokes*, Todd and Dana each earned distinction in their field by warranting a profile in *TV Guide*. And when Todd's story ran and when Dana's story ran, the articles were promoted on the magazine's cover. And when Todd's cover photo was chosen and when Dana's cover photo was chosen, the editors made sure to pick a shot that paired each with Gary. Celebrity-wise, they weren't going anywhere without the little kid.

Pass the Kleenex, right?

You want to hear a real sad-luck story? Talk to the kid who works in a sweatshop for change. Or to the kid who's sold into prostitution by his crack-head parents. In the annals of lousy things that have happened to children, Todd Bridges and Dana Plato getting overshadowed on a long-running prime-time sitcom doesn't really rank. There are worse things than to sign onto a television series and wind up a second-class foil – a warm body kept on salary to feed straight lines to the little guy with the booming voice, lackeys ordered to goad Gary into unleashing a "Whatchu talkin' 'bout?" Yes, there are, we can agree, worse things. Unless, of course, these things are happening to you, in which case, petty or no, they *are* the worst things. Maybe that was the tough thing about being Todd Bridges or Dana Plato on *Diff'rent Strokes* – you had no reason to complain and every reason to want to. You had every reason to believe you were a TV star and every reason to know you weren't. You had every reason to know Gary was just a kid like you and every reason to know (right down to the size of your paycheck – and the size of *his*) that he wasn't.

Issues of jealousy were broached early on. In 1980, Todd's mother, Betty, allowed to *TV Guide* that her son needed some time adjusting to the fact that he wasn't the baby – or being babied – on the *Diff'rent Strokes* set. Todd himself copped to resenting the attention Gary received. "Long time ago, when we first started, it made me mad," he said in the same 1980 article. "But now I don't care. I got used to it." Used to it or no, they continued to tussle. Many of their scrapes were chalked up to

TV-land sibling rivalry, others to plain old bad vibes. In 1982, there was something of a scandal when Todd engaged Gary in what was described as a slap-fight. The referee services of Conrad Bain were required to break the two up. Remembered Shavar Ross, "I think they had made a bet that day on the set that whoever would mess up first would have to pay all this money or whatever. And I think Todd or Gary – one of them, I'm not sure who – messed up their lines but the bet didn't go through and they ended up getting into a little fight. I just remember hearing this slap, you know, in the dressing room on the set and then Gary is crying and Todd is running somewhere and there's this big deal. The next thing it's on the news and stuff. And I didn't see Gary the next week. I think for a couple of weeks he just didn't come on the set." To *People* magazine in 1983, a source on the set described Todd as "bad news." ("I know Gary is scared of him," the mole said.)

And so the show's legend grew. "I remember on the set of *Little House* they used to tell us over and over again, 'Don't play with the children from *Diff'rent Strokes*,' Alison Arngrim, who costarred on the Melissa Gilbert–Michael Landon family drama *Little House on the Prairie* (1974–81), once said. Another child actor who worked on the lot where numerous Norman Lear-backed sitcoms of the early 1980s (*Diff'rent Strokes*, *The Facts of Life*, *One Day at a Time*, *Silver Spoons*, etc.) were produced, agreed that the *Diff'rent Strokes* production home radiated bad vibes. "It was the whole set, it was weird," the actor said. "It was just different, it's different. It had a lot to do with the fact that Gary got so much fame." The insider's take on the dirty, little secret to *Diff'rent Strokes* was the same as the dirty, little secret to Watergate: follow the money. Gary, Todd, and Dana were hardly equals when the show premiered. But one summer later, following Gary's holdout, they were hardly on the same planet – economic- and stature-wise.

At the peak of her earning powers, Dana made less than a third of what Gary made. Granted, there are worse things than making one-third of what Gary Coleman made. Unless you're blessed with otherworldly perspective, though, there aren't worse things when you're the one who's feeling slighted. Dana, for one, tried to put a bright spin on things. She joked that her role on *Diff'rent Strokes*, such as it was, consisted of telling the boys that the bathroom was free. ("Viewers must have thought I slept in there.") And that was fine by Dana. Hey, she said, they'd only originally signed her to appear on seven episodes – getting into six years' worth of them, even for a minute or two, wasn't bad. And, hey, *not* being a TV star (she never considered herself a star) wasn't that bad, either. Stars got typecast, remember? That *Exorcist* thing was a close enough call. Can you imagine if she'd become the name-above-title draw of *Diff'rent Strokes*? Awful. Why, she'd never work again. She'd get stuck as goody-two-shoes Kimberly Drummond and resort to posing in *Playboy* in an ill-advised bid to revive and restructure her career – Oh, that happened anyway? Well, never mind. Dana didn't seem to.

"Dana was so crazy, you know, she was easy to get to know but she was really, uh, bonkers, God rest her soul. The nature of her personality was a little wacky. We used to have these golf carts to go around the studio. Well, she stole one once and went and followed the tram through the Universal [Studios] Tour and got stuck in the tunnel that spins and she was escorted back by security guards and everything. And everyone was just like, 'Yeah, that's Dana.'" (Glenn Scarpelli)

"She always seemed very excited about being on the show. She had just a high energy on the set all the time. She just seemed always happy." (Shavar Ross)

"There was a time toward the end of one season when she went to go skydiving and they asked her to wait until the season had wrapped just in case she hurt herself and she said, 'No, I'll be fine,' and then showed up in a cast for the last show of the season. They had to rewrite everything and put her behind tables and stuff." (Steven Mond)

"She was a free spirit . . ." (Gary Coleman)

The verdict: Dana was, as always, Dana. Which was too bad, because to get ahead on *Diff'rent Strokes* you had to be Gary. As the production catered itself more and more to Gary – extending *his* screen time, meeting *his* salary demands, accommodating *his* personal needs – Todd and Dana moved farther into the background. By the mid-1980s, there were few story lines to be had for the show's young adults, particularly young adults whose mere physical appearance emphasized an uncomfortable point: they'd grown up; Gary/Arnold hadn't. Sure, Willis got a girlfriend (Janet Jackson); and Kimberly once got green hair, but that was about it for the story lines, folks. Gary/Arnold was "Whatchu talkin' 'bout"-ing all the way to the bank; Todd and Dana were looking stuffed and uncomfortable in crew-neck sweaters, boat shoes, and blazers – TV's two most unlikely preppies. Outside of *Diff'rent Strokes*, their opportunities were just as varied. While Gary toplined movie project after movie project, there were no tailor-made projects for Todd and Dana. It wasn't supposed to be that way.

"I think he could grow into a young leading man, a Sidney Poitier." (*Diff'rent Strokes* executive producer Howard Leeds, on Todd, circa 1980)

"She is a fine actress, a ballerina, and she earns a great deal of money. Someday she will be another Liz Taylor or perhaps another Ingrid Bergman." (Journalist/future game-show star Ben Stein, on Dana, circa 1981)

During their *Diff'rent Strokes* careers, the future Sidney Poitier and the future Liz Taylor jointly did a couple of *CHiPs* episodes and appeared (but did not star) in a couple of TV movies (chiefly, 1983's *High School U.S.A.*). Their acting careers – particularly Todd's, which had been so active before the show – were drying up even as they continued to play TV stars. Shut out and all but ignored, Todd and Dana acted like any other disgruntled teens – they acted out. Between them, they had enough spending money to buy themselves a whole lot of trouble.

Todd's police-blotter troubles began in 1983 when he was eighteen. On July 20, he was stopped for speeding and reckless driving in Beverly Hills. Police got a bonus when they checked the glove compartment – found a loaded .45. (Todd had a permit, but it was expired. He ended up pleading guilty to the weapon charge, and agreeing to a $240 fine and a year's probation.) On September 24, the same year, Todd was detained by Los Angeles police for, as he put it, stealing his own car. (As Todd, his brother, and a friend tried to jump-start his Porsche, police tagged the trio as potential thieves and handcuffed Todd until the matter was straightened out.) In November, also of that year, the aforementioned Porsche (license plate TODD B 1) was found torched. Todd posed mournfully beside it for a *People* magazine feature. Investigators suspected revenge (for what, they didn't speculate); Todd said it was his neighborhood, including the local police, ganging up on him because he was young and black. Said his mother, "Todd is now under psychiatric care, and he is in a terrible state." So much for the future Poitier.

Dana's early troubles were not nearly so dramatic, nor publicized. She did not get arrested, à la Todd; she did not get suspended, à la Mackenzie Phillips. In 1984, there was the troubling story about her estranged father, Dean, suing her (unsuccessfully) for support, but that was about it. It was only years later the *other* stories would come out: Al Burton remembering Dana coming to the set "in a daze, in a funk," and otherwise drunk at age fifteen; her onetime manager, Sy Levin, recalling Dana overdosing on valium at age fourteen. Were these the results of the pressures of being on *Diff'rent Strokes*? The pressures of growing up with fame (or not enough fame)? Maybe, maybe not. A family friend said Dana got into drink and drugs even before *Diff'rent Strokes* began. Perhaps Todd Bridges had the goods on Dana all the way back in 1981. "Dana's a good kid," he said, "but she's a girl, so she has lots of problems." What Todd specifically meant was that Dana was always "moonin' about some boy." To be sure, demure Kimberly Drummond drove Dana Plato nuts. Kimberly was such a good-girl with such boring tastes in fashions – always with the ponytail, always with the bangs. "She is obsessed with wanting to look older," judged a 1981 *TV Guide* profile on the actress. In 1984, she perfected the older look – she got pregnant. The giddy announcement to her coworkers came first ("Well, don't you see? When I get the baby I'll never be alone again"); the Vegas wedding, to one Lanny Lambert, followed in April 1984. Next up: the ax. It might have been okay for Kimberly Drummond to counsel a pregnant teen (as was the plot of one Very Special Episode), but it was not okay for Kimberly Drummond to be *with child* herself. In short order, Dana (and Kimberly) disappeared from *Diff'rent Strokes*.

Well, more so than usual.

AND THEN ONE DAY NANCY REAGAN VISITED THE SET

How big was *Diff'rent Strokes*? Or, rather, how big was Gary Coleman? On the episode originally broadcast on March 19, 1983, the guest star was first lady Nancy Reagan. In the annals of TV guest stardom, this was a very big deal. The first lady could

have had her pick of any prime-time series on which to dissemi-
nate her anti-drug, "Just Say No" message. Any old *Gimme a
Break, Silver Spoons,* or *Facts of Life* would do. But they didn't.
Reagan chose *Diff'rent Strokes* because Gary Coleman was *the*
perceived way to reach Kid America. She was the first lady of the
nation; he was the first adolescent of TV. They were meant to do
good together. And so Secret Service agents were called. Photo
ops were ordered. And a $596 check for Nancy Reagan's acting
services rendered was cut. (She donated the money to charity.)

The episode was called "The Reporter." The setup: little
Arnold (as played by the increasingly exasperated-sounding, fif-
teen-year-old Gary Coleman) is looking for a big scoop to win a
local newspaper contest. To the rescue: old friend Robbie.
Explained Steven Mond: "I was the kid with the drug problem.
My whole life was turned around by a thirty-second chat with
Nancy Reagan." Yes, that was the gist of it, all right. Bad-news
Robbie shows Arnold and Dudley an upper ("An upper what?"
asks Dudley, to the delight of the laughtrack); Arnold asks
Robbie to hook him up with his dealer (in the name of investiga-
tive journalism, natch); Arnold writes his exposé; Arnold takes
heat from his doofus of a school principal who claims Arnold
must have made up his story because there couldn't possibly be
drugs on campus; Nancy Reagan saves the day (and Arnold's
reputation) by turning up at Arnold's school and coaxing kids
(Robbie, included) into confessing to prior drug use in front of
the world, federal agents, and that doofus of a school principal.

Along the way, there was the requisite groaner-in-the-making
line (an indignant Kimberly on why Arnold should divulge his
source on the drug story, regardless of whether it involves a
friend: "We're talking about drugs here!"); the inevitable
"Whatchu talkin' 'bout, Mrs. Reagan?" and a surprisingly natural, polished performance by Nancy Reagan (right down to her
big-finale *Reefer Madness* speech: "Let me tell you a true story

about a boy we'll call Charlie . . ."). If it all played like a camp classic by the mid-1990s, in the mid-1980s it was all perfectly perfect. Insiders said Mrs. Reagan was nice, the shoot fun. Dana wasn't pregnant yet; Todd still arrest-free. Only Gary seemed nonplussed by the momentous occasion-ness of it all. To a reporter about the Nancy Reagan visit, Gary said in 1983, "She came in, did her job, and left."

AND THEN ONE DAY IT WASN'T FUN ANYMORE

There was a lot that Gary Coleman's TV riches couldn't buy – health, height, good scripts. *Diff'rent Strokes* was kids' stuff. In the beginning, that was enough. Then the show's original viewers – Gary Coleman's peers – grew up, moved on. There were high-school football games to go to, episodes of *The Love Boat* to baby-sit by. Meanwhile, back on *Diff'rent Strokes*, Arnold was spearheading a drive to save a squirrel and bellowing (still), "Whatchu talkin' 'bout?"

The Nancy Reagan episode, coming at the tail end of season No. 5, represented both the highlight and twilight of his influence. On one hand, he had the ear of the White House; on the other hand, he had a tone-deaf touch for his core audience. No self-respecting fifteen-year-old, with delusions of joining the cool crowd, would shill for Reagan's bumper-sticker platitudes. But Gary Coleman – still playing an elementary schooler, no less – did. The separation from the star and his audience was complete. Arnold Jackson was over. Only, *Diff'rent Strokes* didn't know it. On *Diff'rent Strokes*, Arnold Jackson was eternal. Year after year after year after year. Nothing about Arnold Jackson ever changed. Not his attitude, size, or (barely) his age. When the adventures of the Jackson boys began in 1978, Arnold was an eight-year-old. By the time Mrs. Reagan stopped by six years later, he was all of eleven. "I think our characters actually spent about four years in sixth grade," said Steven Mond. "And I know [Gary] didn't really like that – he didn't like that his character was really stagnating and never really got to age." It troubled viewers, as well. "When is Gary Coleman of *Diff'rent Strokes* going to grow up?" the *New York Post* asked in 1980. "That's a question asked constantly by many of his fans. . . ." The *Post* meant "grow up" in the feet-and-inches sense, of course.

Feet and inches (or lack thereof) were always part of the Gary Coleman equation. At first, they were what helped make him employable. And then they were what helped make him (to our eyes) weird. (Enough with the small Arnold already, all right? Shouldn't he be getting bigger or something?) The powers-that-be at *Diff'rent Strokes* tried to cover up for Gary's lack of a growth spurt. They kept Arnold in grade school; they gave him little (read: younger) friends with whom he could see eye-to-eye. Shavar Ross said he was introduced on the show in 1980 for that very reason – Todd/Willis had shot up; Gary/Arnold needed an inch-wise peer. "I remember [at the audition] they had this big, old photo – life-size photo – of Gary Coleman that they would measure me up against him to see how my height was with him," Ross said. "I think I got [the part] basically because of height."

But there were only so many shorter, younger friends who could be deployed to make Gary/Arnold look, well, not so small. (Not that the producers didn't stop trying. A final, last-ditch ploy came in 1984, when eight-year-old Danny Cooksey joined the cast as Sam McKinney, the pipsqueak son of Phillip Drummond's main squeeze – and future TV wife – Maggie, as originally played by Dixie Carter.) Only once did *Diff'rent Strokes* address the matter of feet and inches (or lack thereof) in an up-front fashion. In the episode entitled "Count Your

Blessings" (originally broadcast on January 7, 1981), a vertically discouraged Arnold goes to see a doctor to determine how much he'll grow. Unfortunately, the answer he gets is: Well, not much. In true, inexplicable *Love Story* fashion, the doctor never says exactly why Arnold won't grow and Arnold never asks. The bottom line is, we're told, he'll top out at five feet – at best. Strangely, the message of the episode isn't: Make good with what you got. It is: See, some people have it worse (aka, count your blessings). In order to cheer up Arnold after the short-person diagnosis, Mr. Drummond summons an old friend who has a wheelchair-bound daughter who's even tinier than Arnold. It works. By the end of the half-hour, Arnold is his usual carefree self.

In real life, Gary said *Diff'rent Strokes* hadn't been fun since season No. 4 – when "my spirit kind of died." The problem was, Gary said, the show became (1) all about the "money, money, money"; and/or (2) "a little boring." Would you call Gary inde-cisive? Not to his face, you wouldn't. As his dissatisfaction grew, his moods darkened. His mother said he yelled at her (but only because he needed to blow off steam, she added). His mother also stressed that Gary could stop acting whenever he wanted (but he didn't *really* want to because "he'd get antsy," she noted). Fact was, Gary didn't stop *Diff'rent Strokes*. Not when he tired of it. Not when he outgrew it. Not when his kidney failed. Not even when he endured major surgery.

On November 10, 1984, Gary Coleman underwent his second career kidney transplant at Los Angeles' UCLA Medical Center. Doctors said the three-hour procedure went beautifully, although they predicted that the sixteen-year-old Gary would probably need about three months off work to recuperate. On January 3, 1985, less than two months later, the "Welcome Back, Gary" banner was hung from the Universal Studios-based *Diff'rent Strokes* set. Gary was back on the job. His return was celebrated with sparkling apple juice. There was relief all around.

As a *Diff'rent Strokes* executive remarked to *People* magazine in 1983 as the waiting game for a new kidney had begun, "What good is he to us dead?"

FINALLY, THE SHOW WAS CANCELED

Call it an early midlife crisis. Call it delayed, inevitable burnout. After the second transplant, Gary Coleman took a good, long, hard look at *Diff'rent Strokes* and didn't like what he saw. All right, he'd *never* liked what he saw. But, now, at age seventeen, he *really* didn't like it. Arnold Jackson was a junior-high kid – a silly thirteen-year-old still subject to being passed around like a prized stuffed animal. Said Gary, "We live in a modern world. Let's live in a modern world." It was the Gary Colemanesque way of saying Arnold and *Diff'rent Strokes* were *not* of the modern world. (If his interviews as a child were brusque, his interviews as a young man were obtuse. He never outgrew being the kid from *The Tonight Show* who dropped three-syllable words to impress.)

Certainly, then-NBC programming chief Brandon Tartikoff seemed to have trouble understanding Gary. Tartikoff said he talked to Gary about his future (and, in turn, the future of *Diff'rent Strokes*) in the spring of 1985. And what Tartikoff heard was that Gary didn't want to come back for an eighth season. Subsequent discussions with Gary's agent Vic Perillo cemented Tartikoff's belief: Gary didn't want to do any more *Strokes*, he wanted to do an action series. (Said Conrad Bain, "He tried to see himself as Mr. T.") Unfortunately, Tartikoff didn't see Gary as Mr. T. He passed on the "Gary Coleman: Man of Action" concept and planned for a schedule without *Diff'rent Strokes*. Then Gary changed his mind – he inked a new contract with Embassy Communications (the Lear-owned parent company of Tandem Productions) and steeled himself for a return engagement as

Arnold Jackson. One problem solved; one problem made. If Gary was now ready to come back, Tartikoff wasn't ready to have him. He said Gary's flip-flop came too late. When the NBC 1985–86 fall schedule was announced that May, *Diff'rent Strokes* wasn't on it. Its longtime 8 p.m. Saturday slot had been awarded to the returning *Gimme a Break* (with that new, little cute kid Joey Lawrence). *Diff'rent Strokes* was done, and Gary was shocked – shocked! – by the turn of events. "NBC acted of its own accord," Gary said. "I was canceled for some strange reason. I'd like to know why."

As it turned out, he wasn't canceled for long. ABC picked up *Diff'rent Strokes* for its revamped, family comedy Friday night lineup. Didn't it know Arnold Jackson was over? Didn't it know Gary Coleman – as far as cute, little kids went – was over? No, it did not. What the network and the producers knew was this: *Diff'rent Strokes* was not going to be over until "you reach a seventeen share," executive producer Ken Hecht told TV reporters in the summer of 1985. And so until it dipped below that must-sell margin, Arnold Jackson was back – and (supposedly) better than ever. On the ABC season, he'd be fifteen. He'd be a high-schooler. He'd get a new TV stepmom (Mary Ann Mobley in place of Dixie Carter, with whom Gary reportedly clashed). And he'd grow a moustache for publicity shots. Perfect, huh? All – or at least some – of Gary's issues addressed, right? Gary must have been happy? Yes?

No. The new season was just a few months old before Gary was griping that he'd only continued with *Diff'rent Strokes* because he'd assumed "some people" (his parents? his agent? his managers who doubled as his parents?) would have been upset if he'd done otherwise. The new season was also just a few months old before Gary's kidney failed (again) and he was readmitted to the hospital in December 1985 to get hooked up to portable dialysis (again). Fans of the show were told not to worry, however, because doctors "predicted the young actor would be on the set of *Diff'rent Strokes* with his concealed [dialysis] unit when taping [resumed] January 15." What a relief. Could you imagine an episode without Gary/Arnold? Or, more specifically, an episode without Gary/Arnold's weary, eye-rolling, just-leave-me-alone attitude (the one that had supplanted the wide-eyed, big-grinned, hug-me look of about four years back)? Well, actually, we could. We could do without a bitter Arnold, a neutered Willis, and an oft-absentee Kimberly, it turned out. We could live without a tired show populated by weary actors. We could tag *Diff'rent Strokes* as one of our childish things and put it away. We could – and we did. *Diff'rent Strokes* was indeed over. It did not help ABC topple *Dallas* over on CBS. It did not get a seventeen share. It did not win renewal.

In the spring of 1986, *Diff'rent Strokes* was canceled – for good, this time. There was no consulting with Gary Coleman Inc. There were no negotiations. ABC owed no allegiance to Gary. It just canceled him.

AND THEN, AND THEN . . .

As they were at the beginning, so were they all there at the end – Gary, Todd, and Dana. (Although she was no longer considered a series regular, Dana was featured in a group photo during the opening credits of the 1985–86 season and was asked back for Very Special Episodes, including one about Kimberly and bulimia.) The trio had been together eight years – a longer run than enjoyed by most TV casts, a longer run than endured by some real families. But as it became clear in 1986 that the series was really, finally near its end, there were no group hugs on the set, no grand Seinfeldian farewell story lines on the screen. Enough was enough was enough. Said Steven Mond: "There was a real feeling among everybody that we're all tired, just let us go, let us go do something else." And so they did. The highlights:

GARY COLEMAN:
- tells his management team (including his parents) he's reviewing their jobs (1987);
- wins a restraining order against his father following a dustup between W.G., Gary, and Gary friend/advisor/ Michael Jackson impersonator Dion Mial on the set of a *Howdy Doody* TV special (1987);
- fires his managers (aka his parents), his business manager (Anita DeThomas), and his agent (Vic Perillo);
- files a lawsuit against his parents and Anita DeThomas, claiming they squandered his then-estimated $7 million TV fortune (1989);
- fights off a counter-defamation lawsuit by DeThomas and a legal bid by his mother to declare him incompetent to handle his own affairs (1989);
- hosts a radio show (*Gary Coleman's Colorado High*) in his new Rocky Mountain home base (1990);
- wins a $1.3 million Los Angeles County Superior Court judgment against his parents and DeThomas after a judge found the trio drained his estate by charging excessive commissions and fees (1993);
- opens a video-game parlor (Gary Coleman's Video Parlor) in Marina Del Rey, California (1994);
- is spotted working as a security guard in the Los Angeles area (1997);
- is arrested for assault on an autograph seeker in a Southern California uniform shop (1998);
- is sued by said autograph seeker for $1 million-plus (1998);

- tells *Us* magazine he's a thirty-one-year-old virgin (1999);
- is arrested at a sobriety checkpoint in Hawthorne, California, for an outstanding warrant (and unpaid $400 fine) related to the fan-bashing case (1999);
- files for Chapter 7 bankruptcy, listing $72,000 in debts and reestimating his onetime fortune at $18 million (1999);
- begins an on-air internship at a Phoenix radio station (1999); and,
- goes on a date with a twenty-three-year-old woman who paid $4,000 for the privilege via an Internet Web-a-thon designed to raise money for him (1999).

TODD BRIDGES:

- files a harassment lawsuit against the Los Angeles Police Department (1984);
- pleads no contest to felony charges of making bomb threats against a Van Nuys, California, auto detailer (1986);
- is arrested (again) on suspicion of reckless driving (80 mph in a 35 mph zone) in Northridge, California, after the Bridges family reports him as suicidal and possibly armed (1988);
- spends Christmas addicted to crack cocaine and contemplating suicide (1988);
- is arrested (again) for allegedly skipping out on a $500 repair bill at a South Los Angeles auto shop and absconding with his BMW at gunpoint (1989);
- is arrested (again) and held on $2 million bail on attempted murder charges for allegedly firing shots at a man at a Los Angeles crack house (1989);
- is acquitted of attempted murder in crack-house case (1989);

- is arrested (again) on a coke-possession charge in North Hollywood, California, in a case that goes nowhere after not enough evidence is found to charge him with a crime (1990);
- is acquitted (again) of assault with a deadly weapon charge in crack-house case (1990);
- establishes Todd Bridges Youth Foundation to help, well, youth (1990);
- resigns as head of Todd Bridges Youth Foundation after being arrested (again) on drug (meth-amphetamines) and weapon (loaded 9 mm Ruger) possession charges stemming from a traffic stop in Burbank, California (1992);
- is arrested (again) on suspicion of attempted murder for the stabbing of a boarder in a rent dispute in his Sun Valley, California, home (authorities decline to file charges) (1993);
- pleads guilty to drug and weapons charges from 1992 Burbank arrest, enters rehab (1993);
- exits rehab clean and sober and reformed (1994); and,
- is arrested (again) for allegedly ramming a friend's car with his car following an argument over a video game in the Los Angeles area (1997).

DANA PLATO:
- endures the death of mother Kay – "the only person I mattered to" (1988);
- divorces husband Lanny Lambert and, in turn, loses custody of son Tyler (1989);
- poses partially nude (see-through tops, no bottoms) for *Playboy* pictorial entitled, "Diff'rent Dana" – says then-personal manager Gary Quinn, "We decided it would be good for her career" (1989);

- moves to Vegas (1989);
- lands job costarring in the revue show "Tropical Heat" at the Rio (1989);
- segues into a $5.75-an-hour wage at Vegas' own Al Phillips dry-cleaning chain (1989);
- applies for a $6-an-hour job picking up trash at her apartment complex, the Anchor Village Apartments, in the Vegas neighborhood the Lakes (1991);
- is rejected for trash-picking job (1991);
- dons baseball cap and sunglasses, arms herself with pellet gun, walks into neighborhood Lake Video store, demands clerk Heather Daly hand over the register money, makes off with $164, leaves a witness – says Daly to police, "I've just been robbed by Kimberly from *Diff'rent Strokes*" (1991);
- is arrested for robbery after returning to scene of crime sans the baseball cap-and-sunglasses "disguise" (1991);
- makes $13,000 bail presumably by, *People* magazine says, "selling her story to the tabloid the *Star*," only to have it later revealed that crooner Wayne Newton was her surprise benefactor – a non-acquaintance who came to her aid "because he knows what it is like to have been a child star";
- works with producers from *The Maury Povich Show* to reunite with her birth mother, Linda Strain, for a Very Special Taping (1991);
- is sentenced to five years' probation and four hundred hours' community service for video-store caper (1991);
- is arrested (again) for forging valium prescriptions (1992);
- is sentenced (again) to five years' probation for the prescription-forging caper (1992);

- forges a career as a B-movie actress with such works as *Bikini Beach Race* and *Night Trap* (1992);
- appears in the unrated would-be threesome romp *Different Strokes: A Story of Jack & Jill . . . And Jill* (1997);
- appears on *Sally Jessy,* stamped with onscreen identifier "Dana Plato: Battled Alcoholism When Show *Different Strokes* Ended" (1998);
- is reported "missing in action" from "her fleabag hotel in central Hollywood" by reputed lover Jennifer Wejbe to the good folks at the *National Enquirer* (1999);
- enlists fellow ex-child star Johnny Whitaker to manage her career (1999);
- buys a Winnebago with an eye toward spending the summer with her son (1999);
- appears on *The Howard Stern Show* in New York City to hype upcoming appearance at alternative-entertainment convention, the Expo of the Extreme, in Chicago, denounce the *National Enquirer* story, and proclaim, "My life is so good now. I've never been happier." (1999);
- when badgered by Howard Stern callers about her professed ten years of sobriety, offers to submit to an on-air drug test and produces a hair sample (1999);
- asks for hair sample back following on-air segment (1999);
- drives to Oklahoma in Winnebago with her boyfriend cum fiancé cum manager of five months, Robert Menchaca, to spend Mother's Day weekend with, first, his family in Moore, then, her ex-in-laws in Tulsa (1999);
- while at the Menchaca household, complains of

feeling sick and tired and retires to the Winnebago (1999);

- is discovered still unconscious at about 9:40 p.m. that night – says Menchaca to his mother, Marcela, a nurse, "There's something wrong with Dana" (1999); and,
- is declared dead at Southwest Medical Center in Oklahoma City at 10:30 p.m. on May 8, 1999.

And then Menchaca supposedly tried to camcorder the deceased at the funeral parlor; and then Dana's remains were sprinkled at sea; and then the Oklahoma coroner's office said the cause of death was suicide – the finding based on Dana's last, lethal "multidrug intoxication" (consisting of the muscle-relaxant Carisoprodol and about seven tablets' worth of the painkiller hydrocodone/acetaminophen, or Lortab) and a "past history of suicidal gestures"; and then the survivors bickered over the rights to the Winnebago (ex-husband Lanny Lambert prevailed in court); and then plans for an Oklahoma-based Dana's Café restaurant/museum were made; and then . . .

And then a fourteen-year-old boy lost his mother. Remembered son Tyler of Dana, "She liked to go to amusement parks. She liked to go on roller coasters."

AND WE SAID THEY ALL LIVED UNHAPPILY EVER AFTER

Did we cover everything? Do you want to know what happened to Gary's millions? Get in line. His parents – back in Zion – said they don't know. Gary said he doesn't really know. If his rags-to-riches life was never all that, perhaps his fortune was never all that, either. Said Gary: "Well, when you have six adults spending your money wildly, you know, to the tune of forty-seven and a half percent, before thirty-five percent taxes, it isn't gonna be a whole lot of anything left."

Do you want to know when the *Diff'rent Strokes* jibes started? When the "jinx" talk took off? Get in line. It's hard to pinpoint a year, actually. There are so many years to choose from. Certainly, by 1989 things were pretty funny – if Gary suing his parents, Todd cooling his heels in jail on an attempted-murder rap, and Dana posing for *Playboy* is "funny." Technically, at that point, of course, only Todd had "gone bad." Gary wasn't accused of any wrongdoing. Dana wasn't accused of any wrongdoing. And then when Dana *was* arrested? Watch out. Said Steven Mond: "Since I was in law school [at the time], it was a big joke that that would be my client base – the people I had worked with. And I figured, yeah, actually, that probably would be pretty steady work." (Ba-du-dum-bum.) Yeah, we know. Gary wouldn't be arrested for another eight-plus years, but why wait? Why let details destroy the big, distorted picture? And then when Gary *was* arrested? Watch out. There had been three *Diff'rent Strokes* kids and, finally, three screwed-up, criminally challenged *Diff'rent Strokes* adults. The numbers were too perfect, the circumstances too perfect, the punchlines too easy. (X-rated Kimberly? Unstable Arnold? Gonzo Willis? . . . What would Mr. Drummond say?)

And so here they are: the star-crossed three. Even after Dana's death, their legacies remain intertwined. Gary, Todd, and Dana. Their misfortunes as dazzling as – no, *more* dazzling than – their once-upon-a-time successes. Not the most special Very Special *Diff'rent Strokes* was half as compelling. The sitcom, after all, was make-believe; these spectacular demises were the real deal. It confirmed what we, the audience, suspected all along about the life of a former child star: it was lousy. And it confirmed what we suspected all along about former child stars themselves: they're losers, at worst; damaged goods, at best.

We set the trap. Gary Coleman, Todd Bridges, and Dana Plato stumbled into it.

At least Dana looked on the bright side.

"It's unfortunate that we were all pretty messed up, but I'm really glad I went through all that stuff because I'm a much better person for it." (Dana Plato)

But were we much better for it?

THE EMMANUEL LEWIS FACTOR

"Clearly, as actor, singer, dancer, Lewis is one of the nation's favorite little people, surpassing Gary Coleman of *Diff'rent Strokes* as TV's most appealing kid."

— UNITED PRESS INTERNATIONAL, ON EMMANUEL LEWIS, CIRCA 1985

Yes, this chapterette is about Emmanuel Lewis, star of screen and, well, *Webster*. But to be artsy (and possibly would-be profound) about it, we're going to start somewhere else. It's November 1999. At a Melrose club called the Gig in West Los Angeles. Onstage: a noted Los Angeles power-pop band name of the Andersons, featuring one Bob Anderson on guitar and vocals. Between songs, Anderson informs the thirtysomething, Nick at Nite-wisened audience of this: "Late-breaking news . . . Robbie Rist has died of a heroin overdose!" The audience laughs. Robbie Rist is, they know, the child actor who played unlucky Cousin Oliver on the final season of *The Brady Bunch*.

Robbie Rist is also, the audience understands, the (not-so) secret identity of Bob Anderson. The OD bulletin is, obviously, a joke. Rist/Anderson/Cousin Oliver isn't really dead. And so the audience laughs. Because it gets the joke.

Oh, does it get the joke.

The audience laughs because it knows that Rist knows that former child actors like him are supposed to be police-blotter funnies.

But what's funnier: the fact that we know he knows; or the fact that he knows that we think the whole freakin' world is *Diff'rent Strokes*?

Oh, all right, we've got our hang-ups. But we're not totally unjustified, either, right? Did you see the last chapter? Three TV kids, three screwed-up adults. What's plainer than that?

What's more complicated than that, of course, is that there were more than three TV kids who grew up on the *Diff'rent Strokes* set. There was Danny Cooksey, who grew up to be a working voice-over actor and musician. There was Steven Mond, who grew up to be an attorney. There was Shavar Ross, who grew up to be a pastor. There was Janet Jackson, who grew up to be the most "normal" member of her eccentric clan. That's not quite three-for-three, is it? Well, no, it's not. In fact, it's not even fifty-fifty.

Which brings us back to this chapterette. This chapterette, as the title indicates, is about Emmanuel Lewis. Consider it a brief aside to the *Diff'rent Strokes* opus. It is about why Emmanuel Lewis is not Gary Coleman. It's also a lot shorter than the *Diff'rent Strokes* chapter because Emmanuel Lewis doesn't have as long a rap sheet.

You saw that joke coming, too, right?

THE CONTROL EXPERIMENT

On paper, Emmanuel Lewis is as big a marked man as Gary Coleman. He's an adult who, by virtue of his size (or lack thereof), can still pass for cute and cuddly. He's a personality who's got sitcom baggage like you wouldn't believe – unless you hung out with him at the mall one day and actually heard the cat-calls ("Hey! It's Webster!"). He's a Friend of Michael Jackson – forever remembered as the tiny one who the pop oddity hoisted onstage at the American Music Awards back in the day. In short (and, where former child stars are concerned, the pun is always intended, isn't it?), he is a pop-culture icon of the cheesiest order.

Except he's not.

Compared to Gary Coleman, Emmanuel Lewis is treated like freakin' Prince Charles, or at least like one of the ex-costars of *M*A*S*H* – say, William Christopher, the guy who used to play Father Mulcahey. Like The Guy Who Used to Play Father Mulcahey, Lewis is a benign, former prime-time player – a man who is either fondly remembered or not quite remembered, but once remembered then fondly thought of. Or to put it another way: If you were organizing a celebrity golf tournament and needed some B-list names to fill out the roster, you could do worse than to get Emmanuel Lewis or the Guy Who Used to Play Father Mulcahey. A lot of your paying customers might even think it's kinda cool to see Webster in person.

How can that be? How does Lewis – Coleman's prime-time doppelgänger – (mostly) escape the jokes, the jibes, and assorted ridicule? Why isn't Lewis fully sharing ownership of the title Ultimate Former Child Star? That's what we're here to find out, and this is what we're here to do: use Emmanuel Lewis as the control experiment to Gary Coleman, in specific, and to troubled ex-TV kids, in general.

If not him, then why Gary Coleman? If not him, then why them?

OUR TEST SUBJECT, PART ONE

Emmanuel Lewis was born March 9, 1971, in Brooklyn, New York. He was the youngest of four children. As he grew in age, he did not grow much in inches. This was not a particularly new problem or concern for the Lewis family. Emmanuel's older brother Roscoe was a mere four feet tall when he was fifteen. By the time Roscoe was seventeen, he was six-foot-two. Clearly, there was hope for Emmanuel. There was also good news (or, at least, no bad news). Unlike Gary Coleman, there was no chronic or dire medical condition that thwarted Emmanuel's growth. He was what he was – short. Emmanuel, who had seen the very literal and painful growing pains that Roscoe went through to crack six feet, wasn't even necessarily anxious to experience them himself. Said a fourteen-year-old Emmanuel, "It doesn't matter to me if I stay very small or grow as fast as Roscoe."

And while that rather sunny disposition made him the attitudinal opposite to Gary Coleman's less-than-sunny disposition, the two were not exactly an odd couple, either. Like Gary Coleman, Emmanuel was a short, cute black kid with enough personality and preternatural camera-ready talent for three full-grown men. Like Gary Coleman, Emmanuel got his start in commercials (the first one when he was eight). Like Gary Coleman (and Rodney Allen Rippy), Emmanuel made his national mark in a burger spot (a 1982 ad for Burger King). Like Gary Coleman, Emmanuel was embraced – not shunned – by Hollywood for his size (the more short kids who can play younger than their real age, the merrier). And like Gary Coleman, Emmanuel was summoned to prime time.

There was one key distinction: Gary Coleman did not become a sitcom star because of Emmanuel Lewis; Emmanuel Lewis became a sitcom star because of Gary Coleman.

In the early 1980s, ABC – saddled with aging comedies (*Happy Days*, *Laverne & Shirley*) and stupid new ones (*Joanie*

Loves Chachi, Too Close for Comfort) – decided it needed NBC's
Diff'rent Strokes. But instead of spending the money to raid the
show (and, in turn, the show's established star salaries), ABC
decided to make its own series and establish its own (cheaper)
stars. Enter the project *Another Ballgame*. As developed by producer Stu Silver (then of ABC's 1982–83 bomb, *Star of the
Family*), the comedy series was to be a Tracy-Hepburnesque star
vehicle for the real-life husband-and-wife team of Alex Karras
and Susan Clark. The two were to play a recently married couple
– ex-jock George Papadopolis and Chicago politico Katherine
Calder-Young. In the grand sitcom tradition, George and
Katherine's world is turned upside down when a plucky orphan
moves into their home. For the role of the plucky orphan, ABC
championed That Cute Kid From the Burger King Commercial,
otherwise known as Emmanuel Lewis.

Emmanuel had three things in his favor: (1) he was adorable;
(2) he could read a line; and (3) he was even shorter than Gary
Coleman. Shorter than Gary Coleman?!? Could it be?!? Well,
when Gary Coleman made his *Diff'rent Strokes* debut (at age
ten), he was forty-three inches tall. When Emmanuel Lewis was
discovered by ABC (at age twelve), he was thirty-six inches tall.
If the American viewing public would be impressed that the
network scouts could find an even smaller, cuter black kid,
think of the incredulous reaction over at the *Diff'rent Strokes*
set. Remembered Shavar Ross: "I couldn't believe it when I
found out [Emmanuel] was the same age as me. For him to be
so short, you know? He's actually smaller than Gary."

And so twelve-year-old Emmanuel Lewis was cast as seven-
year-old Webster Long (Long is short – get it?), the surviving
son of one of George's old football buddies, and *Another Ballgame* was retitled *Webster*. So much for Tracy-Hepburn. This
was *Diff'rent Strokes II*. And like the original, there was no
doubt about the identity of the new show's real star. The theme

song said it all: "Then Came You." Not then came Susan Clark or then came Alex Karras. Then came Emmanuel Lewis.

When *Webster* premiered on September 16, 1983, *Diff'rent Strokes* was entering its sixth season. ABC could be — and was — accused of ripping off NBC's prized property, but in reality, ABC was grave-robbing. It was stealing the *old Diff'rent Strokes* — the one from 1978 or 1979, when Gary/Arnold's pout was funny because it seemed like a temporary put-on rather than a permanent disposition. To keep things fresh, *Webster* stole some of the new, social-minded *Diff'rent Strokes*, too. If there was a child molester on *Diff'rent Strokes*, then you could bet there'd be a child molester on *Webster*. (All in the name of keeping kids safe, of course.) To be fair, *Webster* wasn't a true carbon copy of *Diff'rent Strokes*. For one thing, it was slightly less — how should you say? — dumb. There was a heft to the tentative relationship between Webster and insta-mom Katherine. (Clark even nabbed a Golden Globe nomination out of the deal in 1983, helping immortalize the show as, yes, the Golden Globe-nominated *Webster*.) And for another thing, there were — how should you say? — fewer poor performances. Do the math: one kid regular on *Webster*, three kid regulars on *Diff'rent Strokes*. By virtue of having fewer mouths to feed with punchlines, *Webster* didn't have as much contractually obligated, here-Dana-you-can-say-this-line-this-week dialogue. In that way, *Webster* proved it had learned its lesson well from its predecessor: why mess with the fat (i.e., Todd and Dana), when what audiences really want is the cute, little kid (i.e., Gary Coleman)?

Arguably higher on the artistic scale than *Diff'rent Strokes*, *Webster* (or Emmanuel) never created the stir of *Strokes* (or Gary). It was not the lone (or even leading) prime-time kid series of its day. It was not the highest-rated. And it was not the first. Emmanuel/Webster didn't even have a catchphrase (unless you counted the way he called Susan Clark "Ma'am" instead of "Mom") *Diff'rent Strokes* was the sensation; *Webster* was the serviceable sitcom with a slightly used, if effective, gimmick. The Brandon Tartikoff/Gary Coleman standoff of 1985 would bring the two shows together when ABC took mercy on NBC's wounded cast-off and brought *Diff'rent Strokes* into its fold. Finally, the network had the sitcom it had wanted all along. (Actually, it had wanted the show as it was about three years earlier, but whatever.)

For the 1985–86 season, ABC scheduled *Diff'rent Strokes* on Friday nights, a half-hour time slot away from *Webster*. The differences between Emmanuel and Gary were never so clear as when their shows virtually bumped into each other. At 8 o'clock, it was time for Emmanuel/Webster, the kid who burst into giggles. At 9 o'clock, it was time for Gary/Arnold, the kid who had mastered the disdainful pout. By the end of the season, the pouty kid was shown the door. But the giggly kid wasn't exactly invulnerable himself. The network suits came after Emmanuel/Webster's head a year later, as ABC tired of its invention and prepared its time slot for an all-new, all-smaller kid (or kids') sensation: the *Full House* Olsen Twins. *Webster* ended its network run on September 11, 1987. From there it moved to the career fate worse than death, otherwise known as first-run syndication. Another two years' worth of *Webster* product was cranked out until 1989, when it was time to call it a series. All told, from 1983 to 1989, *Webster* produced 150 episodes, and Emmanuel Lewis grew about five inches. Roscoe Lewis' growth spurt did not transfer to his younger brother. At age eighteen, Emmanuel was about three-foot-five. He was short (still). Short enough to look like seven-year-old Webster Long for the rest of his life. Short enough to likely never land another major role in Hollywood.

Was he bitter? Was he disillusioned? Was he ready for his mug shot?

OUR TEST SUBJECT, PART TWO

Actually, Emmanuel Lewis was ready to move on and move out. After *Webster* ended in 1989, he left Los Angeles and enrolled at Clark Atlanta University in Georgia. In the South, he was still very much the oddity – the instantly recognizable Cute, Little Kid From That Show – but he wasn't very much the joke. Instead of trying to hang on in Hollywood, a town conditioned to kick when down, he found a place where all celebrity is novel, where Webster could be (and was) granted a good write-up for helping open the local Planet Hollywood. But most of all, in Atlanta, Emmanuel found a place to try out the new him: Emmanuel Lewis, civilian. Gary Coleman had tried a new locale, too. Tried to do the hideaway thing in Colorado after *Diff'rent Strokes* ended. But Gary Coleman wasn't much of a hideout guy. His voice was too big to keep quiet. He kept trying to resurface. He did the local radio show. He returned to Hollywood for the guest spots (mostly to parody himself *as* himself on *The Wayans Bros.*, *The Ben Stiller Show*, *MAD TV*, etc.). Emmanuel, meanwhile, said he wanted to "concentrate on my education . . . I just want to be a student." To be sure, he did side projects, too. He costarred in a rappin' kids video (*The New Adventures of Mother Goose: The Great Rhyme Rescue*, from 1995), he contributed vocals to an all-star track ("Yeah") on an Eddie Murphy album (*Love's Alright*, from 1992), he even guested at Elizabeth Taylor's Neverland ranch wedding to Larry Fortensky (1991). Yes, Emmanuel Lewis got around.

Whereas Gary Coleman's world seemed to be forever shrinking (severing ties with his parents, his agent, his costars, his fans), Emmanuel Lewis' was ever-expanding. He was said to have homes in Japan, New York, and Los Angeles. He was always good for a celebrity charity event. And except for the Clark Atlanta campus (where he "just [wanted] to be a student"), he was almost always good for an autograph. ("People want hugs, kisses, and autographs," Emmanuel said of the publicity game during a 1985 location shoot for the TV movie *Lost in London*. "But I don't mind.") For some of his worldliness, Emmanuel owed a debt to Michael Jackson. The superstar pop singer took him into his entourage during the height of his *Thriller* reign. With Brooke Shields, Emmanuel made the perfect awards-show accessory for Jackson. When the three made the scene together they were beyond TV-friendly, spanning nearly every demographic group – kids, adults, whites, blacks, men, women, man-children. As the years went on, it might not have been the best thing, publicity-wise, to be linked to an individual whose reputation was damaged by a child-abuse investigation, but on a private basis, hey, it got Emmanuel an invite to the Liz-and-Larry shindig – a chance to mix it up with former presidents (Ronald Reagan, Gerald Ford) and Roddy McDowall. Emmanuel chose not to talk about the Michael Jackson connection – saying private stuff was private stuff – but he didn't shy away from being seen in public with him, either.

What with all the extracurricular activities, Michael Jackson-related or otherwise, Emmanuel didn't graduate from Clark Atlanta until 1997, but he *did* graduate. Earned a degree in theater arts. Was one of nine hundred undergrads receiving diplomas on May 19, 1997, at the Georgia Dome under the watchful eye of *Cosby Show* mom Phylicia Rashad (a graduation guest speaker) and the chief executive of the United Negro College Fund (another guest speaker). "Don't ever forget that you are not standing alone," UNCF's Bill Gray told the assembly. "You are standing on the shoulders of others and that makes you a debtor. And the way to pay that debt is through service."

A couple months later, Emmanuel was spotted by a tabloid selling car wax out of the back of a van at a Shoney's restaurant in Nashville, Tennessee. Or, as the headline succinctly put it: "TV's Webster Sells Car Wax From Back of Van."

Was this the sign? Was the education thing a sham? Was Emmanuel finally bitter? Was he ready for his *E! True Hollywood Story*?

THE FINDINGS

Hard as it might be to accept, Emmanuel Lewis is not, was not, Gary Coleman. Not even the car-wax scene was made out to be a major tragedy by the tabloid. "It looked like a hard life, but he said he was having a lot of fun," customer Angie Wagner told the *Star*. "And he did seem pretty happy." He seemed "pretty happy"? Do you think Gary Coleman would ever seem – or be portrayed as being – "pretty happy" selling car wax? Think of Emmanuel Lewis as the Teflon Gary Coleman – nothing bad ever seemed to stick. Not bad press, not bad feelings, not bad vibes.

Which brings us back to the original question: Why isn't Emmanuel Lewis Gary Coleman? Isn't he just as doomed with his choice of "adult" acting roles? (Emmanuel plays a space alien on *In the House*, to Gary's turn as Snafu on *Homeboys in Outer Space*)? Isn't he just as forever linked to his old sitcom self by virtue of the fact that he still looks like his old sitcom self? Isn't he just as, you know, cursed?

Based on the evidence above, though, we know that Emmanuel Lewis is not Gary Coleman because:

- We didn't mention anything about him suing his parents because Emmanuel didn't sue his parents because Emmanuel didn't accuse them of stealing his money. Rather, Emmanuel actually seemed to *like* his parents. A 1995 profile in the *Atlanta Journal-Constitution* even noted how twenty-four-year-old Emmanuel arrived at the interview walking hand-in-hand with his mother, Margaret.

- We didn't mention all the health problems Emmanuel endured during the making of *Webster*, because he didn't have any outstanding ones.

- We didn't mention all the TV movies Emmanuel made during his hiatus breaks because he didn't make all that many TV movies. In fact, other than *Lost in London*, he didn't make *any* other TV movies.

- We didn't mention Emmanuel's gripes about Hollywood or *Webster* or the press because he didn't have any — not public ones, anyway. Gripes about the show were reserved for his adult costars who felt overshadowed by the small, happy one. That was their problem, though, not his.

- We didn't mention how *Webster* dragged on (and on and on and . . .) because it had the good fortune to suffer declining ratings before it became a big, slow-moving target.

- We didn't mention his arrest record because he didn't have one.

- We didn't mention his penchant for hanging out with a Michael Jackson impersonator, because Emmanuel hung out with the real thing.

Simply put: Emmanuel thrived in his world; Gary sickened of his. Why? How? Did Emmanuel have "better" parents? Did he have "better" coworkers? Did he have "better" friends? Did he have a "better" (read: more manageable) level of fame? Did he have a "better" education? Maybe it was all those things; maybe it was none of those things. Trying to pinpoint why Emmanuel Lewis is *not* Gary Coleman is like trying to pinpoint why Anissa Jones ended up dead at eighteen. It can't be done. Sometimes things – even good things – just are.

What can be answered more definitively is why we perceive Emmanuel Lewis differently than we perceive Gary Coleman: save a TV guest shot or two, Emmanuel Lewis quietly went away; Gary Coleman didn't. It's pretty simple, actually. If you're gonna get in our faces after you've outlived your usefulness (read: your TV show), then you better be entertaining (read: you better get a *new* TV show) or you better *go away*. Those are the top two choices. Pick one or pay.

CHAPTER SEVEN

PRAYER FOR AMERICA'S LEAST WANTED

"Tony, Tony, rally round. Something's lost
and must be found."

— PRAYER TO SAINT ANTHONY

Did you hear the one about the TV former child star who went
to college and got into real estate? Or the one who went to Yale
(no, not Jodie Foster) and became an author?

Of course not.

Lord, we are a predictable bunch. We can tell you the name
of the guy convicted of masterminding the Oklahoma City federal building bombing and not recall a single face of any of the
one-hundred-plus victims. We can recite the opening weekend
gross of the new Tom Cruise movie and not have a clue as to the
size of the gross national product. We can regale you with the
itty-bitty facts of the *Diff'rent Strokes* story and come up empty
on everything else regarding TV child stars. "We" includes this

book. (Fifty thousand or so words later and we finally acknowledge that, in addition to getting arrested and checking out on drugs, some ex-prime time tykes actually pursued higher education.) All right, we're all guilty. We're weak. We're easily seduced by *Sally Jessy Raphael*. We can't help ourselves.

And we can't help former child stars.

Help them? It's too much fun to revel in scandal or delight in the "dark side" of celebrity. And, frankly, it's one of the few perks of *not* ever being famous – getting to make fun of those who are (or were). So no, there's no real solution to the former child star dilemma. We can analyze this thing from Jackie Coogan to Gary Coleman and back again and it's no use. They're not really our problem; we're *their* problem. What do you do with that? Nothing. There's no real way for them to convince us that they're not what we think they are. All it takes is one police booking to tear down the good of a thousand uplifting "Whatever happened to . . ." stories. We're dealing. We're labeling. They're America's least wanted.

So, let us pray:

> Help us not be obsessed with the salacious and the tawdry and the foibles of certain cast members of *Diff'rent Strokes*. Let us shine our light on those who persevere, who are just fine, thank you. Let us celebrate the ways of Emmanuel Lewis and his kind. Let us leave Gary Coleman alone.

What's a TV former child star to do until that one's answered? Where to seek salvation? Let us consider.

1. GET GONE

This is the Emmanuel Lewis defense. You go away and get another life. You don't necessarily want to do this (because being a TV star is fun), but you do. Because Mickey Rooney told you to. (At least, that was Paul Petersen's story.)

> Paul Petersen: "In 1969 Mickey Rooney came to my house and put it bluntly to me that it was over for me. "
> Question: "How did he seek you out?"
> PP: "Well, my house was one of the few houses in Los Angeles in January of 1969 which was heavily damaged by a thirteen-day rainstorm we had out here. And that news had gotten around. It been on the evening news and [Rooney] actually drove to my house in Encino. Under the pretext of coming to look at the damage, [he] sat me down in my own living room and said — and now, this is Mickey Rooney, to me, giant star — and said, 'Paul, you have to get out of town and get your education 'cause they won't let you work for maybe twenty-five years.' And, of course, he was completely accurate."

Petersen didn't pack his bags immediately, but stuff happened. He sold a *Marcus Welby, M.D.* script and discovered writing to be his lifeline. In 1972, he made good on Mickey Rooney's advice and left Hollywood for the New Haven Motor Inn in New Haven, Connecticut, on a book assignment. The motor inn was located, more or less, across the street from Yale University. Petersen, who'd attended UCLA while on *The Donna Reed Show*, became a college student anew at age twenty-seven. The writing career was underway – he pounded out titles on car racing, on the film *It's a Wonderful Life*, and more. He created a pulp hero – Eric Saveman – and cast the character in a series of novels called *The Smuggler*. In the 1970s, he began a book on former child actors. The working title: *Suffer the Children*.

Glenn Scarpelli also went back to school. After *One Day at a Time*, Scarpelli moved to the unmemorable Ann Jillian-as-aghost sitcom *Jennifer Slept Here* (1982–83), and after *Jennifer Slept Here*, Scarpelli moved to New York to enroll at New York University. "I needed to party and I needed to hang out with people and I needed to cram and stay up all night and look like shit when I go to take my test," Scarpelli said. "And I needed to do something that was somewhat normal – I hate that word, but you know what I mean. I needed that for myself more any anything, I really did. And going to New York was the key for me because you can get a lot more lost in the woodwork in New York than you can in L.A."

At nineteen, Scarpelli was cool with leaving behind what was left of his prime-time career; his people (the managers, the publicist, the agents, etc.) were not. They're "making money," Scarpelli said. "And they're not gonna anymore. And that was a responsibility and it was a tough thing to look at that and know that my career fed their children. My career put food [on their table] and a roof over their heads."

Still, he did it, he went to college. And when college wasn't enough, he got a nose job. ("I need[ed] to change something.") And when the nose job wasn't enough, he went to Belize. As in Central America.

"I was about twenty-three at this point. I needed to get as far away from what is known as America and I needed to be with something else. And this opportunity came — I met this group of people who were going to start this ecological university [in Belize] and I was going to videotape the growth of the university. Well, the university never really happened, but the experience is why I needed to go. 'Cause in all honesty I wasn't too attached to the whole university thing. I really wanted to just live in a Third World country. I wanted to be with people who have different needs, who have different priorities. I needed to learn more about what else is out there and not in a wealthy way. I had to take money out of the picture and I went down there and I lived in this little village [where] there's no running water, there's no electricity, we had an outhouse and we had a thatched-roof hut. And we fished for our food; whatever we caught, that's what was for dinner." (Glenn Scarpelli)

Belize for Glenn Scarpelli; Portugal for Johnny Whitaker. The ex-*Family Affair* munchkin made his way to Europe for a two-year Mormon missionary stint in the late 1970s. This, after *Sigmund* folded, after the fledgling pop career died, and after *Good Morning, America* noted that Anissa Jones had died. "I'd been working for the past fifteen years," said Johnny, who caught the fateful 1976 *GMA* broadcast from his home in Salt Lake City. "I needed to stop and think about what I wanted and what was going on in my life."

Jon Provost, who divorced himself from *Lassie* in 1964, divorced himself from Hollywood (where he'd moved on to film, most notably 1966's *This Property Is Condemned*, with Natalie Wood and Robert Redford) in 1970. It was all in the name of love. He followed a girlfriend to Sonoma State University in Northern California and ended up enrolling (major in psychology; minor in special education).

"This was during the late '60s, early '70s, you know, and it was the height of the hippie times. And I grew my hair very long and fit right into the mainstream, and if somebody would come up and say, 'You know, gee, you kind of look like that kid on . . .' I might say, 'Well, yeah, a lot of people say that — bye.' There was a time there where I kind of skirted the issue because I didn't want it to interfere with where I was at the time. It was a time for me to grow and to play and all of that." (Jon Provost)

And when it was time to stop playing, he got a real-estate

license and worked the real-estate business for a dozen years. Then he got into an escrow company.

Willie Aames, meanwhile, found God in Kansas. Actually, post-*Eight Is Enough* (and post-*Charles in Charge* – his second TV life), the Born Againer founded a production company in the Midwest state and went on to star in and produce a children-oriented Christian video series, *Bibleman*. ("At first I thought the idea was ridiculous. Bibleman? Who is he? What does he do?") Aames came to terms with Bibleman and ended up touring the country in his cowl.

Got another hundred years? There's more. Lots more. In fact, there are more second-career/second-life stories than there are screw-up stories. Not every ex-TV kid winds up with a record or a habit; nearly everyone faces The Choice: stay or go? And Hollywood employment being what it is (lousy), most go. Even if they don't physically leave Hollywood, they get gone from acting. Brandon Cruz hooked up as a film editor. Danny Bonaduce segued into radio. Glenn Scarpelli helped found an audio post-house. Stanley Livingston wrote for theater and launched an educational video series (*Kids in Show*) for a new generation of young Hollywood hopefuls. Tony Dow became a director. Adam Rich became an assistant director. And so on and so and so on . . .

"I'd like to compile a list of the childhood stars who turned out just fine," Susan Olsen, the erstwhile Cindy of *The Brady Bunch*, once said. "The majority of child stars are just fine."

Common sense tells us this is so. (Outside of a prison cell-block, the majority of members in any population are "just fine.") Research tells us this is so. A 1998 Wayne State University survey of former child actors found that three-quarters of the participants felt they led "normal" lives with "normal" relationships with their parents. And empirical evidence tells us this is so. Mike Lookinland's 1997 drunken-driving arrest aside, the

Brady clan, for instance, featured six child actors (seven, if you counted Rist's Cousin Oliver) who were as squeaky clean in real life as in reel life (no matter what the spinmeisters behind Barry Williams' book intimated). *The Facts of Life* – a spin-off of the infamous *Diff'rent Strokes* – featured nearly a dozen young actresses during its decade-long run, none of whom ended up in court or on police blotters. Danny Bonaduce aside, the *Partridge Family* kids were of no interest to the scandal sheets. (And, frankly, Bonaduce's been pretty boring himself for almost a decade now.) Susan Olsen is right. We know she's right, too. But we also think we know this: Something's *got* to be wrong if they're not on TV anymore.

> "I always thought it amusing when people would come up to me after sixteen published books and say well, 'Don't you miss acting?' And I would look at them and think, 'Do you think that being a successful, published author is less than being a bubblegum star on television?'" (Paul Petersen)

Guilty.

2. COME BACK

Emmanuel Lewis might grow into a fine, upstanding citizen; Gary Coleman might unlock the key to cold fusion; the Brady kids might achieve the wonders of personal enlightenment; but the Ricky-to-Rick Schroder metamorphosis is the kind of story we *really* love.

Ricky, the *Silver Spoons* boy turned *NYPD Blue* cop, is who we consider a bona fide Former Child Star Made Good. He is, like that rare Natalie Wood creature before him, revered for being as (or more) famous as an adult than he was as a child. There's nothing harder than that, we say. There's nothing more admirable than that. A once-and-forever celebrity? Now, *that's* a winner.

Richard Bartlett Schroder was born April 13, 1970, in Staten Island, New York, to a telephone-company executive dad, Richard, and a stay-at-home mom, Diane (also formerly with the phone company). With Coleman and Lewis, Ricky would complete the holy trinity of kid TV stars of the 1980s. Of the three, Ricky had the classiest pedigree. He beat out two thousand hopefuls to nab his first onscreen role (not including, natch, commercials) in the 1979 film *The Champ*. (How did the relative novice master the film's prodigious crying scenes? "Well, you gotta think of something real bad and your emotions just sort of fill up and you start to cry," the nine-year-old Rickster explained.) The tear-jerker of a role (opposite Jon Voight) brought him a Golden Globe (as best new male star), a gig presenting at the 1979 Oscars, and comparisons to storied child actors past, à la Jackie Cooper. In 1981, another prestige assignment was secured, with Ricky working opposite William Holden in *The Earthling*. And then, in 1982, because there are only so many prestige assignments for twelve-year-old boys, he headlined the inevitable sitcom. This one was called *Silver Spoons*. It premiered on NBC on September 25, 1982.

In a twist to the tested *Diff'rent Strokes/Webster* format, Ricky's *Silver Spoons* alter ego, Ricky Stratton, was not an orphan – just a spoiled rich kid abandoned by his mom and dumped on his dimwit of a single father, Edward Stratton III (Joel Higgins). On the TV cheese scale, *Silver Spoons* was a mere also-ran to *Diff'rent Strokes* and *Webster*. If possible, it was even more lightweight than the other two. On NBC, it couldn't even hang as a companion to *Diff'rent Strokes*, getting shipped off Saturday nights in its second-to-last network season and paired with, well, *Punky Brewster* in the beyond-G-rated 7 o'clock Sunday night hour.

As a star, Ricky was something of a teenybopper favorite, but overall was neither as dynamic as Gary Coleman, nor as cuddly-bear cute as Emmanuel Lewis. Did any of this mean that, when the time came, there was hope that audiences (and casting agents) would collectively forget Ricky's kiddie TV past? That somehow he'd escape the typecasting trap? Not a chance. He was on a show that ran for four years in prime time (and a fifth in syndication). That's a *long* paper trail. Ostensibly, his career was just as screwed as the other guys'.

To be sure, Ricky had advantages in pursuing adult acting jobs over Gary Coleman and Emmanuel Lewis. For one thing, he was white. (See: any recent report on minority casting in Hollywood – such as it is.) And for another thing, he wasn't height-challenged. Though no linebacker, he actually grew up – got bigger. The fates smiled on him with health and growth hormones. Physically, he fit into the young-adult world in a way that Gary Coleman never would. He got a break. And just like in regular ol' real life, the one with the most breaks wins.

At the time, however, Ricky sure didn't think he was winning. When *Silver Spoons* ended in 1987, he found himself boxed into TV-movies. (Gary Coleman or Emmanuel Lewis should have been so boxed in.) Still, Ricky, who'd taken to billing himself as the less-cutesy Rick Schroder at age eighteen, wanted more. On the glamour scale, the grind-'em-out, made-for-television motion picture is right down there with, say, basic cable original programming. It's a paycheck. It's a credit. It's a chance to entertain couch-bound Cheetos-heads who have nothing better to do on a Tuesday night. "I'm happiest when I'm working productively," Rick once said, "and that wasn't the case."

He was right. He wasn't working productively. Even though he'd done a couple of passable TV movies (including 1988's *Too Young the Hero*, about a World War II fighting teen) and the acclaimed 1989 miniseries *Lonesome Dove*, he wasn't getting ahead. The jobs weren't *Silver Spoons*. Or, more to the spirit, they weren't *The Rick Schroder Show*. They were TV movies. And he was a TV movie star. The problem? Audiences don't bond with TV movie stars. They don't celebrate them. They settle for them. (Nothing else good on that night.) In a different way, at a different level, Rick was facing what every child actor, post-cancellation, eventually faces: indifference. The boy (or girl) who was once the nation's darling becomes, as an adult, Just Another Actor. Egos have been crushed over less. "I was making more money then than I'm making now," Rick griped about the state of his career to *TV Guide* in 1989.

Things got to the point that even Rick tried the old "get gone" escape. After *Lonesome Dove*, he changed his address from Hollywood to Colorado, bought a spread of land in Grand Junction, tried a little college (three weeks' worth), considered a career in ranch management, got married (to Andrea Bernard, a college student he met in Canada during the shoot for the 1991 TV movie, *Blood River*), had a few kids (two boys, one girl – the eldest, Holden, named after Rick's *Earthling* mentor, William Holden), did some more TV movies. To the outside world, Rick said everything was fine. "I have a completely separate life there that's very fulfilling and rewarding for me," he said in 1993, as he hyped yet another telepic (*Call of the Wild*). "I don't derive my self-esteem from my job."

The aforementioned outside world, meanwhile, couldn't have been colder. When asked to describe a teen idol's greatest fear by the *Los Angeles Times* in 1994, then-teen idol (and future former child star) Mark-Paul Gosselaar had a ready response: becoming Rick Schroder. "I look at him now, and I don't take him seriously," Gosselaar said of Rick. This from a kid on the Saturday morning sitcom *Saved By the Bell*.

If his peers were dissing Rick Schroder, producers and directors were discounting him. "There have been times I almost got a persecution complex," Rick said. "I felt like people wouldn't let me grow up."

He said his dream was to do a prime-time series again – preferably, a cop show. Something to show people he wasn't twelve anymore. Finally, in 1998, he caught another break. At the time, *Silver Spoons* was more than a decade in the grave; Rick, more than a decade into his TV movie career as a new generation's Tim Matheson. Meanwhile, over in the Los Angeles production offices of *NYPD Blue*, ABC's Emmy-winning, butt-baring police drama was bracing for the departure of star Jimmy Smits. The show put out the casting net for a new youngish leading-man type to pair up with middle-aged, leading-man type Dennis Franz. Every twentysomething male in Hollywood read for the part (well, at least forty of them), including one who producers would rather have crossed off their list. Said *NYPD Blue* producer Steven Bochco: "I was like, 'C'mon, Rick? Ricky Schroder?'" Protest or no, incredulous or no, Rick was allowed to audition. His New York City roots did him well to conjure the voice of Detective Danny Sorenson; his out-in-the-Colorado-sun wrinkles did him well to pass for a workaday guy. Ricky *Silver Spoons* Stratton? Who was that? This guy at the audition wasn't some sitcom kid; he was a prime-time drama man. The morph had been successful. He got the job.

Rick's first *NYPD Blue* episode aired on ABC on December 1, 1998. And this time, he was taken seriously. There was no laughter, no ridicule, no snide comments from *Saved by the Bell* thespians. There was only praise and a sort of awe that Rick Schroder had done it – made it all the way back from Ricky to Rick. He'd wanted a top-line Hollywood job – he'd done it. He'd wanted the spotlight back – he'd gotten it. A line in a 1999 *TV Guide* profile said it all: "Nicer still [to Rick] has been the opportunity to prove he is not another fading child star."

Yes, God forbid he fade. God forbid he do dinner theater,

or worse, another TV movie. Continued prime time fame, by any means necessary. Even self-described well-adjusted Rick admitted it was fun to be a star again, as opposed to grinding it out as a working actor. "I had a lot of attention and stuff when I was a little boy," he said, "and now to have that attention again as a young man . . . it's really sweet."

No doubt it was sweet. As Paul Petersen once put it: "We all want to be part of the family" – "the family" being Hollywood, the set, the job, and all the stuff ex-kid stars used to have. Nearly everybody wants back in; literally nobody is granted readmittance. Asked a sincere *Parade* magazine, "How . . . had Schroder succeeded when so many other former child performers fail?"

Fair question. Did he try harder? Did he want it more? Did he grow up less funny-looking? Did he luck out? Again the "why" he succeeded can never really be answered. The "how" he succeeded is simple: Rick Schroder succeeded by coming back.

All we ever asked of him, or any other former child star, was to get another series. Preferably, one we liked.

3. BECOME JODIE FOSTER

Saying you want to grow up to be Jodie Foster is like saying you want to grow up to be Cinderella – the lifestyle is seemingly as unattainable as that of the glass-slippered, fairy-tale princess. Two Oscars before she was thirty? Eight-figure picture deals? A lofty ranking on Hollywood power charts? It's all too much, but if you're a kid actor, who do you fix your sights on: I want to be the next Gary Coleman; or, I want to be the next Jodie Foster?

You hear the answer over and over again from the mouths of latter-day prime-time stars: I want to be the next Jodie Foster (Yale class of 1985). To that end, the 1980s and 1990s saw a batch of former prime-time kids enroll at top schools. Fred Savage (*The Wonder Years*) and Danny Pintauro (*Who's the Boss*) to Stanford. Danica McKellar (*The Wonder Years*) and Jaleel White (*Family Matters*) to UCLA. Joey Lawrence (*Blossom*) to the University of Southern California. Scott Weinger (*Full House*) to Harvard. Kellie Martin (*Life Goes On*) and Sara Gilbert (*Roseanne*) to Foster's alma mater. Even TV's Blossom (aka Mayim Bialik) was eschewing the Hollywood scene for neuroscience (at UCLA). In addition to the usual lofty reasons (to explore new worlds, seek new life, find new civilizations, etc.), each arguably enrolled in search of the sort of thing that the glossiest of recruitment brochures neglects to mention: the prestige degree as good-luck charm; the prestige degree as hex-breaker; the prestige degree as Anti-Former Child Star Protection Device.

Will it work? Well, it seemed to work for *her*. But then again, the Jodie Foster story is tough to duplicate.

Jodie Foster (born: Alicia Christian Foster on November 19, 1962) was a freaky kid who read her own scripts by age five, taught herself French and, by age ten, amassed the résumé of a fortysomething character actor. *The Partridge Family*, *The Courtship of Eddie's Father*, *My Three Sons*, *Mayberry R.F.D.*, *Medical Center*, *Gunsmoke*, *Harry O*, *Kung Fu*. Name a prime-time diversion of the Nixon administration, and Foster probably appeared on it. Not quite a star, Foster was very much the reliable hired gun, the affordable Tatum O'Neal. Her two attempts at regular prime-time work – 1973's *Bob & Carol & Ted & Alice* and 1974's *Paper Moon* – lasted a combined six months.

But if anyone didn't need a TV show to keep her busy, it was Jodie Foster. She could carry an after-school special (like 1973's *Rookie of the Year*), handle a bit in a Raquel Welch flick (1972's *Kansas City Bomber*), or hawk Colgate toothpaste. She could work with demi-teen idol Johnny Whitaker one year

(1973's *Tom Sawyer*) and auteur Martin Scorsese the next (1974's *Alice Doesn't Live Here Anymore*). At age thirteen, Foster turned tricks as Iris the prostitute in Scorsese's *Taxi Driver* (1976) and, in the process, definitively separated herself from her peers. Even then, it was clear she would never want for what the Brady kids had. They had a TV show; she had a career (not to mention an Oscar nomination). The cool roles continued all the way up to 1980's *Foxes*, when the eighteen-year-old high-school valedictorian enrolled at Yale University to study literature (and, briefly, to "get gone" from the industry). College, much less the Ivy League, was not then the usual route for the Hollywood kid. The usual route was coping with cancellation, coping with real life, coping with auditions, coping with new career tracks. To kid actors raised on sitcom sets of the 1960s and 1970s, higher education was not part of the big picture. School was something to be tolerated in between camera setups. Post-TV school was something to be endured – a state-sanctioned potential torture chamber where jealous peers cut their famous classmates down to size. And college? Who went to college? Gary Coleman? Todd Bridges? Dana Plato? Anybody?

Jodie Foster.

College, of course, didn't immunize her from growing pains, in life or in Hollywood. There was the matter of John Hinckley (the would-be assassin who claimed he shot President Reagan in 1981 for her love). There was the matter of some underwhelming film work (from 1983's Svengali, a TV movie, to 1984's *Hotel New Hampshire*, to 1988's *Stealing Home*). But through it all, she was still thought of as cool. Why? Because if she wasn't scoring the most prestigious gigs in the mid-1980s, then it appeared to be by choice, as if it was all part of her let's-go-to-college-and-be-normal journey. When she reemerged as the rape victim in 1988's *Accused*, it was time to welcome her back and present her reward – the Best Actress Oscar.

(Another followed for 1991's *The Silence of the Lambs*.) Jodie Foster was set. And others would try to follow.

4. BECOME RON HOWARD

Becoming Ron Howard is a lot like trying to become Jodie Foster, except instead of forging a career as an Oscar-winning actor, you accept that you no longer have onscreen looks or downtime patience and move behind the camera in a bid to become a popular filmmaker (*Splash, Cocoon, Apollo 13*). College is optional. (Dropping out of USC film school to take an acting gig on *Happy Days*, in fact, is okay.) The desire to pay dues in Roger Corman flicks (*Grand Theft Auto*), the ability to remain upbeat about your kid-star past, even in the face of continual "Hey, Opie!" reminders, the talent for keeping early success in perspective ("My parents taught me not to overinvest in fame and success"), and a wide assortment of baseball caps are mandatory. But be warned: becoming a Ron Howard is just as hard as becoming a Jodie Foster or a Rick Schroder. There is, after all, only one Ron Howard, one Jodie Foster, one Rick Schroder. The rest are, well, the rest.

5. GET A SENSE OF HUMOR

Jodie Foster could have earned a master's degree at MIT, returned to Hollywood to win *three* Oscars — and there'd still be a contingent of kid actors who wouldn't follow her lead. College is not everyone's bag. Among civilian non-stars, the academically disinclined develop work skills that (hopefully) will take them as far as their trades allow. Among young Hollywood types, the anti-collegiate develop (hopefully) senses of humor. (Unless they keep getting big-league work, in which case they become Ron Howard. See above.)

In any case, in lieu of trying to convince the public you're worthy of intellectual respect, a sure route to former child star peace of mind (if not economic security) is to crack the joke first. Examples of this method abound: Barry Williams scores a *New York Times* best-seller with his *Brady Bunch* tell-all, turns the thing into a TV movie (also titled *Growing Up Brady*); Danny Bonaduce congenially opens up about his Partridge and post-Partridge life as a drive-time deejay and (once) a TV talk-show host; Butch Patrick secures the Web site URL www.munsters.com to hawk Eddie Munster Woof-Woof dolls; Alison Arngrim, the pigtailed, pigheaded Nellie Oleson from *Little House on the Prairie* (1974–81), goes stand-up with an act based on her days as "the Prairie Bitch." And so on. The more the merrier.

Lesson learned: since we insist on laughing at former child stars, the former child star might as well make us laugh *with* them. (Makes us think they're being useful.)

FORMER CHILD STARS: THE END?

So, this is how you build a better former child star: through higher education, through a new, outside-Hollywood career (or, alternately, through a better, in-Hollywood career), through self-deprecating humor. Could any of these approaches have saved Anissa Jones? Or Trent Lehman? Or Rusty Hamer? Or Dana Plato?

Well, it's nice to think so.

"We learned the mistakes of the previous generation of actors," Fred Savage vowed in 1997.

Well, it's nice to think that, too.

To be sure, Savage, the angel-faced wonder of *The Wonder Years*, was prototypical of TV child stars of the late-1980s and 1990s. Media-savvy. Book-smart. Always talking about backup career plans and alternatives. And as aware as any *Entertainment*

Weekly subscriber of the former child star legacy (read: curse). If it was impossible for the TV kids of the 1950s and 1960s to know the traps that lay ahead, it was impossible for the TV kids who followed *not* to know. (They get the *National Enquirer* in Hollywood, too, you know.) To their eyes, the pioneering child stars must have seemed macabre players – a lost generation trashed by drugs, bad relationships, bad luck, and/or lousy career advice. Actually, the whole mess was a wake-up call to the kids of the 1950s and 1960s, as well.

In 1990, Paul Petersen was at work anew on the child actor book, now *A Minor Consideration*, when Rusty Hamer shot himself to death. Petersen was moved to anger ("They say children in this industry are protected. Bullshit," he once said. "Hollywood would save Bosnia before the life of a single child actor"), and then to action. He shelved the book, borrowed the title, and, in January 1991, established the child-actor advocacy and support group A Minor Consideration. Petersen described the venture as being like Alcoholics Anonymous – minus the anonymous part. Petersen's strategy was to talk publicly, early, and often (and on every talk show that would have him), about the needs and rights of kids in Hollywood. He could paint with broad strokes to make his points – using everyone from Rusty Hamer to Carl "Alfalfa" Switzer (who died because a guy who owed him money shot him in the stomach) as proof of the industry's corrosive touch.

To Petersen, there were no coincidences. And there was no time to let up, no time to be lulled into trusting that latter-day kid stars really had "learned the mistakes" (or that Hollywood really had helped prevent them). Said Petersen: "It's very hurtful to me when people play fast and loose with our lives and don't understand the totality of the impact of early fame. It's too easy to whitewash this. The world is not the way it appears. Kids [from] my era [to] now – until we change the law – are working for money that does not belong to them. This playing field is decidedly tilted." Could a group like A Minor Consideration level the playing field?

Well, it's nice to think so.

By Petersen's own count, there were thirty-seven U.S. states in 1999 that didn't have child labor laws specifically addressing child entertainers. That's a lot of leveling to do. But, conceivably, it could be done. And, conceivably, modern-era child stars could do their part by saying their lines, not bumping into the furniture, and not making headlines. That's a lot of lives to keep straight, but it could be done.

And, conceivably, we – the audience – could do our part by getting a collective life and moving onto another group worthy of our virtual obsessions like, say, the quasi-stars of real-life MTV soap *The Real World*.

Now, wouldn't that be a nice change of pace? Not that we'd ever entirely renounce our claim on Gary Coleman, but it's worth considering. *Real World*ers are so former child star-like anyway – they're people who are famous for acting on instinct and not necessarily talent; they're people who literally grow up (hopefully) before our eyes; and they're people who are prone to outbursts on camera. In some ways, they're even better than TV former child stars. For one thing, they're often easier on the eyes. And for another thing, they're old enough to get in trouble right away. No need to wait around ten years to see how they'll pan out. And think about the hours of fun spent asking: Whatever happened to that actor boy from the London cast? Whatever happened to the stuck-up model from New York? And the inevitable, Gary Colemanesque, Whatever happened to Puck?

We could do it. We, more than any group, have the power. We could single-handedly end the former child star "curse" – and, by way of transference, start a whole new one! Imagine the talk-show panels! The *People* magazine cover stories! The Fox docudramas! The indie film satires! The would-be think-piece books! Goodbye, former child star; hello, former *Real World* roommate. Would it – could it – work?

Well, it's nice to think so, anyway.

In the end, though, there is absolutely nothing "former" about a former child star. They could get lost; we could give them up. But they'd always be found. They are and always will be.

Reruns, after all, are forever.

GARY COLEMAN
2001

"They have forsaken me . . ."

— EVERYMAN, IN EVERYMAN (CIRCA 1485)

Gary Coleman is everywhere.

I've seen him at my local coffee shop – ordering eight strips of bacon and French toast. (He delivered the order to the back row, as it were. You couldn't help but hear the details.) I've seen him patiently signing autographs for about five dollars a pop at his namesake (and now-defunct) video arcade. I've watched him, of course, on Court TV. I've got friends and acquaintances who have sold him TV sets, sold him train sets, bought computers from him, bumped into him at restaurants.

I've stood on the rooftop of a Beverly Hills boutique hotel interviewing him about his potential candidacy for the U.S. Senate. ("I have certain ideas and opinions and beliefs about political issues and how I believe things should be run for citizens and cities and counties and towns and states, but that doesn't *make* me want to be a politician. That's my whole platform, I'm a *non*-politician.") And in this, my first formal face-to-face, I found him less brusque to the press than his clippings had made him out to be. I found him about as tall as I expected (which is not as short as you might think) and I found his manner as Gary Colemanesque as I expected (careful, serious, resigned, emphatic).

Gary Coleman, to sum up, does not disappoint. He *is* Gary Coleman. And he *is* everywhere.

With one exception, perhaps.

Until I started work on this book and began a dogged pursuit of old *Diff'rent Strokes* episodes, I literally had not seen the show in fifteen years. (Not that you could ever really forget that voice, that face. . . .) Among quintessential TV former child star sitcoms, *Diff'rent Strokes*, strangely, is one of the least rerun. (Why mess with the old stuff, apparently, when the new stuff is so much more, you know, interesting?) It's either a credit to the power of Gary Coleman, or to our obsession with Gary Coleman, that most of us don't need to revisit the source of his legend to know why he is our legend. (Once bitten . . .)

Diff'rent Strokes reruns do exist, of course. And if you live in the right TV market, then its star really *is* everywhere. Literally. Figuratively. On our TVs. In our memories. In the tabloids.

Gary Coleman does not go away. He exists in a post-fame purgatory, walking the streets of Hollywood like the hero of a long-ago Medieval drama – forsaken by fans and family and separated from his onetime wealth.

He walks because he refuses to stay down.

"I just happen to be one who has survived, who has survived being chewed upon, and I will always continue to survive being

chewed upon. There's nothing anybody can do me to stop
me." (Gary Coleman)

If Gary Coleman was in charge (as an honorable senator or no),
there would be no more like him, meaning there would be no
more child actors in Hollywood. "I've always said if they can
replicate dinosaurs they can replicate kids," Gary said,
espousing the *Jurassic Park* theory of casting. "They don't need
any human kids to be in this business to get chewed up." Gary
Coleman knows he can take it. He's just not sure about the
others. Not everybody, after all, is Gary Coleman.

At the end of *Everyman*, the title character, deserted by all,
is finally delivered to heaven by his Good Deeds. They were all
that really mattered.

The conclusion of the Every Former Child Star saga is not
yet written. Gary Coleman is still here, still alive.

And awaiting redemption.

Still.

THE END?

SOURCES

Note: Author's interviews with Danny Bonaduce, Gary Coleman, Tony Dow, Billy Gray, Bryan Madden, Billy Mumy, Dana Plato, and Robbie Rist were conducted from 1997 to 2000 for the purposes of journalism articles for *E! Online*, Hollywood.com, and Former Child Star Central (www.formerchildstar.net). For reader clarity, ellipses largely have been eliminated from quotes to indicate when a phrase or sentence has been combined. The below source listings correspond, in chronological order, to all quotes that appear.

CHAPTER ONE:

Author interview with Bryan Madden, January 1999; Marcia Seligson, "Small Wonder: *Diff'rent Strokes* Gets Its Comic Energy From a Sassy 10-year-old," *TV Guide*, March 3, 1999; author interview with Gary Coleman, October 13, 1999; Associated Press, "Gary Coleman Arrested for Allegedly Punching Autograph Seeker," July 31, 1998; Tracy R. Fields lawsuit; Bryan Robinson, "Coleman Says He Struck Fan Out of Fear," Court TV Online,

February 4, 1999; Gary Coleman testimony, Inglewood, Calif., Municipal Court, February 4, 1999; BMI Wire, "Quayle's Back, and So Are the Jokes," *Hartford Courant*, February 10, 1999; Dana Debin, "Radio Appeal Outrage," originally broadcast on *Extra*, September 21, 1999; WPLJ caller, "Radio Appeal Outrage"; Joal Ryan, "Rock Throws Stones at MTV Video Music Awards," *E! Online*, September 9, 1999.

CHAPTER TWO:

"Jackie Coogan Coming for $300,000 Contract," *New York Times*, April 9, 1921; Charles Chaplin, *Charles Chaplin: My Autobiography*, Simon & Schuster, New York, 1964; "Screen People and Plays," *New York Times*, February 13, 1921; review of The Kid, *New York Times*, January 22, 1921; Aljean Harmetz, "Jackie Coogan – Remember?" *New York Times*, April 2, 1972; review of *Peck's Bad Boy*, *New York Times*, April 25, 1921; Jay Rubin, "Jay Rubin Interviews Jackie Coogan," *Classic Film Collector*, Fall 1976; "Jackie Coogan Arrives," *New York Times*, April 17, 1935; Associated Press, "Junior Durkin Dies as Crash Kills 4," *New York Times*, May 5, 1935; Associated Press, "Jackie Coogan Is 21," *New York Times*, October 27, 1935; "Offer Jackie Coogan $500,000 for 4 Films," *New York Times*, January 11, 1923; "Mother Is Sued by Jackie Coogan," *New York Times*, April 12, 1938; Associated Press, "Mother of Coogan 'Hurt' by His Suit," *New York Times*, April 13, 1938; Associated Press, "Coogan's Mother Wins Court Delay," *New York Times*, April 23, 1938; "Child Star Jackie Coogan, 69, Dies," *Variety*, March 7, 1984; Associated Press, "Bargains at Coogan Auction," *New York Times*, January 11, 1939; author interview with Don Stroud, March 8, 2000; Ted Thackrey Jr., "'The Kid,' Jackie Coogan, 69, Dies," *Los Angeles Times*, March 2, 1984.

CHAPTER THREE:

Janet Weeks, "Catch a Falling Star," *Los Angeles Daily News*, March 3, 1995; Mark Goodman with Tom Cunneff, "Nelson, the Next Generation," *People*, August 5, 1991; Walter Ames, "Ricky Nelson, Going Back to TV, Stays Funny Being Natural," *Los*

Angeles Times, September 13, 1953; author interview with Billy Mumy, March 1, 2000; author interview with Billy Gray, March 8, 2000; Cliff Rothman, "Sweet Talker," *Los Angeles Times*, December 30, 1998; author interview with Jon Provost, November 20, 1999; author interview with Tony Dow, February 28, 2000; author interview with Paul Petersen, September 1999; Ralph Blumenthal, "A Guiding Hand for the Child Actor," *New York Times*, September 2, 1997; Sara Davidson, "The Happy, Happy, Happy Nelsons," *Esquire*, June 1971; J.P. Shanley, "Ozzie Nelson: Practical Parent," *New York Times*, June 9, 1957; author interview with Stanley Livingston, October 20, 1999; Fred Bronson, *The Billboard Book of Number One Hits*, Billboard Publications, 1988; author interview with Glenn Scarpelli, October 4, 1999; Hedda Hopper, "Ricky Nelson Can't Get All Shook Up Over Fame at 18," *Los Angeles Times*, October 5, 1958; Myrna Oliver, "Tommy Rettig: Child Star of TV's *Lassie*," *Los Angeles Times*, February 17, 1996; Susan King, "Jeff Comes Home Again to *Lassie*," *Los Angeles Times TV Times*, November 18, 1990; Shaun Considine, "Wow, Has Little Ricky Changed!" *New York Times*, January 23, 1972; *The E! True Hollywood Story: Lauren Chapin*; "TV Actor Convicted on Dope Charge," *Citizen-News*, June 14, 1962; Greg Wustefeld, "Billy Knows Best," *New Times*, December 27, 1974; Boots LeBaron, "Filming of Happy *Donna Reed Show* Buzzes Along at Exhilarating Pace," *Los Angeles Times TV Times*, October 5, 1958.

CHAPTER FOUR:

"Child TV Star Found Dead," *New York Daily News*, October 30, 1976; Wustefeld; Sara Davidson; Joan Dew Schmitt, "The Love Affair Behind *Family Affair*," *Coronet*, March 1970; "ABC: She's Anissa, She's Adorable and She Misses Her Friend 'French,'" *TV Radio Mirror*, March 1967; David Laurell, "An Affair to Remember," *Collecting Online*, May 1998; Cleveland Amory, "Review: *Family Affair*," *TV Guide*, December 24, 1966; Dwight Whitney, "The Great Faffler," *TV Guide*, April 22, 1967; "New Movie," *Extra* (TV), December 13, 1999; Leslie Raddatz, "When

Home Is a Soundstage . . . How Does a Family Really Live?" *TV Guide*, September 7, 1968; Sebastian Cabot, *The Mike Douglas Show*, 1969; Mike Douglas, *The Mike Douglas Show*, 1969; "Inside *Family Affair*," Rona Barrett's Hollywood, June 1970; Carolyn See, "A Family Is a Family Is a Family," *TV Guide*, May 31, 1969; Lisa Reynolds, "Love, Marriage, Widows, Bachelors and Babies," *Photoplay*, September 1967; Peer J. Oppenheimer, "Johnny Whitaker and Anissa Jones of *Family Affair*: Nice Kids or Spoiled Stars?" *Citizen News Family Weekly*, February 18, 1968; News Bureau, "Sealed With a Kiss," *New York Daily News*, November 13, 1968; Greg Davis and Bill Morgan, "Classic TV Memorabilia: *Family Affair*'s Biggest Little Star," *Collecting Online*, April 1997; Ruth Rockwell, "What Their TV Kids Know About Them That Their Real Kids Don't," *TV Radio Mirror*, April 1969; Polly Terry, "The Many Faces of Love: Anissa Jones," *Photoplay*, February 1968; Mike Hughes, Gannett News Service, June 24, 1996; Gregg Kilway, "Johnny Whitaker: A Self-Rated G," *Los Angeles Times*, May 23, 1973; "Pill Overdose Apparently Killed TV Actress, 18," *Los Angeles Times*, August 30, 1976; "Death of Ex-Child TV Star Laid to Accidental Drug Overdose," September 14, 1976; Annisa Jones' death certificate, State of California, Department of Health, September 16, 1976.

CHAPTER FIVE:

Susan Wloszczyna, "Star-Crossed Kids: Child Actors Face Pain After Fame," *USA Today*, February 12, 1990; "Today's *People*," *San Diego Union-Tribune*, September 14, 1985; Rick Sandack, "After the Laugh Track Fades: Why Do So Many Kids Who Made It Big in Hollywood Become Troubled Young Adults?" *San Francisco Chronicle*, June 6, 1993; author interview with Provost; author interview with Gray; Guy Nicolucci, "Where Are They Now: Billy Gray," *Us*, February 19, 1990; Wustefeld; Leonard Maltin, *Leonard Maltin's Movie & Video Guide*, 1997 Edition, Signet, 1996; "Maltin's Mea Culpa," *Mr. Showbiz*, April 20, 1998; "Brief," *Rolling Stone*, December 25, 1980; Oliver; "*Lassie*'s First Master Accused of Cocaine Karma," *Village Voice*, January 5, 1976;

"Tommy Rettig, Ex-Child Star of *Lassie*, Arrested in Cocaine Raid," *Los Angeles Times*, May 31, 1980; Judith Michaelson, "Bonaduce, Tuned In," *Los Angeles Times*, October 20, 1999; Brad Darrach, with Eleanor Hoover and Dan Knapp, "Life After *Ozzie & Harriet*: The Battle for Rick Nelson's Son Tears the Harmon Family Apart," *People*, September 7, 1987; Mary Murphy, "Time After Time," *TV Guide*, March 13, 1999; UPI, "Gig Goes Sour for Former Scion of Munster Clan," *San Diego Union-Tribune*, November 4, 1990; Butch Patrick biography, www.munsters.com; Greg Johnson, "Ex-Child Stars Squandered and Lived to Sell the Tale," *Los Angeles Times*, July 16, 1999; Blumenthal; author interview with Brandon Cruz, May 9, 2000; Richard Warren Lewis, "The Poor Relation," *TV Guide*, March 28, 1970; Andy Furillo, "Last Days of 'Brilliant Child Actor,'" *Los Angeles Herald-Examiner*, January 29, 1982; Wally Burke, "Former Child Star, 20, 'Depressed,' Hangs Himself," *New York Post*, January 19, 1982; Aline Mosby, "Aline Mosby in Hollywood," *News Life*, March 9, 1954; Burt A. Folkart, "Obituaries: *Make Room for Daddy* Child Star Rusty Hamer," *Los Angeles Times*, January 20, 1990; Kathleen Fearn-Banks, "Ex-Child Stars Say There's No Substitute for Happy Families," *Dallas Morning News*, June 23, 1994; "Actor Hamer Wounded," *Los Angeles Herald Examiner*, December 28, 1966; Associated Press, "*Make Room*'s Hamer Dead at 42," *Daily Variety*, January 22, 1990; Hank Grant, "Jon Provost Becomes a Millionaire Today," *Hollywood Reporter*, March 12, 1971; author interview with Petersen; Hopper; author interview with Scarpelli; Marcus Errico, "Jury Says Mouseketeer Is Racketeer," *E! Online*, December 11, 1998; Darlene Gillespie, "Once a Mouseketeer, Always a Mouseketeer . . . ," *Los Angeles Times*, July 14, 1985; Mack Reed, "Jury Finds Grown-up Mouseketeer Guilty of Shoplifting," *Los Angeles Times*, August 21, 1997; David Rosenzweig, "Ex-Mouseketeer Sentenced to Prison," *Los Angeles Times*, March 12, 1999; King; Steve Bornfeld, "Ex-Child Star Explains His Troubled Life: 'I Was Sexually Abused,'" *New York Post*, February 14, 1994; Aleene MacMinn, "People Watch," *Los Angeles Times*, April 22, 1991; author interview with

Livingston; Patty Duke and Kenneth Turan, *Call Me Anna: The Autobiography of Patty Duke*, Bantam, 1987; Lauren Chapin with Andrew Collins, *Father Does Know Best: The Lauren Chapin Story*, Thomas Nelson Publishers, 1989; William Heller, "Remember James at 15? Well, Now He's 38 and Helping People Like Him Kick Drugs," *Star*, July 13, 1999; Weeks; Philip Potempa, "Teen Idol Star of Eight Is Enough Has Changed His Life and Career to Religion and Education," *The Times*, September 15, 1998; Dewey Webb, "Help Sought for Child Actors," *San Diego Union-Tribune*, November 27, 1990; *Dennis the Menace Revealed: The Jay North Story, The E! True Hollywood Story; Danny Bonaduce*, "My Life as a Has-Been," *Esquire*, August 1991.

CHAPTER SIX:

Opening title card, After *Diff'rent Strokes: When the Laughter Stopped*, Fox TV, 2000; Joe Stein, "Oscars: Billy Crystal Stole Light From the Stars," *San Diego Union-Tribune*, March 26, 1991; The Coleman Family and Bill Davidson, *Gary Coleman: Medical Miracle*, Coward, McCann & Geoghegan, New York, 1981; "The High Price of Fame: Chat With Former Child Star Gary Coleman, ABCNEWS.com, May 19, 2000; author interview with Gary Coleman, May 11, 2000; Bella Strumbo, "A Tale of a Falling Star," *Los Angeles Times Magazine*, May 20, 1990; Sue Ellen Jares, "Game, Gifted Gary Coleman, 11, Survived a Kidney Transplant to Become NBC's Hottest New Star," *People*, May 14, 1979; "Remember Gary?" *20/20 Downtown*, December 30, 1999; Bornfeld; Antoniette Marsh, "Todd Bridges: Older Is Better," *Black Stars*, June 1979; Edwin A. Kiester Jr., "Me! A Corporation!" *TV Guide*, December 6, 1980; Ashley Samuels and Erik Sterling, "Black Stars Visits: Todd Bridges," *Black Stars*, September 1980; "Diff'rent Dana," *Playboy*, June 1989; Bill Davidson, "For Dana Plato of *Diff'rent Strokes* Being a Star and a Teen-Ager Sometimes Produces Painful Conflicts," *TV Guide*, July 14, 1981; Matt Slovick, "William Peter Blatty: Author, Screenwriter, Director," *WashingtonPost.com*; William Peter Blatty, e-mail to author, May 5, 2000; Diane Anderson-Minshall, "What You Talkin' Bout,

Dana?" *Cafe Eighties*, 1999; Marcia Seligson, "Small Wonder: *Diff'rent Strokes* Gets Its Comic Energy From a Sassy 10-Year-Old," *TV Guide*, March 3, 1979; Cleveland Amory, "Review: *Family Affair*," *TV Guide*, December 24, 1966; Helen Dorsey, "Gary Coleman, the Mighty Mite," *New York Post*, April 23, 1980; Ann Guarino, "Gary Coleman: He's 13, Quickly Going on 31," *New York Daily News*, July 22, 1981; Marie Moore, *"Diff'rent Strokes'* Gary Coleman on 'Right Track,'" *New York Amsterdam News*, October 17, 1981; Arthur Unger, "TV's Gary Coleman: Please Don't Call Him Cute," *Christian Science Monitor*, July 2, 1979; author interview with Shavar Ross, December 4, 1999; author interview with Steven Mond, February 4, 1999; Robert P. Laurence, "Gary Coleman Will Stay Cute Until His TV Ratings Go Down," *San Diego Union-Tribune*, August 25, 1985; 20th Century Fox press release for *On the Right Track*, 1981; Montgomery Brower, with Malcolm Boyes, "Racial Harassment and Violence Shatter the *Diff'rent Strokes* World of Actor Todd Bridges," *People*, December 5, 1983; Ben Stein, "Being Beautiful Is Just Not Enough," *Los Angeles Herald-Examiner*, January 30, 1981; Conrad Bain on *The E! True Hollywood Story: Diff'rent Strokes*; Lois Armstrong, "For Gary Coleman, Acting With the First Lady Is 'No Big Deal,' But Finding a New Kidney Is," *People*, March 1983; "Gary's Troubles Grow,", December 30, 1980; Andrea Darvi Plate, "The Growing Pains of Gary Coleman," *TV Guide*, February 1, 1986; Associated Press, "Cast Welcomes Coleman Back on the Job," *San Diego Union-Tribune*, January 4, 1985; Associated Press, "Dumped Coleman Speaks Out," *New York Daily News*, May 3, 1985; UPI, "Coleman to Be Home for Holidays," *San Diego Union-Tribune*, December 24, 1985; Andy Meisler, "It's a Good Nudes, Bad Nudes Game," *TV Guide*, August 26, 1989; George Seminara, *Mug Shots*, St. Martin's Griffin, 1996; Elizabeth Sporkin, with Tom Cunneff, Todd Gold, Lois Armstrong, Doris Bacon, Vickie Bane, Lynn Emmerman, *"Diff'rent Strokes'* Fallen Stars," *People*, March 25, 1991; Aleene MacMinn, "Peoplewatch: Newton Bails Out Plato," *Los Angeles Times*, March 21, 1991; *Sally Jesse Raphael*, March 12, 1998; Jesse Oppenheimer,

"Diff'rent Strokes' Cute Missing After Deadly Cocaine Binge," *National Enquirer*, March 2, 1999; Joal Ryan, *"Diff'rent Strokes* Kid Dana Plato Dead," *E! Online*, May 10, 1999; Dana Plato autopsy report, Oklahoma Office of the Chief Medical Examiner; author interview with Gary Coleman, October 4, 1999; author interview with Dana Plato, April 5, 1997.

CHAPTER SIX AND A HALF:

Vernon Scott, *"Growing Pains* Could End Party for Tiny 'Webster,'" *San Diego Union-Tribune*, September 4, 1985; Robbie Rist, *The Gig*, November 1999; Drew Jubera, "TV Interview: The New Adventures of Mother Goose: The Great Rhyme Rescue," *Atlanta Journal-Constitution*, May 18, 1995; Lyle Harris, "Around Town: We'll Never Forget Old What's His Name," *Atlanta Journal-Constitution*, March 3, 1994; Colin Dangaard, "Emmanuel Lewis: This Got a Lot of Power From Those Burgers," *San Francisco Chronicle*, November 17, 1985; Gail H. Towns, "Graduation Day: A Debt to Be Repaid, with Service," *Atlanta Journal-Constitution*, May 20, 1997; Susan Goldfarb, "TV's Webster Sells Car Wax From Back of Van," *Star*, August 26, 1997.

CHAPTER SEVEN:

Prayer to Saint Anthony, Domestic-Church.com; author interview with Petersen; author interview with Scarpelli; "Where Are They Now: Johnny Whitaker: The Tragic Death of His TV Twin Helped Him Take Stock of His Life," *People*, November 28, 1994; author interview with Provost; "An Interview with Willie Aames," Dan & Angie's Home Page, www.geocities.com/Heartland/Farm/5645/willieaames.html; Paige Smoron, "The Littlest Brady, All Grown Up," *Chicago Sun-Times*, June 7, 1998; chat with Paul Petersen, Biography.com, August 19, 1999; Brodie Hemel, "Coke and Potato Chips," *Soho Weekly News*, April 5, 1979; Shelley Levitt, "Blue's Coup," *TV Guide*, January 16, 1999; Bill Davidson, "Over the Hill at 15? Boy, Was Ricky Mad!" *TV Guide*, May 13, 1989; Lori E. Pike, "Call of the Camera: Rick Schroder at 22 Says He's

Ready to Direct," *Los Angeles Times TV Times*, April 25, 1993; N.F. Mendoza, "Heartthrob Heaven," *Los Angeles Times*, July 24, 1994; Tom Seligson, "I Wanted This So Bad, It Hurt," *Parade*, March 5, 2000; Ann Oldenburg, "Schroder: From Child Star to *NYPD Blue*," *USA Today*, February 4, 1999; Patrick Goldstein, "Ron Howard Making a Big Splash," *Los Angeles Times*, March 26, 1984; Marilyn Beck and Stacy Jenel Smith, "Savage Attacks Prejudices about Child Actors," *The News-Times*, October 1, 1997; Ken Black, "When Early Acting Careers Careen to an End," *Los Angeles Times*, January 5, 1994.

POSTSCRIPT:

Anonymous, Everyman, www.luminarium.org/medlit/ everytext.htm; author interview with Coleman, May 11, 2000; author interview with Coleman, October 13, 1999.

BIBLIOGRAPHY

ARTICLES

Adalian, Josef. "Coleman on Culkin: 'Slap His Behind!,'" *New York Post*, May 1, 1996.

Alexander, Shana. "A Gradual Clean Sweep" (re: Tommy Rettig/Jon Provost *Lassie* transition), *Life*, November 25, 1975.

Ames, Walter. "Ricky Nelson, Going Back to TV, Stays Funny Being Natural," *Los Angeles Times*, September 13, 1953.

Amory, Cleveland. "Review: *Family Affair*," *TV Guide*, December 24, 1966.

Anderson-Minshall, Diane. "What You Talkin' Bout, Dana?" *Cafe Eighties*, 1999.

Arar, Yardena. "Jackson, Alabama Takes Top Awards" (re: Michael Jackson, Emmanuel Lewis at American Music Awards), Associated Press (as published in *San Diego Union-Tribune*), January 17, 1984.

Armstrong, Lois. "For Gary Coleman, Acting With the First Lady Is 'No Big Deal,' But Finding a New Kidney Is," *People*, March 1983.

Associated Press:

"Junior Durkin Dies as Crash Kills 4; Jackie Coogan Is Injured and Father Is One of the Dead in California Wreck," *New York Times*, May 5, 1935.

"Jackie Coogan Is Sued for Fatal Auto Crash," *New York Times*, June 22, 1935.

"Jackie Coogan Is 21," *New York Times*, October 27, 1935.

"Jackie Coogan to Wed," *New York Times*, December 3, 1935.

"Coogan and Fiancée Robbed in Chicago," *New York Times*, February 13, 1936.

"Jackie Coogan Wins Suit," *New York Times*, April 9, 1936.

"Betty Grable Is Wed to Coogan in West," *New York Times*, November 21, 1937.

"Mother of Coogan 'Hurt' By His Suit," *New York Times*, April 13, 1938.

"Coogan's Mother Wins Court Delay," *New York Times*, April 23, 1938.

"Bargains at Coogan Auction," *New York Times*, January 11, 1939.

"Agreement Gives Coogan $126,000," *New York Times*, August 17, 1939.

"Child Actors Placed Under State's Wing," *Los Angeles Times*, August 18, 1939.

"Sues Coogan for $30,000" (re: entertainer, Princess Luana, suing Jackie Coogan), *New York Times*, August 22, 1939.

"Is There Life after *Beaver*?" *Los Angeles Times*, October 11, 1979.

"Tommy Rettig, Ex-Child Star of *Lassie*, Arrested in Cocaine Raid," *Los Angeles Times*, May 31, 1980.

"Dumped Coleman Speaks Out" (re: cancellation of *Diff'rent Strokes*), *New York Daily News*, May 3, 1985.

"Heater Blamed for Death of Rick Nelson," *San Francisco Chronicle*, May 29, 1987.

"Make Room's Hamer Dead at 42," *Daily Variety*, January 22, 1990.

"Ex-Child Star Enters Plea of Innocent" (re: Todd Bridges), *San*

Diego Union-Tribune, March 13, 1993.

"Actor Who Played Bobby Brady Charged with DUI After Rollover Near St. George," *Salt Lake Tribune*, November 13, 1997.

"Coleman Lawyer Blasts Plaintiff," August 6, 1998.

"Actress Plato Dies of Overdose," *Washington Post* Web site, May 9, 1999.

"Gary Coleman Rights His Legal Troubles with a Clean Stroke," Court TV Online, July 28, 1999.

Atlanta Journal–Constitution (unbylined): "People, etc.: Fayette County: Webster's Back with Fairy Tales for Modern Times" (re: Emmanuel Lewis), *Atlanta Journal–Constitution*, April 20, 1995. "Peach Buzz: Stars Honor Vinings' Pyle" (re: Emmanuel Lewis), *Atlanta Journal–Constitution*, November 14, 1997.

Barron, James. "Jackie Coogan, Child Star of Films, Dies at 69," *New York Times*, March 2, 1984.

Beck, Marilyn and Stacy Jenel Smith. "Savage Attacks Prejudices about Child Actors," *The News-Times*, October 1, 1992.

Bender, Eric. "dBase, Come Home" (Tommy Rettig profile), *PC World*, June 1987.

Biegel, Jerry. "Children's TV Stars Face Life Audience" (review of Johnny Whitaker, Brady Bunch kids concert), *Los Angeles Times*, August 1, 1973.

Biography (unbylined). "Lisa Loring," *Biography*, 1998.

Black, Kent. "When Early Acting Careers Careen to an End" (re: Paul Petersen's work with A Minor Consideration), *Los Angeles Times*, January 5, 1994.

Blumenthal, Ralph. "A Guiding Hand for the Child Actor" (re: Paul Petersen's work with A Minor Consideration), *New York Times*, September 2, 1997.

BMI Wire, "Quayle's Back, and So Are the Jokes" (Jay Leno joke about Gary Coleman), *Hartford Courant*, February 10, 1999.

Bogert, Bob. "The Kids Were All Right" (Video roundup, including item on *The Kid*), *Bergen County (NJ) Record*, November 20, 1992.

Bonaduce, Danny. "My Life as a Has-Been," *Esquire*, August 1991.

Bornfeld, Steve. "Ex-Child Star Explains His Troubled Adult Life: 'I

Was Sexually Abused'" (re: Todd Bridges's revelation), *New York Post*, February 14, 1994.

Brasher, Joan. "Willie & Maylo Aames," *Marriage Partnership*, Fall 1996.

Brower, Montgomery with Malcolm Boyes. "Racial Harassment and Violence Shatter the *Diff'rent Strokes* World of Actor Todd Bridges," *People*, December 5, 1983.

Burke, Wally. "Former Child Star, 20 'Depressed,' Hangs Himself" (re: Trent Lehman), *New York Post*, January 19, 1986.

Cart., "Child Star Jackie Coogan, 69, Dies; Always Remembered for *The Kid*," *Variety*, March 7, 1984.

Cerone, Daniel. "Winsome Winnie: The Actress Behind the Girl Behind the Boy," *Los Angeles Times*, May 6, 1990.

Champlin, Charles. "*Tom Sawyer* Set to Music," *Los Angeles Times*, May 23, 1973.

Ciaccia, Maria. "Where Are They Now? All in the *Family*," *People*, June 1997.

Citizen-News (unbylined): "TV Actor Convicted on Dope Charge" (re: Billy Gray pot possession case), *Citizen-News*, June 14, 1962. "*Lassie* Star Gets $50,000" (re: Jon Provost's new contract), *Citizen-News*, November 30, 1962.

City News Service, "Gary Coleman's Attorney: Bus Driver Seeks 'Fame and Fortune' With Lawsuit," CNS, August 13, 1998.

Connelly, Michael. "TV Actor Accused of Driving Recklessly" (re: Todd Bridges arrest), *Los Angeles Times*, January 19, 1988.

————."Bridges Freed; Prosecutor Refuses to File Drug Charges," *Los Angeles Times*, May 9, 1990.

Considine, Shaun. "Wow, Has Little Ricky Changed!" (Ricky Nelson profile), *New York Times*, January 23, 1972.

Cook, Bruce. "Coogan Gets Goodbye from the Gang," *Los Angeles Daily News*, March 6, 1984.

Current Biography (unbylined). "Jodie Foster," *Current Biography Yearbook*, 1992.

Dan & Angie. "An Interview with Willie Aames," Dan & Angie's Home Page ("Did You Know They Were Christians?"), http://www.geocities.com/Heartland/Farm/5645/willieaames.html.

Dangaard, Colin. "Emmanuel Lewis: This Dynamo Got a Lot of Power from Those Burgers," *San Francisco Chronicle*, November 17, 1985.

Darrach, Brad, with Eleanor Hoover and Dan Knapp. "Life After *Ozzie & Harriet*: The Battle for Rick Nelson's Son Tears the Harmon Family Apart," *People*, September 7, 1987.

Davidson, Bill. "For Dana Plato of *Diff'rent Strokes* Being a Star and a Teen-Ager Sometimes Produces Painful Conflicts," *TV Guide*, July 4, 1981.

———. "Over the Hill at 15? Boy, Was Ricky Mad!" (Rick Schroder profile), *TV Guide*, May 13, 1989.

Davidson, Sara. "The Happy, Happy, Happy Nelsons," *Esquire*, June 1971.

Davis, Greg and Bill Morgan. "Classic TV Memorabilia: *Family Affair*'s Biggest Little Star" (re: Mrs. Beasley), *Collecting Online*, April 1997.

Dorsey, Helen. "Gary Coleman, the Mighty Mite," *New York Post*, April 23, 1980.

Dunn, Clif H. "Whatever Happened To . . .? Brandon Cruz Goes from TV Tyke to Punk Rock Dad," *Star*, March 7, 2000.

Eggers, Dave. "The Last Laugh" (re: Adam Rich's *Might* hoax), *City Paper*, June 12, 1996.

Elliott, Stuart. "Jello-O Dishes Up Classic Cosby Ads" (re: Emmanuel Lewis Jell-O commercial) *USA Today*, October 26, 1988.

Errico, Marcus. "Jury Says Mouseketeer Is Racketeer," *E! Online*, December 11, 1998.

Fearn-Banks, Kathleen. "Ex-Child Stars Say There's No Substitute for Happy Families" (re: Angela Cartwright), *Dallas Morning News*, June 23, 1994.

Fitzsimmons, Barbara. "Public Eye: Mickey on the Stand" (re: Darlene Gillespie), *Los Angeles Times*, April 28, 1990.

Folkart, Burt A. "Obituaries: *Make Room for Daddy* Child Star Rusty Hamer," *Los Angeles Times*, January 20, 1990.

Foster, Jodie. "Why Me?", *Esquire*, December 1982.

Furillo, Andy. "Last days of 'Brilliant' Child Actor" (re: Trent Lehman), *Los Angeles Herald-Examiner*, January 29, 1982.

Gautschy, Dean. "Brian Keith: 'God Gave Me 16 Children to Love'," *TV Radio Mirror*, July 1967.

Gillespie, Darlene. "Memories of Walt's Place: Once a Mousekeeter, Always a Mousekeeter," *Los Angeles Times*, July 14, 1985.

Gliatto, Tom. "Little Girl Lost" (Dana Plato profile), *People*, May 24, 1999.

Goldfarb, Susan. "TV's Webster Sells Car Wax from Back of Van," *Star*, August 26, 1997.

Goldstein, Patrick. "Ron Howard Making a Big *Splash*," *Los Angeles Times*, March 26, 1984.

———. "Pop Eye" (re: Emmanuel Lewis attending Al Green concert with Michael Jackson), *Los Angeles Times*, April 13, 1986.

Goodman, Mark with Tom Cunneff. "Nelson, The Next Generation: Rick's Twin Sons, Matthew and Gunnar, Brighten the Family Star," *People*, August 5, 1991.

Grant, Hank. "Jon Provost Becomes a Millionaire Today," *Hollywood Reporter*, March 12, 1971.

Guarino, Ann. "Gary Coleman: He's 13. Quickly Going on 31," *New York Daily News*, July 22, 1981.

Haller, Scot with Joyce Wagner. "I Was Crying All The Time" (Kristy McNichol profile), *People*, April 3, 1989.

Harmetz, Aljean. "Jackie Coogan – Remember?", *New York Times*, April 2, 1972.

Harris, Lyle. "Around Town: We're Never Forget Old What's His Name" (re: Emmanuel Lewis), *Atlanta Journal–Constitution*, March 3, 1994.

Hart, Jon. "The Olivier of Porn" (re: Lisa Loring's ex-husband, Paul Siederman/Jerry Butler), *Green Magazine*, March 22, 2000.

Heimel, Brodie. "Coke and Potato Chips" (interview with Ricky Schroder), *Soho Weekly News*, April 5, 1979.

Heller, William. "Remember *James at 15*? Well, Now He's 38 and Helping People Like Him Kick Drugs," *Star*, July 13, 1999.

Herz, Steve. *Diff'rent Strokes* Star Gets a Different Job – as a Security Guard," *National Enquirer*, February 10, 1998.

Hollywood Reporter (unbylined). "Jon Provost Picks Up Minority *Lassie* Money," *Hollywood Reporter*, March 15, 1971.

Hopper, Hedda. "Ricky Nelson Can't Get All Shook Up Over Fame at 18," *Los Angeles Times*, October 5, 1958.

Huff, Richard. "Coleman's Cash Plea Enrages PLJ Listeners," *New York Daily News*, September 21, 1999.

Hughes, Mike. (Johnny Whitaker profile), Gannett News Service, June 24, 1996.

Jack & Jill (unbylined). "Young Stars of *Family Affair*," *Jack & Jill*, October 1967.

Jares, Sue Ellen. "Game, Gifted Gary Coleman, 11, Survived a Kidney Transplant to Become NBC's Hottest New Star," *People*, May 14, 1979.

Jarvis, Jeff with reporting by Malcolm Boyes and Karen G. Jackovich. "Caught in a Terrifying Spiral of Depression, Kristy McNichol Is Rescued by Big Brother Jimmy," *People*, May 9, 1983.

Johnson, Greg. "Ex-Child Stars Squandered and Lived to Sell the Tale" (re: Jon Provost, Paul Peterson, Brandon Cruz being hired as spokesmen for SunAmerica Inc.), *Los Angeles Times*, July 16, 1999.

Jones, Jack. "Rick Nelson Killed in Plane Crash," *Los Angeles Times*, January 1, 1986.

Jubera, Drew. "TV Interview: *The New Adventures of Mother Goose: The Great Rhyme Rescue*" (re: Emmanuel Lewis), *Atlanta Journal–Constitution*, May 18, 1985.

Kiester Jr., Edwin. "Me! A Corporation!" (Todd Bridges profile), *TV Guide*, December 6, 1980.

Kilway, Gregg. "Johnny Whitaker: A Self-Rated 'G'," *Los Angeles Times*, May 23, 1973.

King, Susan. "Jeff Comes Home Again to *Lassie*," *Los Angeles Times TV Times*, November 18, 1990.

——. "The Savage Within," *Los Angeles Times*, May 5, 1996.

——. "Schroder: A Long Way from 'Silver' to Blue," *Los Angeles Times TV Times*, November 29, 1998.

Landis, David. "Conductor to Retire" (briefs, including one on Eddie Murphy/Emmanuel Lewis recording project), *USA Today*, June 12, 1992.

Laurell, David. "An Affair to Remember" (about Johnny Whitaker),

Collecting Online, May 1998.

LeBaron, Boots. "Filming to Happy *Donna Reed Show* Buzzes Along at Exhilarating Pace," *Los Angeles Times TV Times*, October 5, 1958.

Levitt, Shelley (with Joyce Wagner). "Debilitated by Manic-Depressive Illness, Kristy McNichol Temporarily Flees 'Empty Nest: Down, Not Out,'" *People*, October 26, 1992.

——. "Blue's Coup" (Rick Schroder profile), *TV Guide*, January 16, 1999.

Lewis, Richard Warren. "The Poor Relation," (re: *Nanny and the Professor*) *TV Guide*, March 28, 1970.

Litwin, Susan. "Goodbye, Cute Child Star – Hello, Troubled Young Man," *TV Guide*, April 1, 1989.

Los Angeles Herald-Examiner (unbylined): "Actor Hamer Wounded," *Los Angeles Herald Examiner*, December 28, 1966.

"'Happiest' Club Graduate" (re: Paul Petersen), *Los Angeles Herald Examiner*, August 28, 1967.

"*Lassie* Star Files for Bankruptcy" (re: Tommy Rettig), *Los Angeles Herald-Examiner*, September 6, 1979.

Los Angeles Times (unbylined): "Coogan Suit Pact Approved," *Los Angeles Times*, August 17, 1939.

"Dancer Sues Jackie Coogan for $30,000 Over Remarks" (about entertainer Princess Luana suing Jackie Coogan), *Los Angeles Times*, August 22, 1938.

"Rettig Now Leading Man," *Los Angeles Times*, May 22, 1969.

"Brief," *Los Angeles Times*, April 4, 1975.

"Former Child TV Star Guilty of Drug Charge" (re: Tommy Rettig), *Los Angeles Times*, January 30, 1976.

"Ex-Child Actor Rettig Sentenced in Drug Plot," *Los Angeles Times*, February 24, 1976.

"Brief" (re: Tommy Rettig getting suspended sentence for marijuana possession), *Los Angeles Times*, March 19, 1976.

"Pill Overdose Apparently Killed TV Actress, 18" (re: Anissa Jones), *Los Angeles Times*, August 30, 1976.

"Death of Ex-Child TV Star Laid to Accidental Drug Overdose" (re: Anissa Jones), *Los Angeles Times*, September 14, 1976.

"Ex-Actor Freed of Drug Charge" (re: Tommy Rettig), *Los Angeles Times*, March 27, 1979.

"Ex-Actor Trent Lehman Hangs Self on Fence," *Los Angeles Times*, January 19, 1982.

"Cocaine, Marijuana Found in Blood of Rick Nelson," *Los Angeles Times*, February 4, 1986.

"Local News in Brief: $2 Million Bail Set for Todd Bridges," *Los Angeles Times*, March 3, 1989.

"Names in the News: Partridge Alumnus Sentenced" (re: Danny Bonaduce), *Los Angeles Times*, July 17, 1990.

MacIntyre, Diane. "The Silents Majority: Before 'The Kid' Could Talk," The Silents Artists Index (www.mdle.com/ClassicFilms/FeaturedStar/index.htm).

MacMinn, Aleene. "Anissa Jones: *Family Affair's* Tiny Tot Knows Arts and Flowers," *Los Angeles Times*, July 31, 1967.

———. "People Watch: Newton Bails Out Plato," *Los Angeles Times*, March 21, 1991.

———. "People Watch" (re: Adam Rich), *Los Angeles Times*, April 22, 1991.

Maksian, George. "Little Gary Gets the Big Bucks," *New York Daily News*, July 31, 1979.

———. "Gary & Geraldo Don't See Eye-to-Eye on *20/20*," *New York Daily News*, October 27, 1979.

Marguilies, Lee. "17 Years Later . . . Things Father Didn't Know" (*Father Knows Best* reunion), *Los Angeles Times*, May 13, 1977.

———. "No More *Happy Days* For Howard," *Los Angeles Times*, July 18, 1980.

Marion, Jane. "Celebrity Dish: Sunday Super Best" (Elinor Donahue profile), *TV Guide*, January 30, 1999.

Marsh, Antionette. "Todd Bridges: Older Is Better," *Black Stars*, June 1979.

Marx, Andy. "Lost and Found: Making Change" (re: Gary Coleman's video game parlor), *Variety*, August 22, 1994.

McDougal, Dennis. "'We Are the World' Spawns New Feed-Africa Efforts" (re: Emmanuel Lewis participating in kid recording project), *Los Angeles Times*, May 4, 1985.

McGraw, Carol. "Court Report Due on Gary Coleman Conservatorship," *Los Angeles Times*, January 31, 1990.

Meisler, Andy. "It's a Good Nudes, Bad Nudes Game" (re: Dana Plato's *Playboy* shoot), *TV Guide*, August 26, 1989.

Memories (unbylined). "Billy Gray," *Memories*, June/July 1989.

Mendoza, N.F. "Heartthrob Heaven" (Mark-Paul Gosselaar on Ricky Schroder), *Los Angeles Times*, July 24, 1994.

Michaelson, Judith. "Bonaduce, Tuned In," *Los Angeles Times*, October 20, 1999.

Miller, Samantha. "No Kidding" (Fred Koehler profile), *People*, November 8, 1999.

Moore, Marie. *"Diff'rent Strokes* Gary Coleman on 'Right Track,'" *New York Amsterdam News*, October 17, 1981.

Moran, Julio. "Actor Rich Gets Suspended Sentence," *Los Angeles Times*, August 4, 1992.

Morrison, Mark. "A Little Schroder. A Little Wiser," *USA Weekend*, July 9, 1999.

Mosby, Aline. "Aline Mosby in Hollywood" (re: death of Rusty Hamer's father), *News Life*, March 9, 1954.

Mr. Showbiz (unbylined). "Maltin's Mea Culpa" (re: Leonard Maltin's apology to Billy Gray), *Mr. Showbiz*, July 20, 1998.

Murphy, Mary. "Time After Time" (Mackenzie Phillips profile), *TV Guide*, March 13, 1999.

National Enquirer (unbylined). "Who's a Has-Been?" (re: Gary Coleman's altercation with a fan), *National Enquirer*, August 18, 1998.

New York Daily News (unbylined): (News Bureau), "Sealed With a Kiss" (Anissa Jones meets LBJ), *New York Daily News*, November 13, 1968.

"Child TV Star Found Dead" (re: Anissa Jones), *New York Daily News*, August 30, 1976.

New York Post (unbylined). "TV" (*Diff'rent Strokes* episode, "Short but Sweet"), *New York Post*, December 30, 1980.

New York Times (unbylined): "The Screen" (review of *The Kid*), *New York Times*, January 22, 1921.

"Screen People and Plays" (re: Jackie Coogan), *New York Times*,

February 13, 1921.

"Jackie Coogan Coming for $300,000 Contract," *New York Times*, April 9, 1921.

"Jackie Coogan III Here," *New York Times*, April 17, 1921.

"Shower Gifts on *The Kid*," *New York Times*, April 19, 1921.

"The Screen" (review of *Peck's Bad Boy*), *New York Times*, April 25, 1921.

"Offer Jackie Coogan $500,000 for 4 Films," *New York Times*, January 11, 1923.

"Metro Gets Jackie Coogan," *New York Times*, January 12, 1923.

"Jackie Coogan Arrives," *New York Times*, July 17, 1935.

"Jackie Coogan Not to Wed Now," *New York Times*, December 14, 1935.

"Mother Is Sued by Jackie Coogan," *New York Times*, April 12, 1938.

"Co-Star in Television Series Found Dead in California" (re: Anissa Jones), *New York Times*, August 30, 1976.

Newman, Bruce. "Ron On . . .," *TV Guide*, March 13, 1999.

Nicolucci, Guy. "Where Are They Now: Billy Gray," *Us*, February 19, 1990.

Oldenburg, Ann. "Schroder: From Child Star to *NYPD Blue*," *USA Today*, February 4, 1999.

Oliver, Myrna. "Tommy Rettig; Child Star of TV's *Lassie*," *Los Angeles Times*, February 17, 1996.

O'Neill, Anne Marie with Ken Baker, Champ Clark, Gabrielle Cosgriff and Ward Morehouse III. "Update: Seeking Serenity" (re: Dana Plato funeral), *People*, June 7, 1999.

Oppenheimer, Jesse. "*Diff'rent Strokes* Cute Missing After Deadly Cocaine Binge" (re: Dana Plato), *National Enquirer*, March 2, 1999.

Oppenheimer, Peer J. "Johnny Whitaker and Anissa Jones of *Family Affair*: Nice Kids or Spoiled Stars?," *Citizen News Family Weekly*, February 18, 1968.

People (unbylined): "TV's All-American Boy Scores the Hard Wary — As a Writer" (Paul Petersen profile), *People*, date not known, circa mid-1970s.

"Passages" (Rusty Hamer obit), *People*, February 5, 1990.

"Where Are They Now: Emmanuel Lewis," *People*, November 28, 1994.

"Where Are They Now: Johnny Whitaker," *People*, November 28, 1994.

Pike, Lori E. "Call of the Camera: Rick Schroder at 22 Says He's Ready to Direct," *Los Angeles Times TV Times*, April 25, 1993.

Plate, Andrea Darvi. "The Growing Pains of Gary Coleman," *TV Guide*, February 1, 1986.

Pool, Bob. "New Rules on Child Actors Applauded," *Los Angeles Times*, August 12, 1997.

Potempa, Philip. "Teen Idol Star of *Eight Is Enough* Has Changed His Life and Career to Religion and Education" (re: Willie Aames), *The Times*, September 15, 1998.

Puit, Glenn. "Actress Plato From *Diff'rent Strokes* Dies," *Las Vegas Review-Journal*, May 10, 1999.

Raddatz, Leslie. "When Home Is a Soundstage . . . How does a 'Family' Really Live" (re: Anissa Jones and her family), *TV Guide*, September 7, 1968.

Rauzi, Robin. "Period of Turmoil Paved Way for Chaplin Masterpiece *The Kid*," *Los Angeles Times*, May 16, 1996.

Reed, Mack. "Jury Finds Grown-Up Mouseketeer Guilty of Shoplifting" (re: Darlene Gillespie), *Los Angeles Times*, August 21, 1997.

Reilly, Sue. "At Sweet 16, Kristy McNichol Is Up to Her Neck, But in Hot Properties, Not Water," *People*, November 20, 1978.

Rein, Richard K. "*The Champ* Ferries Ricky Schroder, 9, From Staten Island to Starland," *People*, May 7, 1979.

Reynolds, Lisa. "Love, Marriage, Widows, Bachelors and Babies" (interviews with Anissa Jones, Johnny Whitaker), *Photoplay*, September 1967.

——. "The Many Faces of Love: Johnnie Whitaker," *Photoplay*, February 1968.

Richmond, Ray. "Jay North's Slow Road to Recovery," *San Francisco Chronicle*, June 23, 1993.

Robinson, Bryan. "Coleman Says He Struck Rude Fan Out of Fear," *Court TV Online*, February 4, 1999.

___. "Coleman Pleads No Contest to Disturbing the Peace and Receives 90-Day Suspended Sentence," Court TV Online, February 4, 1999.

Rockwell, Ruth. "What Their TV Kids Know About Them That Their Real Kids Don't" (profile of Anissa Jones, Johnny Whitaker, Marc Copage), *TV Radio Mirror*, April 1969.

Rolling Stone (unbylined). "Brief" (quote from Tommy Rettig saying "LSD saved my life"), *Rolling Stone*, December 25, 1980.

Rona Barrett's Hollywood (unbylined). "Inside *Family Affair*," *Rona Barrett's Hollywood*, June 1970.

Rosenzweig, David. "Ex-Mouseketeer Sentenced to Prison" (re: Darlene Gillespie), *Los Angeles Times*, March 12, 1999.

Rothman, Cliff. "Sweet Talker: Elinor Donahue Has Taken a Lighthearted Approach With Her First Book, a Mix of Recipes and Show-Biz Memories. . . .," *Los Angeles Times*, December 30, 1998.

Rottenberg, Josh. "Little Big Man" (re: Gary Coleman), *Us*, February 1999.

Ryan, Joal. "The *Diff'rent Strokes* Kids: Cursed?," *E! Online*, August 22, 1998.

___. "*Diff'rent Strokes* Kid Dana Plato Dead," *E! Online*, May 10, 1999.

___. "Gary Coleman: Bankrupt," *E! Online*, August 18, 1999.

___. TV Scoop column on "C'Mon Get Happy: *The Partridge Family Story*," E! Online, November 1999.

___. "What Would Gary Coleman Do?" (re: Coleman's potential run for the U.S. Senate), Hollywood.com, June 20, 2000.

___. "Former Child Stars in Space" (re: sci-fi film featuring Tony Dow, Billy Gray, Billy Mumy), Hollywood.com, July 6, 2000.

Samuels, Ashley and Erik Sterling. "Black Stars Visits: Todd Bridges," *Black Stars*, September 1980.

San Diego Union-Tribune (unbylined): "Today's People" (re: Danny Bonaduce arrest), *San Diego Union-Tribune*, September 14, 1985. "Public Eye" (re: Jackie Coogan's grandson Keith Mitchell-Coogan), *San Diego Union-Tribune*, November 8, 1986. (Tribune Wire Services). "Names in the News" (briefs, including item about Emmanuel Lewis participating in celebrity softball tournament), *San Diego Union-Tribune*, February 23, 1988.

Sandack, Rick. "After the Laugh Track Fades: Why Do So Many Kids Who Made It Big in Hollywood Become Troubled Young Adults?" (re: Jay North, Lisa Loring, Butch Patrick, Paul Petersen), *San Francisco Chronicle*, June 6, 1993.

Sanz, Cynthia with Nancy Matsumoto. "Where Are They Now? The Boys Grow Up" (*My Three Sons* feature), *People*, September 7, 1992.

Schmitt, Joan Dew. "The Love Affair Behind *Family Affair*", *Coronet*, March 1970.

Schruers, Fred. "A Kind of Redemption" (Jodie Foster profile), *Premiere*, March 1991.

Scott, Vernon. "*Growing Pains* Could End Party for Tiny 'Webster,'" *UPI Arts & Entertainment*, September 4, 1985.

———. "Scott's World" (Jon Provost profile), *UPI Arts & Entertainment*, October 17, 1999.

See, Carolyn. "A Family Is a Family Is a Family" (re: *Family Affair*), *TV Guide*, May 31, 1969.

Seligson, Marcia. "Small Wonder: *Diff'rent Strokes* Gets Its Comic Energy from a Sassy 10-year-old," *TV Guide*, March 3, 1979.

Seligson, Tom. "I Wanted This So Bad, It Hurt" (Rick Schroder profile), *Parade*, March 5, 2000.

Shanley, J.P. "Ozzie Nelson – Practical Parent," *New York Times*, June 9, 1957.

Simpson, Lee. "Who's the Hustler?" (Rick Schroder profile), *Time Out New York*, July 1, 1999.

Slate, Libby. "Provost Comes Home," *Los Angeles Times*, April 7, 1990.

Slovick, Matt. "William Peter Blatty; Author, Screenwriter, Director" (Danny Pintauro profile), *WashingtonPost.com*.

Smith, Cecil. "From Superteen to Supersick Role" (re: Rick Nelson), *Los Angeles Times*, January 27, 1972.

Smith, Steven. "Cooler Than Mr. Freeze" (Q&A with George Clooney, Chris O'Donnell joking about Gary Coleman, Emmanuel Lewis), *Los Angeles Times Calendar*, June 19, 1997.

Smoron, Paige. "The Littlest Brady, All Grown Up" (Susan Olsen profile), *Chicago Sun-Times*, June 7, 1998.

Smyth, Mitchell. *"Family Affair* Ended Sadly" (re: Anissa Jones's death), *Toronto Star*, April 4, 1993.

Snow, Shauna. "Morning Report: People Watch" (re: Gary Coleman winning court judgment against parents), *Los Angeles Times*, February 24, 1993.

Sporkin, Elizabeth with Tom Cunneff, Todd Gold, Lois Armstrong, Doris Bacon, Vickie Bane, and Lynn Emmerman. *"Different Strokes*, Fallen Stars," *People*, March 25, 1991.

Stein, Ben. "Being Beautiful Is Just Not Enough" (re: Dana Plato), *Los Angeles Herald-Examiner*, January 30, 1981.

Stein, Joe. "Oscars: Billy Crystal Stole Light From the Stars" (Billy Crystal joke about *Diff'rent Strokes*), *San Diego Union-Tribune*, March 26, 1991.

Strumbo, Bella. "A Tale of a Falling Star" (re: Gary Coleman), *Los Angeles Times Magazine*, May 20, 1990.

Taylor, Dan. "All Grown Up and Ready to Start Again" (Jon Provost profile), *Press Democrat*, July 26, 1987.

Terry, Polly. "The Many Faces of Love: Anissa Jones," *Photoplay*, February 1968.

Thackrey Jr., Ted. "'The Kid,' Jackie Coogan, 69, Dies," *Los Angeles Times*, March 2, 1984.

Thomas, Karen. "Rich's Arrest; Bonaduce's Denial," *USA Today*, April 8, 1991.

———. (with Jeannie Williams). "Liz and Larry Join in Wedded Blitz" (re: Emmanuel Lewis at Taylor/Fortensky nuptials), *USA Today*, October 7, 1991.

Time (unbylined). "Stay-at-Homes" (re: TV cutting into movie attendance), *Time*, February 13, 1950.

Towns, Gail H. "Graduation Day: A Debt to Be Repaid, With Service" (re: Emmanuel Lewis), *Atlanta Journal–Constitution*, May 20, 1997.

Trebbe, Ann and Arlene Vigoda. "Two Young Celebs Face Drug Charges" (re: Danny Bonaduce), *USA Today*, March 12, 1990.

Tresniowski, Alex and Samantha Miller with Irene Zutell and Amy Brooks. "Where Are They Now? The Facts of Wife" (re: Lisa Whelchel), *People*, July 6, 1998.

TV Guide (unbylined). "Stanley Livingston – And No Cracks, Please!", *TV Guide*, May 26, 1962.

TV Radio Mirror (unbylined). "ABC: She's Anissa, She's Adorable and She Misses her Friend 'French,'" *TV Radio Mirror*, March 1967.

Unger, Arthur. "TV's Gary Coleman: Please Don't Call Him Cute," *Christian Science Monitor*, July 2, 1979.

United Press International: "Coogan Kin, 16, Who Ran Away Is Found Safe," *San Diego Union-Tribune*, November 7, 1986.

"Gig Goes Sour for Former Scion of 'Munster' Clean" (re: Butch Patrick arrest), *San Diego Union-Tribune*, November 4, 1990.

USA Today (unbylined). "Briefly . . ." (re: Emmanuel Lewis working on record project with Michael Jackson) *USA Today*, September 21, 1995.

Variety (unbylined): "Former Child Actor Apparent Suicide" (re: Trent Lehman), *Daily Variety*, January 19, 1982.

"Trent Lawson Lehman," *Variety*, January 20, 1982.

Village Voice (unbylined). "Lassie's First Master Accused of Cocaine Karma," *Village Voice*, January 5, 1976.

Warner, Tom. "The Kids Are Alright. Really, They Are" (re: child star-related urban legends), *City Paper*, June 12, 1996.

Webb, Dewey. "Help Sought for Child Actors" (about Jay North, Paul Petersen), *Union-Tribune*, November 27, 1990.

Weeks, Janet. "Catch a Falling Star" (Paul Petersen profile), *Los Angeles Daily News* (as published in the *St. Louis Dispatch*), March 3, 1995.

Whitney, Dwight. "The Great Faffler" (re: Sebastian Cabot), *TV Guide*, April 22, 1967.

Wilson, Jeff. "Ex-Child Stars Sell Sad Tales of Squandered Riches" (re: Jon Provost, Paul Petersen, Brandon Cruz being hired as spokesmen for SunAmerica Inc.), *Dayton (Ohio) Daily News*, September 2, 1999.

Wloszczyna, Susan. "Star-Crossed Kids; Child Actors Can Face Pain After Fame," *USA Today*, February 12, 1990.

Wustefeld, Greg. "Billy Knows Best" (Billy Gray profile), *New Times*, December 27, 1974.

Zamora, Jim Herron. "Ex-TV Star Charged with 2 Felonies" (re: Todd Bridges), *Los Angeles Times*, January 7, 1993.

Zeller, Steven. "Chip & Ernie Meet 'Dorian!': Stanley and Barry Livingston," *Drama-Logue*, June 19, 1986.

BOOKS

Applebaum, Irwyn. *The World According to Beaver*. Bantam Books, 1984.

Black, Shirley Temple. *Child Star*. Warner Books, 1988.

Bronson, Fred. *The Billboard Book of Number One Hits*. Billboard Publications, 1988.

Chapin, Lauren with Andrew Collins. *Father Does Know Best: The Lauren Chapin Story*. Thomas Nelson Publishers, 1989.

Chaplin, Charles. *Charles Chaplin: My Autobiography*. Simon & Schuster, 1964.

Chaplin Jr., Charles with N. and M. Rau. *My Father, Charlie Chaplin*. Random House, 1960.

The Coleman Family (W.G., Sue and Gary) and Bill Davidson. *Gary Coleman: Medical Miracle*. Coward, McCann & Geoghegan, 1981.

Duke, Patty and Kenneth Turan. *Call Me Anna: The Autobiography of Patty Duke*. Bantam Books, 1987.

Maltin, Leonard (editor). *Leonard Maltin's Movie & Video Guide 1997 Edition*. Signet, 1996.

McNeil, Alex. *Total Television: Fourth Edition*. Penguin Books, 1996.

Phillips, John. *Papa John: An Autobiography*. Dell Publishing, 1986.

Seminara, George (compiled by). *Mug Shots*. St. Martin's Griffin, 1996.

Williams, Barry with Chris Kreski. *Growing Up Brady: I Was a Teenage Greg*. HarperPerennial, 1999.

INTERVIEWS

William Peter Blatty, May 5, 2000 (email correspondence to author).

Danny Bonaduce, November 10, 1999 (for TV Scoop column on "C'Mon Get Happy: 'The Partridge Family' Story," *E! Online*,

November 1999).

Gary Coleman, October 13, 1999 (for article: "Saving Gary Coleman?," *E! Online*, November 15, 1999.); May 11, 2000 (for article: "What Would Gary Coleman Do?," Hollywood.com).

Brandon Cruz, May 9, 2000.

Tony Dow, February 28, 2000 (for article: "Former Child Stars in Space," Hollywood.com, July 6, 2000).

Billy Gray, March 8, 2000 (for article: "Former Child Stars in Space," Hollywood.com, July 6, 2000).

Jeremy Licht, November 1999.

Stanley Livingston, October 20, 1999.

Bryan Madden, January 1999 (Q-and-A for Former Child Star Central).

Steven Mond, February 14, 2000.

Billy Mumy, March 1, 2000 (for article: "Former Child Stars in Space," Hollywood.com, July 6, 2000).

Paul Petersen, September 1999 (for article: *"Diff'rent Strokes* Kid Dana Plato Dead," *E! Online*, May 10, 1999).

Dana Plato, April 5, 1997 (Q-and-A for Former Child Star Central).

Jon Provost, November 20, 1999.

Robbie Rist, January 7, 1999 ("Up Close" Q-and-A for Former Child Star Central).

Shavar Ross, December 4, 1999.

Glenn Scarpelli, October 4, 1999.

Don Stroud, March 8, 2000.

Johnny Whitaker, April 5, 1997 (Q-and-A for Former Child Star Central); May 9, 1999. (for article: *"Diff'rent Strokes* Kid Dana Plato Dead," *E! Online*, May 10, 1999).

Barry Williams, September 1999 (for article: "The 'Lost Bradys,'" *E! Online*, September 24, 1999).

ONLINE RESOURCES

Anissa Jones Page (death certificate) — www.tyler.net.tambbs/anissa.htm.

Dana Plato Cult (autopsy report) — www.danaplatocult.com.

Domestic-Church.com (Prayer to Saint Anthony) – www.domestic-church.com.

Electric Library – www.elibrary.com.

Google – www.google.com.

Internet Movie Database – www.imdb.com.

MadisonOnline.com ("Television History")
(quote from ad ex talking about opportunities in TV) – www.madisononline.com/faqanswers/tvhistory/TV_index.html.

Munsters.com (Butch Patrick bio) – www.munsters.com.

Nick at Nite's TV Land – www.nick-at-nite.com/tvretro.

Partnership for a Drug-Free America (drug usage stats: National Household Survey: Trends in Monthly Users of Illegal Drugs) – www.drugfreeamerica.org.

Remember Anissa Jones – www.geocities.com/CollegePark/Field.3554/anissa.html.

Rock and Roll Hall of Fame and Museum ("Ricky Nelson – 1987, Performer") – www.rockhall.com.

Sitcoms Online – www.sitcomsonline.com.

The Text of *Everyman* – www.luminarium.org/medlit/everytext.htm.

Welcome to My *Family Affair* Page – http://members.tripod.com/maryanne2/.

TRANSCRIPTS

ABCNEWS.com online chat with Gary Coleman, "The High Price of Fame: Chat with Former Child Star Gary Coleman," May 19, 1999.

Biography.com chat with Paul Petersen, August 19, 1999.

Disney.com chat with Mackenzie Phillips, "JoeBiz and Gwenny G Welcome Mackenzie Phillips," October 6, 1999.

Disney.com chat with Kim Richards, "Chat with Disney Film Actress Kim Richards!," Disney.com, August 13, 1999.

Gary Coleman testimony, Inglewood, Calif., Municipal Court, February 4, 1999.

People Online chat with Dick Van Patten, "People Online Hosts

Actor Dick Van Patten" (about Adam Rich as assistant director), April 1, 1997.

TV SHOWS/FILM

Access Hollywood (Gary Coleman feature, "Remember Gary?" (December 16, 1999)

The Adventures of Ozzie & Harriet (various episodes)

After 'Diff'rent Strokes': When the Laughter Stopped (2000)

20/20 Downtown (December 30, 1999)

Diff'rent Strokes (Dana Plato feature) (1997)

Diff'rent Strokes episodes ("Moving In," "The Reporter," "Short but Sweet," "Sam's Missing")

The E! True Hollywood Story: "Dennis the Menace."

The E! True Hollywood Story: "Diff'rent Strokes."

The E! True Hollywood Story: "Family Affair."

The E! True Hollywood Story: Lauren Chapin.

Extra (Gary Coleman feature) (September 21, 1999)

Extra (*Family Affair* feature: "New Movie") (December 13, 1999).

Family Affair (various episodes)

Here Come the Nelsons (1950)

The Jeffersons (guest star: Gary Coleman) (1978)

Jimmy the Kid (Gary Coleman feature) (1983)

Lassie (various episodes with Tommy Rettig and Jon Provost)

The Kid from Left Field (Gary Coleman TV movie) (1979)

The Kid with the Broken Halo (Gary Coleman TV movie) (1982)

Leeza (various episodes devoted to Dana Plato) (1999)

The Mike Douglas Show (guest host: Anissa Jones) (1969)

Sally Jessy Raphael (Dana Plato tribute, "Death of a Child Star") (May 1999)

Unauthorized 'Brady Bunch': The Final Days (2000)

The Unknown Chaplin: The Great Director (1980)

Every other TV show and/or movie I've ever watched (unfortunately, too long a list to list).

MISCELLANEOUS

Autopsy report: Dana Plato, Office of the Chief Medical Examiner, Oklahoma City, OK (issued May 21, 1999).

Christmas card: Anissa Jones (circa 1975) (posted on Kay's Toys and Other Fun Stuff, http://www.kaystoys.com/).

Death certificate: Anissa Jones, State of California, Department of Health (issued September 16, 1976).

Lawsuit: Tracy R. Fields v. Gary Coleman, Los Angeles County Superior Court (filed August 3, 1998).

Press releases:

MGM press material for *Talk About a Stranger* (1952), featuring Billy Gray.

Stanley Livingston ABC bio ("Stanley Livingston: Chip in ABC-TV's *My Three Sons*") (1961).

Anissa Jones, CBS bio (circa 1969–70).

Trent Lehman, ABC bio (circa 1970).

Filmway Pictures press material for *The Earthling* (1981), featuring Ricky Schroder.

20th Century Fox press material for *On the Right Track* (1981), featuring Gary Coleman.

Screen Actors Guild. "Screen Actors Guild-Sponsored Bill Protecting Child Performers Signed Into Law" (about Coogan Law), Screen Actors Guild, October 12, 1999.